THE
HUMAN HEART

Rudolf Joseph Lorenz Steiner
February 27, 1861 – March 30, 1925

FROM THE WORKS OF DR. RUDOLF STEINER

THE HUMAN HEART

SUPERSENSIBLE ORGAN OF PERCEPTION

Dr. Douglas J. Gabriel

Our Spirit, LLC
2024

OUR SPIRIT, LLC

P. O. Box 355
Northville, MI 48167

www.ourspirit.com
www.neoanthroposophy.com
www.gospelofsophia.com
www.eternalcurriculum.com

ISBN: 978-1-963709-00-1

CONTENTS

The World Changes When Our Hearts Do 1

Physiological Aspects of the Human Heart 13

- Heart/Brain Coherence 14
- Secrets of the Heart 15
- The Electrical Axis of the Heart 23
- The Ideal Heart Axis 25
- The Heart Sac—'Fifth Chamber' of the Heart 25
- Auricles of the Atria—'6th & 7th Chambers of the Heart' 27
- The Vagus Nerve 29
- Heart Rate Variability 32
- Frequency Rate of the Human Heart 33
- The Heart's 'Pacemaker'—Sinoatrial Node 34
- The Anatomical 'Box Around the Heart' 37
- The Four Parts of the Mediastinum 38
- Blood Types 39
- Blood Types and Nutrition 41

Three Fields of Force 43

- The System of Chakras 44
- Heart Chakra 44
- Head Chakra 46
- Lower Chakras—Metabolic System 47

A Cup of Golden Light 48

Plasma Generators in the Human Body 50

Great Thoughts About the Heart 53

Rudolf Steiner on the Human Heart 103

The Heart as a Supersensible Organ of Perception 103

The Heart is Not a Pump 105

Mysteries of the Human Heart 128

The Heart is the Temple of the Human Spirit 190

The Etheric Heart and Blood 226

Heart Thinking as Living Thoughts 248

Dodecahedron Universe 265

Historical Review of the Centrality of the Heart 273

Ancient Indian Wisdom of the Heart 273

Heart Research in Egypt 288

The Heart According to the Greeks 289

Alexandrian Period 292

Roman Period 293

Byzantine Period 294

Islamic Period 295

The 'Eye of the Heart' in Sufi Tradition 296

European Period 297

The Christian Desert Fathers 298

Eastern Wisdom of the Etheric Heart 303

The Box Around the Wish Fulfilling Stone 305

The Wishing Fulfilling Tree—Cintamani Jewel 305

Heart: Chinese Fire-Energy 306
Traditional Pulse Diagnosis 307
The Heart Channel Pathway via Acupuncture Points 308
Eternal Para-Bindu Drops 310
The Drum of Shiva 311

Conclusion 313

Bibliography 317
About Dr. Rudolf Steiner 323
About the Author, Dr. Douglas Gabriel 325
Translator's Note 327

The World Changes When Our Hearts Do

Any undertaking to describe the human heart in all its glory is bound to be limited in its scope because the heart has been evolving along with humanity and will continue to do so into the future as its nature, over time, is unlimited. Any comprehensive expose on the human heart would have to go back in time to witness the embryological development of the heart and project into the future an attempt to describe what the heart will become. Even with a comprehensive historical perspective on what great thinkers have 'discovered' about the heart, we cannot wrap our arms around this central core of the human being. The ideas of what the heart will become has been speculated upon by doctors and philosophers with mysterious stories of the future fifth, sixth, and seventh chambers of the human heart yet to be discovered.

These speculations shed light on a few parts of the unfolding heart mystery. Indeed, the ancients focused on the heart as the seat of human consciousness and speculated that the involuntary muscle of the heart will become a voluntary muscle that will someday be completely controlled by human willpower that is charged with moral forces. Many philosophers say the voice of the heart is the moral conscience of the individual, a type of super-organ that can perceive everything, both inner and outer.

There is no limit to the power and majesty of the cardiovascular system working together with respiration. As Christopher Fry tells us in his play, *A Sleep of Prisoners*: "The human heart can go to the lengths of God." In fact, spiritual scientists, old and new, agree that the heart is a sense organ that can listen to and understand the language of the divine. Some would go so far as to claim that the human heart is the Holy Grail that is the treasure found by the worthy knight who suffers the quest for the Grail for the sake of others. Or as Walter J. Stein tells us in his book, *The Ninth Century*: "The Holy Grail is the consummation of the heart's desire, its root and blossoming . . . paradisical, transcending all earthly perfection."

Throughout our presentation we will be seeking answers to many questions about the heart from the ancient Hindu *Vedas* to cutting edge modern research on heart rate variability. Many misconceptions will be outlined in a timeline that reflects the evolution of heart knowledge over the course of history. One of those gross errors in understanding the heart and its function is the myth that the heart is a pump. The true view of blood circulation is much more complicated and has only become accepted by cardiologists in recent times. Dr. Rudolf Steiner's teachings contend that: "*The heart is not a pump; the heart is an organ of perception.*" As a matter of fact, he believes that the heart is the most important organ of perception that can be trained to become a supersensible organ of perception of both the outside world and the inside world of the human being. The heart is the organ that can commune with the divine through a language of the spirit that is unique to the heart.

The mechanisms that develop this supersensible organ will be the major theme of this book. We intend to show that a thorough examination of the heart will unveil numerous 'heart mysteries' that have been known since time immemorial; but little understood by modern science. Even though, the most current heart research demonstrates that the ancients, and spiritual scientists like Rudolf Steiner, had the story correct all along.

Some of the mysteries that have come to light concerning the heart are leading doctors and scientists to rethink and reimagine the profound centrality of the heart and its effects on all aspects of human physiology and health. Some ideas from the past will sound somewhat unfounded or magical; but over time they have come to be the new view that is being adopted by mainstream science. A few of those heart mysteries are:

- The nature of the seven chambers of the heart
- The connection between heart and brain coherence
- The etherization of the blood through the 'front spinal column' (vagus nerve)
- The importance of the axis of the heart in utero and as an adult
- The predictive capacities of heart rate variability to determine longevity and illness
- The electrical nature of the heart and its torus field of energy
- The nature of the human "I Am" found in the heart
- The central focus of the human mind in the heart—not the head
- The capacity to develop heart-thinking through warmed-up thoughts
- The secret 'box' in the heart that records karma from one life to another
- The role of the heart 'chakra,' its nature and function
- The etherization of the blood and its ability to nourish the pineal and pituitary glands
- The development of morality through the supersensible organ of the heart
- The true shape of the heart in current times and its shape in the future
- Heart perception as an alchemical process involving sulfur/mercury/salt
- The mystery of the 'jewel in the heart of the lotus'—the cintamani stone
- The mystery of the 'wish fulfilling tree'—the world tree planted in Eden

- The awakening of the heart as the tool that defines and controls all perception, both outer and inner
- The heart is created by two interpenetrating vortices
- Perception is written into the blood
- There is a cognitive path of heart-perception

This list of heart mysteries is not exhaustive, and many other hidden truths will come forth as we look at the literature concerning the heart. We find many of these insights and inspirations in every type of writing, from sacred texts to modern poetry. Everywhere we look, we will find aspects of the heart being described as the most profound center of human consciousness, evolution, and love. The ancients often lumped the heart together with other key components of human self-development by linguistics and association. The heart is clustered together with ideas about the hearth (seat of fire), the ear (hearing), the home, heaven, and mother. When you think about the heart, the most important human thoughts also come to light. The seat of life and consciousness find their home in the heart as the throne of love that reflects the divine love of Heaven onto Earth. The heart is the mystical source and crucible of love, the 'august master binding of all.' As the *Chaldean Oracles* state: "Having mingled the spark of soul with two, with breath and mind divine, he added to them a third, pure love, the august master binding of all."

It is now time in human evolution to start thinking with the mind of the heart. Or as Van Morrison puts it in one of his lyrics: "If my heart could do my thinking, and my head begin to feel, I would look upon the world anew, and know what's truly real." This poetic injunction is the key mission of humanity as it develops moral (warmed-up) thinking instead of brain-bound, cold, dead thinking that leads to the void of materialism. The head is the past. The heart is the past, present, and future where we learn to speak with Spiritual Beings and receive cosmic nourishment from the exchange of love between humans and the divine. Or as Meister Eckhart has told us: "God is born in the heart and the heart is born in God."

When warm and loving hearts merge with higher thinking, it can develop into living imaginative thinking that is based in reality—not cold-hearted scientific materialism that leads to nihilistic despair. Living thoughts are born in warm-hearted thinking that has a life of its own, fired through and through by spiritual, hierarchical beings who share those Moral Imaginations and Moral Inspirations with humans. Learning the 'Language of the Spirit' is basically learning the language of the moral heart. Often this 'Language of the Heart' is spoken in poetry that can stretch the human imagination to 'the lengths of God.' The great poet and writer, Novalis (Georg Philipp Friedrich von Hardenberg, May 2, 1772–March 25, 1801) gives us the insight that: "The human heart is the universal field of beings. It is the field where all faculties of the mind—understanding, reasoning, imagination, and feelings, are integrated. Human beings can feel with their heart using a language indicative of love."

Novalis also tells us that it is only the human heart that can satisfy this unquenchable desire to commune with our higher nature that is found in the divine. He tells us: "Building worlds is not enough for the deeper urging mind; but a loving heart sates the striving spirit."

Khalil Gibran agrees with Novalis that the heart is where the secrets of love are found: "All these things shall love do unto you that you may know the secrets of your heart, and in that knowledge become a fragment of life's heart." Or as Johann Wolfgang von Goethe put it: "What is uttered from the heart alone will win the heart of others to your own." Goethe predicated the perception of the world upon the capacity of the individual's heart content: "A man sees in the world what he carries in his heart." Thus, the heart is the key to perceiving the world either as heaven or hell, depending on what each person carries in their heart. We see the world through the lens of the heart. It seems that to change our view of the world, we simply need to change the content of our hearts. The great Sufi poet Kabir insinuates the same wisdom when he said: "Lift the veil that obscures the heart, and there you will find what you are looking for."

We must learn to seek the answers about the world, and ourselves, inside the heart as the poet Rainer Maria Rilke tells us: "The work of the eyes is done. Go now and do the heart-work on the images imprisoned within you. All the soaring of the mind begins in the blood." This teaches us that our conscious mind needs to realize that the depth of heart-wisdom never ends. Rilke tells us in another passage: "I would like to beg of you, dear friend, as well as I can, to have patience with everything that remains unsolved in your heart. Try to love the questions themselves, like locked rooms and like books written in a foreign language. Do not now look for the answers. They cannot now be given to you because you could not live them…At present you need to live the question. Perhaps you will gradually, without even noticing it, find yourself experiencing the answer some distant day."

Poets have given us the ability to transcend brain-bound thinking with a few simple words that open the heart to its truly divine nature. Whatever you consider the divine to be, we find its source and end in the human heart. As the Sufi poet Rumi tells us: "Only from the heart can you touch the sky. Your heart knows the way. Run in that direction. If light is in your heart, you will find your way home." So, we begin and end in the heart, which sometimes is unfamiliar to the secular humanist who 'believes' in modern materialistic science. Human consciousness transcends the limits of the five senses upon which modern materialistic science is based. There are higher senses that reveal our divine nature that is to be found in the quiet beating of the heart.

Rumi points to the source and finds it to be never ending. He gives us the injunction: "Why are you knocking at every door? Go, knock at the door of your own heart. Whoever has the heart's door wide open, could see the Sun itself in every atom. Surely there is a window from heart to heart: they are not separate and far from each other. And now the time has come to turn your heart into a temple of fire." This temple of fire is the source of fiery wisdom that connects us directly to our higher self and the divine self of the Universe. Rumi gives us the formula in the following lines: "When you seek love with all your heart you shall find its echo in the Universe. When love for God has been doubled in your heart, there is no doubt that God has love for you."

But modern poetry takes its lead from the wisdom of the ancients found in every sacred book or text of the past. In ancient India, a profound understanding of the heart was known as a central principle of spiritual teachings that go back to the first writings of humanity. The heart was always given the highest praise and was placed on a throne that was unequal to anything but the divine beings themselves. In the *Chandogya Upanishad* we are told: "As great as the infinite space beyond is the space within the lotus of the heart. Both Heaven and Earth are contained in that inner space, fire and air, Sun and Moon, lightning and stars. Whether we know it in this world or know it not, everything is contained in that inner space. The heart is the center of the perception process of the soul and the sensory environment of the human being. In the heart, these sense impressions are perceived, detected, bound together, and thus first truly felt and understood. The heart is the starting point for all sensory impressions."

This view of the heart is far beyond the pseudoscientific nonsense that the heart is simply a muscle that is a 'pump' that forces blood through the cardiovascular system. To underestimate the heart is a grave mistake that veils the true nature of what a human being will become in the future through the evolution of the heart. Even Aristotle, in his *On the Generation of Animals*, has a more profound view of the heart than our top heart doctors: "We are justified in seeing the heart as the source of the being's life, shape, and organization. Blood and its blood vessels are the original source of life. All other parts of the body depend on the heart and have their source, or origin, in the heart."

We need to listen to the ancients and glean the wisdom they developed thousands of years ago concerning the importance of the heart as a highly developed sense organ. The primary place of the heart is beautifully described by Aristotle and only now is coming to be understood as the king or queen of all organs.

The capacity for the human heart to be an organ of knowledge that produces our concepts that are connected to our perceptions is often ignored by science, medicine, and philosophy. Over eight hundred years ago, Thomas Aquinas informed his students that a concept is a 'word of the heart' that forms after perceptions are digested by the heart. Concepts in the modern world have been relegated to the brain where they are said to be stored within nerve cells. Some new research on heart/brain coherence has demonstrated that Aquinas was correct when he wrote in *Summa Theologica* that: "The heart is related to the higher cognitive activities, which take place after sensory perception and the development of imaginative images. Something takes place in people whenever they perform an act of perception. This is the act of receiving and conceiving the perceived object. This concept designates the sound, and the concept itself is called a word of the heart. This thought process takes place in the individual penetration and unification of the act of perceiving with what is being perceived. Sense perception is the tool for the spiritual and intellectual activity of thought. The human heart is an organ of knowledge and love, mediating between Heaven and Earth, thinking and willing, human being and environment."

Theosophists, who study the wisdom of God, also give the highest praise to the heart as the home of god in the human being. The heart is the center of the Universe and is a perfect reflection of the Cosmos. Helena P. Blavatsky wrote in *The Secret Doctrine*: "In the heart is the only manifest God. The first born are life, the heart, and pulse. Shiva is the being in the heart, the lowest aspect of Brahma—*force or mind.* Shiva is the Lord of the Pulse, the only direct manifestation of spirit in matter. It is the heavenly breath and the rhythm of the Infinite. The pulse point is also termed the 'drum of Shiva.' The heart is also the great mountain of the divine rising above the four elements into the ether concealing a spirit so vast that the Universe can scarcely contain it."

The great spiritual scientist, Dr. Rudolf Steiner, points out that the human being has evolved to the point where hearts must begin to have conscious thoughts—warm, imaginative, living thoughts. He is also one of the strongest proponents of the idea that the human heart is a sensing organ, a type of eye for the divine beings to work through. Steiner tells us in *The Michael Letters*: "Hearts begin to have thoughts, that is the new way of thinking with the heart. The newly developed heart-organ slowly transforms into an eye or a sensing-heart-eye-organ."

Ehrenfried Pfeiffer, one of the closest students of Rudolf Steiner, was directly taught some of the greatest secrets of the heart by his teacher. Pfeiffer has written a great deal about the Etheric Heart, its fifth chamber and the necessity to develop the heart as a new supersensible organ of perception that can perceive the working of the Etheric Christ. These mysteries were guarded by Pfeiffer and others due to their sensitive nature which describes evolutionary aspects of the heart that were well-guarded secrets of the ancient mystery schools. The mystery of the fifth chamber of the heart was central to why Steiner's life was somewhat 'cut-short,' according to Pfeiffer. But even though Pfeiffer indicated these secrets were to be still hidden in the present time, he revealed as much as he could about the fifth chamber to help change the current view of materialism that believes that the 'heart is a pump.' Pfeiffer further clarified his point-of-view in December 1950, by writing:

> "The radiation from this etheric organ of the heart is actually developing into a spiritual sense organ. A new sense organ is developing in this Etheric Heart, and this is the only organ by which man is able to sense and to recognize the Etheric Christ."

Another Anthroposophist, named Karl *König*, agreed with Pfeiffer and described the Etheric Heart and the etherization of the blood in his book, *Earth and Man*. *König* reaffirms Pfeiffer's ideas and adds to them the future condition of the Etheric Heart that loosens itself from the physical heart. *König* tells us:

> "The heart is concerned with warmth and light within the blood. Rudolf Steiner describes how into the heart—on account of its being a sensory organ—streams all the activities of our metabolic system, all the activities of our limbs, arms and legs, where we go, what we do, and how we do it. All this is stored up in the heart, as in a casket. This now, going through life between death and rebirth, becomes the whole of our karma in our next incarnation. Since the year 1720, the heart has altered its condition and loosened its connection from the physical structure of the heart and very great changes in the whole life and existence of man have come about."

Even though Rudolf Steiner's lecture, *The Human Heart* (May 26, 1922) is not usually combined with his pedagogical lectures, it is a key for Waldorf teachers to unlock the secrets of the etheric bodies of elementary aged students. My teachers in Waldorf education asked that I make sure to include this lecture in our materials necessary for Waldorf teacher training. It is imperative that Waldorf teachers understand the evolution of the physical, etheric, and astral components of the human heart as it develops from birth through age fourteen. Only when the teacher can work with the incarnating Etheric Heart and help birth the incarnating Astral Heart, can the teacher understand the true task of education. Teachers are the midwives of numerous births in the growing child and a complete cosmology, pedagogy, and psychology can paint the full picture of what a child is and what they are becoming. In Steiner's *The Human Heart*, we find a guide to these delicate processes and are given the insights that allow the teacher to offer each child what they need in a developmentally appropriate fashion.

Many mysteries of the heart are revealed in Steiner's, *The Human Heart*. Here are relevant selections from his book:

> "All that happens in the moral life, and all that happens physically in the world, the moral and the physical, are found

in their real union when we learn to understand all the configurations of the human heart.

"When puberty occurs, man's own Etheric Heart is so far formed that it can receive these forces that develop out of our activity in the outer world. Thus, from puberty onwards man's whole activity becomes inserted, via the astral body, in his Etheric Heart—out of the pictures of the stars, out of the images of the Cosmos—this is a phenomenon of untold importance. At the same place where our own Etheric Heart—has formed itself, we now have an astral structure too, which gathers together all our actions. And so, from puberty a central organ is created wherein all our doing is centered. The etheric-astral structure wherein the heart is floating, so to speak, contains all that man takes with him into his further life of soul and spirit; wherein, he can hand over his entire karma to the Cosmos.

"In the heart, as far as the etheric Universe is concerned, you have a Cosmos gathered up into a center; and a gathering together of all that man does in the world. This is the point where the Cosmos—the cosmic process—is joined to the karma of man—this intimate correspondence of the astral body with the etheric body is to be found nowhere in the human organism except in the region of the heart.

In our time there are certain changes taking place in the heart, by which gradually a fifth chamber will develop. In this fifth chamber man will have a new organ which will allow him to control life forces in a different way than is possible at the moment."

The lucid insight of Dr. Steiner concerning the human heart is unparalleled in any time of history. He gives the reader the ability to understand human development so that the teacher can become a knowledgeable person assisting the cosmological aspects of human evolution developing in the growing child. When the teacher first knows what to look for, then the sense organs can be developed to perceive the subtle and invisible forces at work in the physiological and psychological development of the child that recapitulates the development of humanity. Each child relives the development of its ancestors and must be given the proper building blocks to create the modern human being anew. Each stage of development has a corresponding curriculum that feeds the needs of the growing human heart. The many secrets of karma are found, and placed, into the Etheric Heart through the integration of the astral desires of the individual. The 'casket' or 'little box' in the heart-of-hearts holds the treasures each child brings with them from the past. The point of education is to nurture this 'jewel in the heart of the lotus' that carries with it the eternal "I Am" of the child that wishes to be born again with new opportunities to gain wisdom and ascend the path of human evolution.

Physiological Aspects of the Human Heart

It is only recently that the intelligence system of the heart was discovered. The heart is not a pumping machine. It is an intelligence system. It is the most intelligent system of all our brains, with its own receptors, its own electromagnetic force, from 45 to 70 times more powerful than the brains of the neocortex, and the only force capable of changing our own DNA. It can turn the mortal into immortal, glial cells into heart cells, mortal center into immortal walls in any cell. It is, in fact, the heart that turns each one of us from dying cells into living cells. No one of us is human until the heart beats. And vice versa, as it is that first beat of the heart that makes us human.

The heart contains its own nervous system and nerve ganglia that process information and send it to the neocortex. The heart is a hormonal gland producing its own neurotransmitters, dopamine, epinephrin, norepinephrin, the catechlomines, which affect the kidneys, the adrenal gland, the circulatory system and the neocortex. The heart generates from 45 to 70 times more amplitude electrically than what we call the brain, plus all emotions alter the heart's electrical field. Electricity emanating from the heart of a person can be detected and measured in the brain waves of others near or touching the person. Cellular memory resides in the heart cells, as can be seen from transplant cases. DNA can be altered in the hands of a person practicing head/heart 'entrainment,' or that which was taught in ancient yoga techniques.

The amygdala, in the midbrain, starts forming immediately after the heart's first beat. It stores all the memories of our life in the womb, with the placenta, the water, the fluids of life, and the terror of losing them, and also the joy of being fed, of bouncing, of moving. But the amygdala also stores the life of the mother, her depressions, her fears, her joy. This accumulation of memories goes on in us until the age of three. Which means that all this time we have lived, our life has been recorded for us in the amygdala. After the age of three, the hippocampus matures in us. In it, conscious memories are stored, and we have access to them. However, the hippocampus has no access to the memories and the life we lived in the amygdala of the previous three years, even if from this point on amygdala and hippocampus converse with each other. What happens to the memories of the amygdala? They become our individual nightmare, the invisible conditioning of all our actions, the blind spot of our lives, the origin of our terrors, the unknown reason why we do what we have done even when we do not know why we do it.

The conditioning of the amygdala can only be removed by the intelligence system that was developed prior to it, which is the heart with its electromagnetic force and its power of transformation. Otherwise, the amygdala can act on its own bypassing the intelligence centers of the neocortex.

Heart/Brain Coherence

Modern science has discovered that when the heart and brain work together, magical things happen. Heart/brain coherence seems to make the human being highly aware of everything happening in the person's environment—inside and outside. HeartMath technology is an innovative approach to improving emotional well-being and triggering capacities that were thought not to be available to waking human consciousness. It can teach one to change your heart rhythm pattern to create physiological coherence, a scientifically measurable state characterized by increased order and harmony in our mind, emotions, and body.

In other words, the heart overrules the amygdala. HeartMath research has demonstrated that different patterns of heart activity (which accompany different emotional states) have distinct effects on cognitive and emotional function. During stress and negative emotions, when the heart rhythm pattern is erratic and disordered, the corresponding pattern of neural signals traveling from the heart to the brain inhibits higher cognitive functions. This limits our ability to think clearly, remember, learn, reason, and make effective decisions. This helps explain why we may often act impulsively and unwisely when we're under stress. The heart's input to the brain during stressful or negative emotions also has a profound effect on the brain's emotional processes, serving to reinforce the emotional experience of stress.

In contrast, the more ordered and stable pattern of the heart's input to the brain during positive emotional states has the opposite effect—it facilitates cognitive function and reinforces positive feelings and emotional stability. This means that learning to generate increased heart rhythm coherence, by sustaining positive emotions, not only benefits the entire body, but also profoundly affects how we perceive, think, feel, and perform.

Secrets of the Heart

One secret of the heart that science is researching is the nature of vortices in the heart and their relationship to the axis of the heart. This new field of study is revealing aspects of blood flow through the heart that previously were never imagined. The heart is not only two interpenetrating vortices; but it also has numerous vortices within the heart itself. Heart vortex rings are created by the flow of blood in the different chambers of the heart. Cardiologists have found numerous vortex rings and found that each one has a specific frequency that it attunes to, creating harmonious blood flow. When heart vortices are mis-shaped or do not form fully, heart problems begin. Likewise, this is the case with the axis of the heart both in utero and throughout life. The angle of the axis and the health of the vortices can predict the health of the body. The optimal degree of inclination mimics the Earth's axis. The heart is based on the curve of the diaphragm; but the axis is inclined at an angle of 23 degrees. Likewise 23 degrees is the axial tilt or mean obliquity of the Earth as it orbits the Sun; which, in-turn, is responsible for the variation of the seasons during the course of the year.

Dr. Rudolf Steiner pointed out that there were two major vortices that work together to create the angle of the axis of the heart using forces from above and below the human body. In *Man: Hieroglyph of the Universe, a* cycle of 16 lectures given in Dornach between April 9-May 16, 1920 (GA 201), Rudolf Steiner describes these whirlwinds in the following fashion:

> "Imagine, if you will, a wind whirling from above downwards with a certain velocity, and another from below upwards so that they whirl into one another. Assuming that the difference in velocity of the downward streaming force is such that we can say: the relation of the velocity of the up-flowing stream to that of the downflowing stream gives us the same ratio as the ratio of the velocity of the motion of the stars to that of the Sun, then, if they are whirling into each other, a condensation will be produced by their whirling and will assume a particular form, the silhouette of the human heart. If we take the difference of velocity between the downward and the upward current, relating the latter to the former in such a way that a difference in velocity results bearing the same relationship as the difference in velocity between the stellar time and the solar time, then through the rotation a condensation arises which receives its own distinct form. One whirls downwards, and because the other whirls upwards driving with a greater

> velocity, the lesser velocity would be that driving downwards, which gives here through the collision a condensation, a certain figure. This figure, disregarding imperfections, is a silhouette of the human heart."

Some years before Rudolf Steiner told us about these vortices, the esoteric Christian author Charles G. Harrison, early in 1893 delivered a series of lectures to the Berean Society in London; which were published in 1894 as: *The Transcendental Universe: Six Lectures on Occult Science, Theosophy, and the Catholic Faith*; wherein he describes the working of vortices and adds further details:

> "Now the forces on different planes of consciousness which go to make up man ultimately resolve themselves into two vortices which represent his higher and lower nature." (pg. 117)
> "The double vortex is a manifestation in time, or the plane of illusion ['Maya'], and is the result of cyclic aberration on the plane of spirit..." (pg. 137)

> "...Now the first material race (the third root race of this 'round') were in a very real sense the first men, for, though the ethereal races who preceded them had developed will, the spiritual forces (which, manifesting vortically downwards towards the next, or human, plane of consciousness, were the immediate or efficient causes of man's will) were themselves radiations from the Unconditioned Cause—the Divine Will projected in Maya. Not until the fourth 'round,' was the human personality, so to speak, born, or detached from the life of its parents the Elohim. Man, to have an independent existence, must be self-centered, or free to originate his own actions, and it is evident that this could not be if the evolution of his reason had proceeded on the same lines. Hence the necessity for a readjustment whereby his personality, or fifth principle,

might become itself a controlling impulse. The mystery of free-will is, in truth, the mystery of human personality, and this, as we have seen, has its source in the Divine Love, which requires an object in order that it may become manifest. We can only conceive of will as the dynamic effect of personality manifesting objectively. In itself it has no existence, for it is neither subject nor object but a middle category necessitated by the laws of thought. In all finite personalities the will is the center of gravity,—a mathematical point. In God, the Infinite Personality, there is no center, or rather the center is everywhere, for in Him subjective and objective are One, and, in manifestation, both comprehend all that is. It is easy to see, therefore, that the projection of will in Maya must be accompanied by a projection of mayavic personality in order that it may become manifest or present an objective side. The center must be located; hence the apparent opposition between the will of man and the Will of God. As the Will of God is the center from which force radiates, passing in turn through every plane of consciousness, this apparent opposition will disappear when the personality, or fifth principle, of man shall be sufficiently developed to obtain full control over the forces which have thrown into objectivity his lower principles, and which have resulted in the anomaly of the double vortex,—an anomaly because its center resides in the fourth, or illusory, principle corresponding to the fourth, or mayavic, stage of the Divine Idea concerning him.

"Our investigations have therefore led us to this point; that man, as he is at present constituted, is the resultant of two vortices manifesting dynamically on the plane of illusion, and proceeding originally from two separate streams of tendency, the one representing Divine Love, and the other, the Divine Wisdom, which, meeting on the plane of human consciousness, coalesce into an objective personality, imperfect as a reflexion of the Divine Personality, inasmuch as its centre is located in maya [illusion]. This imperfection is due to a disturbance of the medium through which it manifests and is the temporary result of the impact of the two vortices, as the reflexion of a light in water is duplicated when the surface is disturbed..." (pgs. 140-142)

"Let us first consider what is called the 'torsion of impact,' or the effect produced when two vortices meet whose axes impinge at an angle. If the medium of the two be of equal density, and their velocity be also equal, they coalesce and form a parabolic figure, but if their velocity be not equal, they form two conical spheroids revolving in opposite directions, corresponding to the figure of 8 which we have selected as the symbol of man's evolution. This, it will be seen, meets the conditions involved, for it will be remembered that the ascending Dhyanis [ascending hierarchy] of the former period complete their evolution, in this cosmic manvantara [306,720,000 year cycle, according to Hindu cosmology], under the law of acceleration, whereas the Dhyanis [descending hierarchy] who manifest as the Powers of Light are on the *descending* arc of their cycle, and are subject to the law of retardation. Accordingly, the vortices which respectively represent their activities are of unequal velocity..." (pgs. 119-120)

"...We see, therefore, that it was Love which drove man from Paradise to the earth, and called into existence free-will by attaching his fourth principle, or body of desire, to the earth by a bond sufficiently strong to balance the centrifugal impetus. Up to the time when he began to develop intelligence, the action of man's will had been purely automatic, the plane of its energies, so to speak, coinciding with the axis of the original vortex. But in the newly-objectivised double vortex, the lower nature required to be consolidated in order to preserve it from absorption into the Eighth Sphere. Free-will in man may therefore be defined as the point of equilibrium between his fifth, or intellectual principle, and his fourth, or body of desire. Man thus became a responsible being with faculties capable of adapting themselves to the law of Love which called him into existence. He is the seed of the Divine Love fructifying in the womb of Maya the great Abyss, or the *Illusion of the Is-not* made pregnant by the Divine Love. This is the Mystery of mysteries which no wisdom of the creature can ever fathom, but which was revealed (though 'as in a glass darkly') when the Word became Flesh and dwelt among us. He took on Himself a body that He might redeem our bodies by grafting them with His own in order that the Universe might become the perfect expression of the Divine Love…

"In bringing this course of lectures to an end I may say that it has been my endeavour to supply materials whereby the true gnosis may be distinguished from the 'oppositions of science falsely so called.' The agnosticism which is the characteristic of modern thought is an indication that the times are ripe for imparting truths which, twenty years ago, would have been as seed falling on the wayside. The remedy for evils which spring from ignorance is knowledge, but until the ignorance is confessed, the remedy cannot be applied. So long as men were satisfied with mechanical authority in religion; so long as it was considered scientific to call the unknown the Unknowable; in other words, while men preferred darkness to light nothing could be done. But we have lately witnessed a reaction from agnosticism and a revival of gnosticism in one of its most dangerous forms. It is, therefore, of the highest importance that we should learn to distinguish the truths to which it bears witness from the falsehoods with which they have been artfully blended." (pgs. 160-163)

Modern scientific research focuses on heart vortices and have discovered that health and illness are directly connected to the proper interaction of heart vortices and axial deviation. Makato Amaki tells us in *Vortex Formation in Decompensated Heart Failure,* about these mysterious rings of frequencies:

> "What are vortices and why do they form? The cardiovascular system's dynamic contours create time-varying and spatially complex patterns of blood flow. Flow coming in from different directions is melded into a compact, nonturbulent mass of fluid and channeled towards preferential flow lines, often in the form of vortices, ring-shaped regions of rotating blood flow. Mitral leaflets and the trabeculated endocardium further modulate the flow, facilitating continuous asymmetric redirection of blood flow to the outflow tract.
>
> "Vortices have different formation time, size, shape, strength, depth, and direction depending on the time of the cardiac cycle, as well as valve and chamber geometry. Which characteristic of the vortex is most important is not clear, but a tightly compact, persistent ring seems to provide the best flow propagation. Interestingly, vortex properties depend on chamber function, but vortices also modulate diastolic LV wall lengthening and recoil. Vortex characteristics may thus be a signature of myocardial health and disease.
>
> "A distinguishing feature of cardiac blood flow is the presence of vortices, which are ring-shaped regions of rotating flow motion. Vortices are well-known entities in fluid dynamics, characterized by instability that can markedly influence mechanical function. More than 500 years ago, Leonardo da Vinci introduced the concept of circular flow formation in the sinus of Valsalva. Such a fluid structure that possesses circular or swirling motion is defined as a vortex. Vortices are considered as reservoirs of kinetic energy. In vitro

experiments have demonstrated that fluid transport can be laminar, vortical or turbulent. Within these patterns, vortex ring formation is the most efficient for periodic changes in the direction of the flow.

"Vortices, whether in tubes, aquatic motion, or nature, seem to transport fluid more efficiently than in a straight jet by providing a compact hydrodynamic channel. Vortices help multidirectional streams of blood merge without collision and energy loss. Their ability to add volume to the LV without a significant increase in pressure benefits chamber compliance.

"Vortices have been exhaustively studied in the field of fluid dynamics, and they possess many remarkable qualities. An extremely energy-efficient platform for transport of fluids, they allow the seamless merging of multiple streams without energy loss. Changes in direction of flow are achieved with similar conservation of power while creating compact zones of flow with uniform directionality and tremendous velocity. The characteristics of vortices have powerful applications in the context of cardiac structure and function.

"The most intriguing advantages of vortex formation may be to couple flow, stretch, and cellular response. Fluid forces and vortices are epigenetic modulators in the development of cardiac chambers and valve geometry, and vortices may help distribute flow-related stress loads.

"Blood motion in the heart features vortices that accompany the redirection of jet flows towards the outlet tracks. Vortices have a crucial role in fluid dynamics. The stability of cardiac vorticity is vital to the dynamic balance between rotating blood and myocardial tissue and to the development of cardiac dysfunction. Vortex dynamics immediately reflect physiological changes to the surrounding system and can provide early indications of long-term outcome. The evaluation of blood flow presents a new paradigm in cardiac function analysis, with the potential for sensitive risk identification of cardiac abnormalities.

"The pattern of flow in the human heart changes dramatically during one cardiac cycle. However, flow is redirected within the cardiac chambers through vortex formation, which avoids excessive dissipation of energy and facilitates the efficient passage of blood. Visualizing multi-directional flow using echocardiographic techniques may open up new possibilities in assessing cardiac blood transport efficiency in health and disease."

The Electrical Axis of the Heart

New research has discovered the importance of the heart axis for optimal health. The axis of the human heart changes over time and eventually mimics the axis of the Earth in relation to the Sun. The electrical axis of the human heart is the net direction in which the wave of depolarization travels. It is measured using an electrocardiogram (ECG). Normally, this begins at the atrioventricular node (AV node); from here the wave of depolarization travels down to the apex of the heart. Anthony H. Kashou tells us:

> "One of the key steps in interpreting an electrocardiogram (EKG) is determining the electrical axis of the heart. Being able to determine the electrical axis can give insight into underlying disease states and help steer the differential diagnosis towards or away from certain diagnoses.
>
> "The axis of the ECG is the major direction of the overall electrical activity of the heart. It can be normal, leftward (left axis deviation, or LAD), rightward (right axis deviation, or RAD) or indeterminate (northwest axis). The sum of all the individual vectors generated by the depolarization waves makes up the electrical axis. Because each myocyte can produce an action potential, an axis for each wave and interval

of the cardiac cycle can be determined. Knowing the axis of each and how they interact can reflect certain pathology.

"When the electrical axis is discussed and taught, the ventricular axis is typically used in common clinical practice, although the atrial axis can be quite useful in clinical situations. Since the left ventricle makes up most of the heart muscle under normal circumstances, it generates the most electrical force visible on the EKG. The normal ventricular axis is thus directed downward and slightly towards the left.

"There is some disagreement on the exact degrees that define each type of electrical axis, but there are some general cutoffs that can be used for the Ventricular (QRS) Axis. The QRS axis moves leftward throughout childhood and adolescence and into adulthood. At birth, the normal QRS axis lies between +30 degrees and +190 degrees. Between the ages of 8 to 16 years, the axis moves leftward with normal lying between 0° degrees to +120 degrees. The normal adult QRS axis is between -30 degrees and +90 degrees, which is directed downward and to the left. This adult range is sometimes extended from -30 degrees to +100 degrees.

"Determining the electrical axis on an electrocardiogram can help narrow the differential diagnosis and lead to an efficient diagnostic approach for the patient. This will help decrease the time needed to arrive at the right diagnosis and improve patient outcomes. An interprofessional team of clinicians, nurses, and technicians trained in the interpretation of an EKG is needed to achieve this goal. Documenting the approximate degree itself of the axis is the bottom line to study the association with the levels of various possible risk factors."

Axis Deviation:

If the electrical axis falls between the values of -30° to +90° this is considered normal.

If the electrical axis is between -30° to -90° this is considered left axis deviation (LAD).

If the electrical axis is between +90° to +180° this is considered Right Axis Deviation RAD). RAD is associated with: Fascicular block, Lateral myocardial infarction, right ventricular hypertrophy, Pre-excitation syndromes, Ventricular tachycardia. Ventricular Ectopy and LAD is associated with: Wolff-Parkinson-White syndrome, ostium primum atrial septal defect, glucose intolerance, atherosclerosis, fibro-degeneration, diabetes, Chagas disease.

The Ideal Heart Axis

The axis of the heart is critical in heart health, and it begins in the womb. In one study, cardiac position and axis were evaluated by ultrasound in 183 normal fetuses; both position and axis were found to be constant throughout gestational life. In the four-chamber view of the fetal heart, the normal axis lies at a 45-degree angle (range 22-75 degrees) to the left of an anteroposterior line drawn from the spine to the anterior chest wall. The normal position of the posterior portion of the heart can also be defined. The axis or position of the heart deviated from the established normal range in 15 cases. Abnormal axis was associated with 50% mortality: abnormal position with 81% mortality. Deviation from the normal position of the fetal heart should initiate a search for an intrathoracic mass, whereas an abnormal axis is an indication for fetal echocardiography. Axis and position of the fetal heart are easily evaluated during a standard obstetric scan and can be a useful tool to determine heart health. Thus, the axis of the heart is a key determining factor for heart health, as well as overall health.

The Heart Sac—'Fifth Chamber' of the Heart

In Anthroposophy, much is made of the nature of the 'fifth chamber' of the heart. This secret has been kept since ancient times but now is the focus of the next step in understanding the true nature of the human heart in its future development. It is our belief that the pericardium, the 'sac' around the heart is indeed this fifth chamber that holds the secrets of proper heart evolution.

University of Calgary researchers were the first to discover a previously unidentified cell population in the pericardial fluid found inside the sac around the heart. The discovery could lead to new treatments for patients with injured hearts. Researchers found that a specific cell, a Gata6+ pericardial cavity macrophage, helps heal an injured heart. The cell was discovered in the pericardial fluid within the human pericardium of people with injured hearts, confirming that the repair cells offer the promise of a new therapy for patients with heart disease.

Heart doctors had never before explored the possibility that cells just outside the heart could participate in healing and repair of hearts after injury. Unlike other organs, the heart generally has a limited capacity to repair itself which is why heart disease is the number one cause of death in North America.

This discovery will open the door to new therapies and hope for the millions of people who suffer from heart disease. Doctors now know that pericardial fluid is rich with healing cells. These cells may hold the secret to repair and regeneration of new heart muscle.

The pericardium (pericardial sac) is a double-walled sac containing the heart and the roots of the great vessels. The pericardial sac has two layers, a serous layer, and a fibrous layer. It encloses the pericardial cavity which contains pericardial fluid. The pericardium fixes the heart to the mediastinum, gives protection against infection, and provides lubrication for the heart.

The pericardium has a tough double layered fibroelastic sac which covers the heart. The space between the two layers of serous pericardium, the pericardial cavity, is filled with serous fluid which protects the heart from any kind of external jerk or shock. There are two layers to the pericardial sac: the outermost fibrous pericardium and the inner serous pericardium. The fibrous pericardium is the most superficial layer of the pericardium. It is made up of dense and loose connective tissue which acts to protect the heart, anchoring it to the surrounding walls and preventing it from overfilling with blood.

The serous pericardium, in turn, is divided into two layers, the parietal pericardium, which is fused to and inseparable from the fibrous pericardium, and the visceral pericardium, which is part of, or in some textbooks synonymous with, the epicardium. Both of these layers function in lubricating the heart to prevent friction during heart activity.

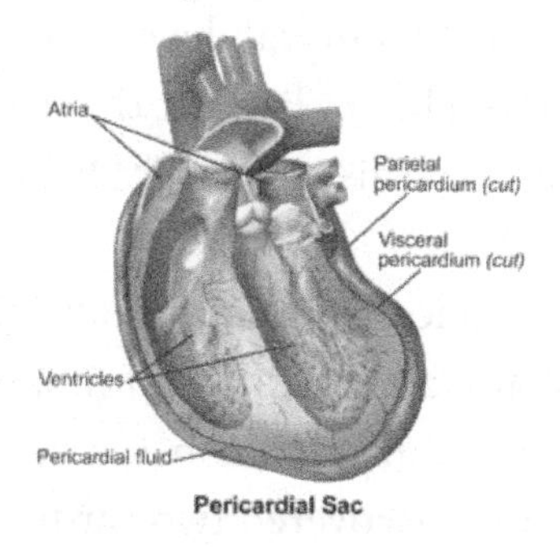

Pericardial Sac

When the visceral layer of serous pericardium comes into contact with the heart it is known as the epicardium. The epicardium is the layer immediately outside of the heart muscle proper. The epicardium is largely made of connective tissue and functions as a protective layer. During ventricular contraction, the wave of depolarization moves from the endocardial to the epicardial surface. The pericardial sac also:

- Sets the heart in the mediastinum and limits its motion,
- Protects it from infections coming from other organs,
- Prevents excessive dilation of the heart in cases of acute volume overload, and
- Lubricates the heart.

Auricles of the Atria—'6th & 7th Chambers of the Heart'

In the future, the sixth and seventh chambers of the heart (auricles) will develop to take on a more central role in heart function. At this point, the auricles insinuate that the 'capacity' of the heart can be expanded when necessary. The auricles have been generally ignored by science and their place in heart function is little understood. We believe that the auricles are another part of the sensory mechanism of the heart that listens to (senses) venous and arterial blood and then can respond appropriately. The auricles are like wings on the heart, which is an image of the heart used by the ancients for millennia.

They are sometimes referred to as the 'ears' of the heart—as their name implies. Is it possible that moral development can expand the heart's capacity to become a better listener that can react to blood flow in an extraordinary fashion? This is a part of heart evolution yet to be understood or developed.

The first speculation concerning cardiac auricles were findings from Ancient Egyptian archaeological studies. It is believed that Diocles of Carystus (4th century BC) considered the role of the heart as a leader of the body and discovered two cardiac ears or auricles. He described the ability of the heart to listen and understand by these ears or auricles. He also attributed a sensory role to these appendages.

Herophilus of Alexandria (300 BC) and later Rufus of Ephesus (1st Century AD) were the first persons who described auricles and distinguished them from ventricles. This clarification was continued by Persian physicians in the Golden Age of Islam (9th-12th Century AD). During the Renaissance, William Harvey (1578-1657 AD), a British physician, noticed auricles and emphasized their function of contracting before the ventricles.

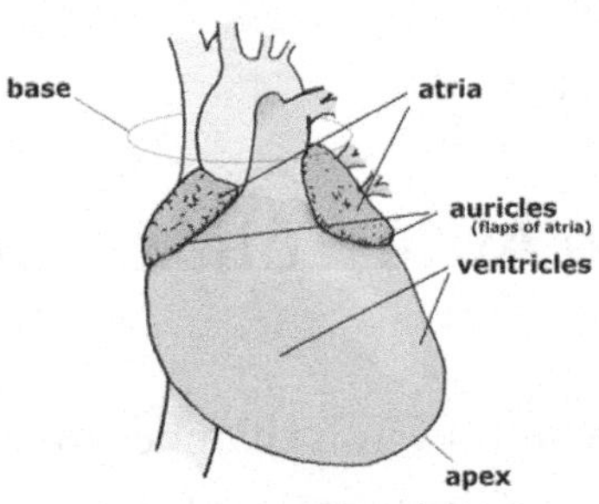

The Auricles of the Atria

In Egyptian sculptures, paintings, and writings the heart was the symbol of faith and courage. Ancient Egyptians used hieroglyphs for the heart with ear-shaped auricles in the symbols and paintings. They saw these ear-like parts of the heart, the auricles, but we do not know if they were aware of their role and function because we cannot find any mention of them in their texts or other written documents.

Today, in anatomy, auricles are known as part of the human heart which is roughly cube-shaped except for these ear-shaped projections. Auricles are pectinate tubular muscle walls that are positioned at the root of the pulmonary vein on the left and externally overlap the ascending aorta, on the right. But the true role of the auricles is still little understood today and their role in the future is not understood at all.

The Vagus Nerve

Rudolf Steiner spoke many times about what he called, 'the frontal spinal column' in contradistinction to the regular spinal column which is associated with the standard chakras of the Hindu/Buddhist system of spiritual development. This frontal spinal column has often been misunderstood by spiritual scientists. The simple reality is that the vagus nerve accomplishes the exact tasks that Steiner attributes to the frontal spinal column. The front column is obviously the vagus nerve that gathers information from all the organs below the heart and gathers them together into the vagus nerve running through the human heart. Then, from the heart and through the throat and brow, the vagus nerve reaches up to the crown of the head and there interacts with the energy arising from the normal spinal column which bathes the pineal gland. The front and back spinal columns merge in the fourth ventricle of the midbrain and unite the ascending and descending columns into a cyclic flow of regenerating energy. Descriptions of these two columns are found throughout spiritual literature concerning ascension practices.

We will describe this phenomenon in the later parts of this book as the 'wish-fulfilling stone,' or the 'cintamani' tree, or the 'jewel in the heart of the lotus.' The front column is well-known as a ruyi stone, which is generally pictured as a specter-like device with multiple stones that represent the heart, throat, brow, and crown chakras. The ruyi stone is a common ritual scepter used by Tibetan Buddhist monks in their daily practices. Speculation runs wild when Westerners try to define or understand this vajra tool. Much more is known about the regular spinal column which is connected to the major chakras. But it is clear to the initiated that the ruyi is a 'spiritual tree' for 'bringing down the heavenly dew' that nourishes the nerves and circulatory systems of the human body.

Let's examine what science tells us about this ruyi stone—or the vagus nerve. The vagus nerve, also called the tenth cranial nerve, starts in the brain and runs down the trunk of the body, with branches innervating the major organs. A major component of the autonomic nervous system, it interfaces with the parasympathetic nervous system and helps to regulate the heart, lungs, and the digestive system. It is a bi-directional nerve, meaning it both sends signals from the brain to the organs and the organs send messages back to the brain. The vagus nerve runs from gut to brain directly through the sinoatrial node, the pacemaker of the heart.

The vagus nerve is an important sensor and regulator of basic functions including breathing, heart rate, the relaxation response, the gut-brain connection, and the formation of memories. The motor vagus nerve normally holds inhibitory influence over both systemic inflammation and some autonomic functions such as heart rate. It exerts stimulatory effects on gastric motility, detrusor contraction, pupillary activity, salivatory secretion, and tear secretion and it is also involved in pancreatic exocrine function.

The vagus nerve is a bi-directional nerve, so both the afferent (sensory) and efferent (motor) branches have important functions: afferent pathways mediate anti-inflammatory responses and the release of corticosteroids from the adrenal glands, whereas efferent pathways mediate anti-inflammatory processes via direct effects on immune cells or through the splenic sympathetic nerve. The vagus nerve is important for maintaining homeostasis and preventing an over-reactive immune response. It can send a signal into the brainstem that triggers both glial cell activation within the central nervous system as well as the general innate immune response, sometimes called the sickness response.

Vagal tone is a measure of the constitutive output of the motor branch of the vagus nerve. The vagus nerve is responsible for the autonomic changes that allow us to go from lying down to standing up without fainting. With a loss of vagal tone, both the anti-inflammatory pathway and parasympathetic inhibition over autonomic systems are diminished.

The vagus nerve is so named because it 'wanders' like a vagabond, sending out sensory fibers from your brainstem to your visceral organs. It is the longest of the cranial nerves and it controls your inner nerve center—the parasympathetic nervous system. It oversees a vast range of crucial functions, communicating motor and sensory impulses to every organ in your body.

The neurotransmitter acetylcholine, elicited by the vagus nerve, tells your lungs to breathe. You can stimulate your vagus nerve by doing abdominal breathing or other breath exercises. The vagus nerve is responsible for controlling the heart rate via electrical impulses to specialized muscle tissue—the heart's natural pacemaker—in the sinoatrial node, where acetylcholine release slows the pulse.

Your gut uses the vagus nerve to tell your brain how you're feeling via electric impulses called 'action potentials.' Your gut feelings are carried to the heart and then to the brain. Vagal syncope is when your body, responding to stress, overstimulates the vagus nerve causing your blood pressure and heart rate to drop. During extreme syncope, blood flow is restricted to your brain, and you lose consciousness and faint. Thus, the importance of the vagus nerve cannot be over-emphasized, and it does all that the ancients said the frontal spinal column accomplishes.

Heart Rate Variability

The importance of heart rate variability cannot be overestimated because it is a clear indicator of heart health and longevity. One can even buy a device that measures heart rate variability that will fairly accurately assess the entire health of the body and make predictions about the length of life and the likely organ or systems that will break down first and lead to death. This amazing discovery is eerily accurate and is the first of its kind to 'predict' the health outcomes of the person being assessed.

Heart rate variability is a measure of the variation in the time between each heartbeat controlled by the autonomic nervous system. It works regardless of our desire and regulates, among other things, our heart rate, blood pressure, breathing, and digestion. Heart rate variability is a non-invasive way to identify autonomic nervous system imbalances. If a person's system is in more of a fight-or-flight mode, the variation between subsequent heartbeats is low. If one is in a more relaxed state, the variation between beats is high. In other words, the healthier the autonomic nervous system, the faster you are able to switch gears, showing more resilience and flexibility. Research has shown a relationship between low heart rate variability and depression or anxiety. A low heart rate variability is associated with an increased risk of death and cardiovascular disease.

People who have a high heart rate variability tend to have greater cardiovascular fitness and are, more resilient to stress. Heart rate variability can provide personal feedback about your lifestyle and help motivate steps toward a healthier life. Heart rate variability changes as you incorporate more mindfulness, meditation, sleep, and especially physical activity into your life. It can track how your nervous system is reacting, not only to the environment, but also to your emotions, thoughts, and feelings.

To determine your heart rate variability you analyze an electrocardiogram or use apps and heart rate monitors that do something similar and download a free app to analyze the data.

Other methods used to detect heart rate variability include blood pressure, ballistocardiograms, and the pulse wave signal derived from a photoplethysmograph.

Reduced heart rate variability has been shown to be a predictor of mortality after myocardial infarction. A range of other outcomes and conditions may also be associated with modified (usually lower) heart rate variability, including congestive heart failure, diabetic neuropathy, post cardiac-transplant depression, susceptibility to Sudden Infant Death Syndrome, and poor survival in premature babies.

Heart rate variability is the measure of the inconsistent gaps between each heartbeat and is used as an index for different aspects of psychology. It is reported to be an index of the influence of both the parasympathetic nervous system and the sympathetic nervous systems. Different aspects of psychology represent the balance of these two influences. For example, high heart rate variability is shown by proper emotion regulation, decision-making, and attention, and low heart rate variability reflects the opposite. The parasympathetic nervous system works quickly to decrease heart rate, while the sympathetic nervous system works slowly to increase heart rate. Heart rate variability has provided a window to the physiological components associated with our emotional regulation.

It has been suggested that increased attention has been linked to high heart rate variability and increased vagus nerve activity. The vagus nerve activity reflects the physiological modulation of the parasympathetic and sympathetic nervous system.

A reduction of heart rate variability has been reported in several cardiovascular and non-cardiovascular diseases, such as: Myocardial infarction, Diabetic neuropathy, Cardiac transplantation, Myocardial dysfunction, Liver cirrhosis, Sepsis, Sudden cardiac death, and Cancer.

Frequency Rate of the Human Heart

Much is made of the measure of heart vibrations and frequencies. The ancients believed that the heart had a standard frequency that could be stimulated for enhancing health and longevity. There is much debate about which frequency is the ideal and what techniques and mechanisms can 'tune' the heart to the cosmic frequency of the Schumann Wave, the cosmic frequency of the revolving Earth. Tibetan bowls are tuned to the individual chakras and claim to create the proper resonance and coherence for the development of human consciousness.

The resting heart rate of a normal adult is between 60-100 beats per minute, depending on age and fitness level. This is calculated upon the heartbeat frequency (Heart Rate Per Minute /60). That translates to 1-1.67 beat(s) per second, or 1-1.67 Hz, based solely upon the frequency of the human beat. If you are talking about the electrical signals that cause the human heart to beat, the P and T wave frequency generally ranges between 0.5 and 10 Hz and QRS complex frequency between 4 and 20 Hz. If you are talking about the heart sound frequency, it is generally between 20 to 500 Hz. During sleep, the ideal breath to heartbeat rate is 1:4.

The Heart's 'Pacemaker'—Sinoatrial Node

Ancient Hindu philosophy refers to a 'thumb of fire' within the heart that is the spiritual flame of the individual. This flame is created through the interaction resulting from the lungs bringing oxygen (fire) to the heart. It is this flame that constitutes the 'seat of consciousness,' or the mind of the individual. It is said that this flame is the cause of the heartbeat and is a replication of the Cosmic Fire found throughout the Cosmos. Modern science has theories about the sinoatrial node causing this flame through the interaction of sodium and potassium interacting on the surface of this node. A full examination of the sinoatrial node will not satisfy the questions about where and how the warmth (fire) of the heart is created. A more thorough and comprehensive theory is needed to truly understand the warmth in the blood and the heart and lung's participation in creating this warmth.

The human heart beats more than 3.5 billion times in an average lifetime. The heartbeat of a human embryo begins at approximately 21 days after conception, or five weeks after the last normal menstrual period, which is the date normally used to date pregnancy in the medical community. The electrical depolarizations that trigger cardiac myocytes to contract arise spontaneously within the myocyte itself. The heartbeat is initiated in the pacemaker regions and spreads to the rest of the heart through a conduction pathway. Pacemaker cells develop in the primitive atrium and the sinus venosus to form the sinoatrial node and the atrioventricular node respectively. Conductive cells develop the bundle of His and carry the depolarization into the lower heart.

The human heart begins beating at a rate near the mother's, about 75-80 beats per minute (bpm). The embryonic heart rate then accelerates linearly for the first month of beating, peaking at 165-185 bpm during the early 7th week. After peaking at about 9.2 weeks, it decelerates to about 150 bpm (+/- 25 bpm) during the 15th week. After the 15th week the deceleration slows reaching an average rate of about 145 (+/ -25 bpm) bpm at term.

The vagus nerve, historically cited as the pneumogastric nerve, is the tenth cranial nerve, and interfaces with the parasympathetic control of the heart, lungs, and digestive tract. The vagus nerves are normally referred to in the singular. It is the longest nerve of the autonomic nervous system in the human body.

Parasympathetic innervation of the heart is partially controlled by the vagus nerve and is shared by the thoracic ganglia. Vagal and spinal ganglionic nerves mediate the lowering of the heart rate. The right vagus branch innervates the sinoatrial node. In healthy people, parasympathetic tone from these sources are well-matched to sympathetic tone. Hyperstimulation of parasympathetic influence promotes arrhythmias. When hyper-stimulated, the left vagal branch predisposes the heart to conduction block at the atrioventricular node.

The sinoatrial node is a group of cells located in the wall of the right atrium of the heart. These cells have the ability to spontaneously produce an electrical impulse (action potential), that travels through the heart via the electrical conduction system causing it to contract. In a healthy heart, the sinoatrial node continuously produces action potential, setting the rhythm of the heart and so is known as the heart's natural pacemaker. The rate of action potential production (and therefore the heart rate) is influenced by nerves that supply it.

The electrical conduction system of the heart transmits signals generated usually by the sinoatrial node to cause contraction of the heart muscle. The pace-making signal generated in the sinoatrial node travels through the right atrium to the atrioventricular node, along the Bundle of His and through bundle branches to cause contraction of the heart muscle. This signal stimulates contraction first of the right and left atrium, and then the right and left ventricles. This process allows blood to be moved throughout the body.

In order to maximize efficiency of contractions and cardiac output, the conduction system of the heart has: 1) Substantial atrial to ventricular delay. This will allow the atria to completely empty their contents into the ventricles; simultaneous contraction would cause inefficient filling and backflow. The atria are electrically isolated from the ventricles, connected only via the atrioventricular node which briefly delays the signal. 2) Coordinated contraction of ventricular cells. The ventricles must maximize systolic pressure to force blood through the circulation, so all the ventricular cells must work together.

Ventricular contraction begins at the apex of the heart, progressing upwards to eject blood into the great arteries. Contraction that squeezes blood towards the exit is more efficient than a simple squeeze from all directions. Although the ventricular stimulus originates from the sinoatrial node in the wall separating the atria and ventricles, the Bundle of His conducts the signal to the apex. Depolarization propagates through cardiac muscle very rapidly. Cells of the ventricles contract nearly simultaneously.

The action potentials of cardiac muscle are unusually sustained. This prevents premature relaxation, maintaining initial contraction until the entire myocardium has had time to depolarize and contract.

After contracting, the heart must relax to fill up again. Sustained contraction of the heart without relaxation would be fatal, and this is prevented by a temporary inactivation of certain ion channels.

The paired cardiac centers located in the medulla oblongata of the brain innervate the heart via sympathetic cardiac nerves that increase cardiac activity and vagus nerves that slow cardiac activity. Calcium ion levels have a great impact on heart rate and contractility: increased calcium levels cause an increase in both. High levels of calcium ions result in hypercalcemia and excessive levels can induce cardiac arrest. Drugs known as calcium channel blockers slow heart rate by binding to these channels and blocking or slowing the inward movement of calcium ions.

The Anatomical 'Box Around the Heart'

The most ancient stories of the Tibetans tell of a fiery box that fell from Heaven to Earth bringing down the first treasures of their religion. Four objects were contained in this box that became the foundation of their beliefs. This box contained the begging bowl of Buddha, the cintamani stone (the 'jewel in the heart of the lotus'), a book of wisdom, and the original design of the first stupa (temple). Until recently, few understood that this box is a reference to human anatomy that is often overlooked. Around the heart is a series of organs that enclose it like a box and indicate that the ancients were onto a profound secret of the human heart that we now call the mediastinum.

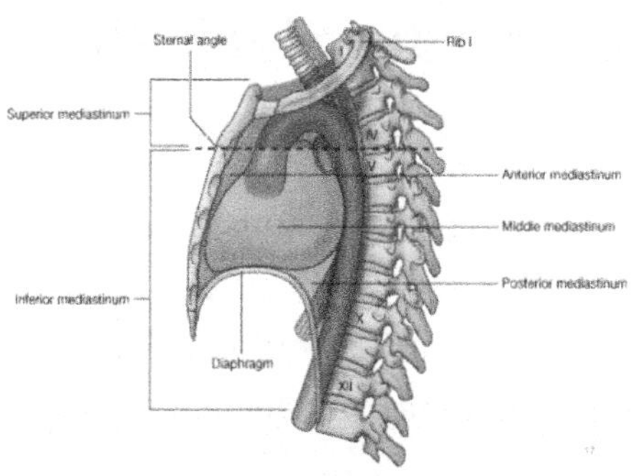

The 'Box' Around the Heart

This 'cube' around the heart is the current 'shape' of the heart container with its six sides defined by the directions of up/down, right/left, and forward/backward. In the future, this cube will evolve into a dodecahedron which has twelve sides that align with the twelve divisions of the Zodiac. From the current shape of the cube to the future shape of the dodecahedron, we find the morphological path that the heart will follow in its development. This sacred shape, inscribed by the cube, is the inviolable home of the human mind that is referred to as the 'jewel in the heart of the lotus,' or the 'cintamani stone.' It is the 'rock' that human consciousness is built upon, the cornerstone of the holy of holies in the heart-of-hearts.

The mediastinum lies within the thorax and is surrounded by the chest wall in front, the lungs to the sides and the spine at the back, essentially creating a 'box' around the heart. It extends from the sternum in front to the vertebral column behind and contains all the organs of the thorax except the lungs.

The four directions of the heart are: above/below (up-down), front/back (forward-behind), and the chambers of the heart representing left/right working with the lungs. Thus, the heart is surrounded by a virtual 'cube' that is indicated in the 'box' of the mediastinum's component parts listed below: 1) superior mediastinum - above the pericardium 2) inferior/middle mediastinum - holds the pericardium from below 3) anterior mediastinum - in front of the pericardium 4) posterior mediastinum - behind the pericardium.

The Four Parts of the Mediastinum

In GA 205 (July 2, 1921) Rudolf Steiner says:

> "You can imagine what a tremendous difference there is, between that which lives in our heart during this incarnation and the condition in which we find ourselves in a new life after having gone through a long development in the time

between death and a new birth. And yet when you look into your innermost heart you can assess quite well, of course in a hidden way only, not in a fully developed imagination, what you will do in your next life. One can, you see, not only say in an abstract way, my next life is being prepared today in all karmic detail, but one can point to the 'little box' in which the karma rests, awaiting the future."

Blood Types

While everyone's blood is made up of the same basic parts, there is a lot of variety in the kinds of blood that exist. There are eight different blood types, and the type you have is determined by genes you inherit from your parents. What makes your blood different from someone else's is your unique combination of protein molecules, called antigens and antibodies. Antigens live on the surface of your red blood cells. Antibodies are in your plasma. The combination of antigens and antibodies in your blood is the basis of your blood type.

Blood typing is particularly important for blood transfusions because certain antigens on blood cells can trigger a person's immune system to attack the donated blood. People who are Rh-negative can only receive Rh-negative blood, but people who are Rh- positive can receive either Rh-positive or Rh-negative blood.

What's more, type A blood can be used for transfusions for patients with type A or type AB blood; type B blood can be used for patients with type B or type AB blood; and type AB blood can be used for patients with type AB blood. People with type O blood are called 'universal donors' because this type can be used for patients with any blood type.

Type O blood is often in short supply in hospitals, due to demand for this universal donor type. In particular, type O-negative blood is in high demand because it's the one most often used for emergencies, when there may not be time to determine a patient's blood type.

Here are some general heart facts:

- Most people have about 4-6 liters of blood.
- Your blood is made up of different kinds of cells that float in a fluid called plasma.
- Your red blood cells deliver oxygen to the various tissues in your body and remove carbon dioxide.
- Your white blood cells destroy invaders and fight infection.
- Your platelets help your blood to clot.
- Your plasma is a fluid made up of proteins and salts.

There are four major blood groups and eight different blood types called the ABO Blood Group System. The groups are based on whether or not you have two specific antigens—A and B:

- Group A has the A antigen and B antibody.
- Group B has the B antigen and the A antibody.
- Group AB has A and B antigens but neither A nor B antibodies.
- Group O doesn't have A or B antigens but has both A and B antibodies.

In general, the rarest blood type is AB-negative and the most common is O-positive. There's also a third kind of antigen called the Rh factor. You either have this antigen (meaning your blood type is 'Rh+' or 'positive'), or you don't (meaning your blood type is 'Rh-' or 'negative'). So, from the four blood groups, there are eight blood types:

- A positive or A negative
- B positive or B negative
- AB positive or AB negative
- O positive or O negative

Blood Types and Nutrition

Peter J. D'Adamo, N.D. does a marvelous job of aligning blood type with nutritional needs and lifestyle in his book, *Eat Right 4 Your Type.* We have extracted a summary of his insight in the selection below.

Blood type, with its digestive and immune specificity, is a window on a person's probable susceptibility to or power over disease. For example, Type O's are the most likely to suffer from asthma, hay fever, and other allergies, while Type B's have a high allergy threshold, and will react allergically only if they eat the wrong foods. Type B's are also especially susceptible to autoimmune disorders, such as chronic fatigue, lupus, and multiple sclerosis. Type AB's tend to have the fewest problems with allergies, while heart disease, cancer, and anemia are medical risks for them.

With arthritis, Type O's, again, are the predominant sufferers because their immune systems are 'environmentally intolerant,' especially to foods such as grains and potatoes which can produce inflammatory reactions in their joints. Types A and B are the most susceptible to diabetes, while types A and AB have an overall higher rate of cancer and poorer survival odds than the other types.

Type O—People with type O blood fare best on intense physical exercise and animal proteins and less well on dairy products and grains. The leading reason for weight gain among Type O's is the gluten found in wheat products and, to a lesser extent, lentils, corn, kidney beans, and cabbage. Ideal exercises for Type O's include aerobics, martial arts, contact sports, and running.

Type A—Those with blood type A, however, are more naturally suited to a vegetarian diet and foods that are fresh, pure, and organic. As Type A's are predisposed to heart disease, cancer, and diabetes. Type A's can derive significant benefit from calming, centering exercise, such as yoga and tai chi.

Type B—Type B's have a robust immune system and a tolerant digestive system and tend to resist many of the severe chronic degenerative illnesses, or at least survive them better than the other blood types. Type B's do best with moderate physical exercise requiring mental balance, such as hiking, cycling, tennis, and swimming.

Type AB—Blood type AB, the most recent, in terms of evolution, of the four groups and an amalgam of types A and B, is the most biologically complex. For this group, a combination of the exercises for types A and B works best.

Three Fields of Force

To study the heart, one must also study the heart chakra and its nature. Modern science has yet to fully embrace these teachings of the ancients, though research continually affirms the axioms of ancient spiritual wisdom. Tyla Gabriel N.D. has done an excellent job of merging modern science and ancient wisdom in her trilogy entitled: *The Gospel of Sophia*, and specifically in Volume 2, *A Modern Path of Initiation*. Dr. Gabriel tells us: "The heart is an energy dynamo producing plasma-generated magneto-hydrodynamic force. Gratitude and love strengthen the field of force around the heart, while the opposite emotions deplete it."

We can find few better renditions of the path of ascension, which intimately involves the human heart and its moral development, than in *The Gospel of Sophia*. We quote at length from Volume 2 below.

The ancients have always taught that the human body has different foci of energy that need to be harmonized. They believed that the unfortunate person who cannot successfully link his three morphic fields of thinking (brain), feeling (heart), and willing (lower three chakras) is doomed to mental instability, unfulfilled feelings, and incoherent behaviors. Only through alignment of these three fields of force can the aspirant find the full potential of energy and nourishment that the human body can provide. A person in harmony with his environment can go even further, expanding his personal field of energy to encompass the entire Universe.

The fields of energy can be discussed in many ways, such as:

- Energy centers of bio-electromagnetic force
- Morally driven spiritual chakras

- Clusters of nerve ganglia
- Stages of initiation
- Stages of philosophical and intellectual development
- Religious symbols
- Bio-electromagnetic toroidal fields

The System of Chakras

Whatever terminology one uses to describe them, the head, heart, and lower chakras (metabolic system) create three separate worlds that must be integrated and coherent for successful spiritual development. All of the images, symbols, and technical explanations agree that for health, longevity, and evolution in physical, psychological and spiritual terms, the energy centers of the body should work together in harmony. Then, the earthly and cosmic nutrition streams can feed both the gods' and the aspirant's spiritual needs.

Heart Chakra

The heart is the organ that produces the most energy, as measured by an EKG. Its bio-electrical current is fifty times stronger than that of the brain, and it can be detected extending far from the body. The heart also demonstrates capacities that science calls the 'little brain of the heart.' Amazingly, it gathers information, communicates, and possesses its own intelligence. We now know that the heart has the power to modulate brain activity and optimize its functioning.

When the heart and brain are working together, this is called cardiac coherence. The brain and heart are synchronized, creating benefits in health, energy levels, and personal relationships. Emotions of the heart can trigger the release of hormones in the blood stream that produce powerful effects in the soul.

In the Vedas of Ancient India they have spoken of a little-known center called Ananda Kanda ('the root of bliss'), a 'sacred chamber' located just below the 12-petalled heart *chakra* 'Anahata' ('unstruck'; In the Vedic tradition, 'Anahata Nad' refers to the 'unstruck sound of the celestial realm'). It was said that once you connected to the flame burning on *Ananda Kanda*—the sacred altar of your heart—you would gain access to the *Kalpavriksha* the divine 'wish-fulfilling tree.'

This flame of the heart is the threefold flame or Trinity Flame. It starts from a white Mother flame and then burns as three flames. The flame in the middle is golden and represents wisdom. Once the wisdom flame has expanded, the human being knows that all the knowledge he ever needs converges on the heart and that the heart becomes his inner guru. The flame on the right side is blue and represents the masculine aspect of Divinity—God the Father or Shiva. The flame on the left is pink and represents the feminine aspect of God as Divine Mother. These three flames should be balanced and expanded for a personality to be centered. A person who is very powerful but not loving is thus unbalanced. So also, a very loving person whose pink flame is dominant but whose blue flame of power is weak, will turn out to be weak.

The ideal is to have the wisdom to express love in a powerful way. That is, the golden flame gives you the wisdom as to when to allow the nurturing feminine part of you to connect to others, and also when you need to allow the powerful masculine part of you to look out for the self's needs. Life is about balancing the threefold flame, thus balancing the masculine and feminine aspects (yin and yang) in ourselves. Once the flame is balanced, it spins and shines as a flame helping our evolution and creates a force-field that will help in attaining enlightenment, nirvana or ascension.

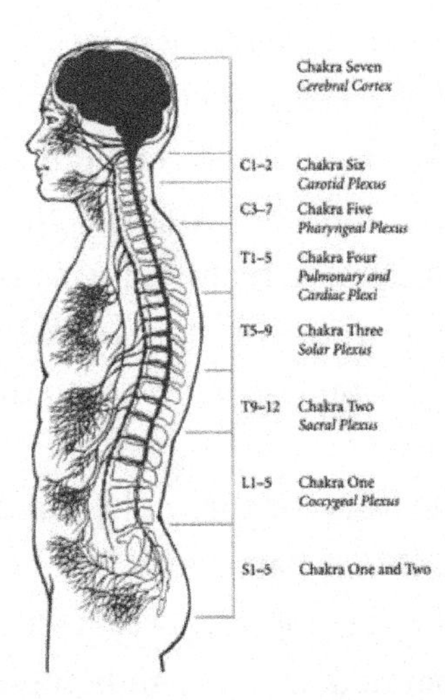

Western View of the Chakras as Nerve Centers

Once you connect to your heart flame and then visualize something you want to achieve, with great intent at your third eye, your desire will manifest soon. That is why they say that if you wish for something from the bottom of your heart, it will manifest soon. The spiritual heart is just below the heart chakra. This is the nature of the wish-fulfilling stone (tree).

Babaji says, “The heart center where God resides is everywhere but is manifest in different parts of the heart area in different individuals and you have to locate it intuitively or with the help of a guru. Once you locate this center and connect to it, you know that your inner guru or God has been there all along inside your heart. You only did not see him there because you were so caught up in Maya. The guru is the inner one who shows us that we have the Universe in us and all answers in us, and the outer guru is but a reflection of the inner God in all our hearts.”

Head Chakra

The torus field created by the head is well known. For a long time, it was thought to be the only generator of bio-electrical energy. The cluster of nerves in the brain was assumed to be the battery, computer, and wires for the human electrical system. These older views then evolved into theories of bioenergetics, where adenosine triphosphate transfer was considered the electrical function of most every cell. Together, the body as a whole produced bioenergy.

This type of bioenergetics is now known to cause far too little energy to drive the bio-electrical functions of the brain. The ancients have always known that in the human head great forces of earthly and spiritual energy are produced and a powerful bio-electromagnetic field emanates. The head also creates a plasma generator capable of producing a tremendous amount of electrostatic and bio-electromagnetic energy that extends a far distance from the body. Still, the human heart is more powerful than the brain, for it can override and entrain the brain to its own rhythms.

Lower Chakras—Metabolic System

The bio-electromagnetic fields generated in heart and head also connect with the foundational energies arising in the lower abdomen from the lower chakras: 1) Hara chakra, just below the naval; 2) Sex chakra, gonads or ovaries; 3) Foundation chakra, sacrum/tail bone.

In Kundalini yoga, it is believed that near the tip of the spine a fiery pit gives rise to the serpent power (kundalini). This energy travels up the spine through the six other chakras to the brow chakra, where a 'hooded serpent' is said to be located in the central spot—the 'third eye' on the forehead.

Often misunderstood, this lowest center of energy generation is attributed to the sex drive, as the Kundalini ('coiled serpent') a form of divine feminine energy (or Shakti) located near the base of the spine, in the muladhara chakra where it is said Kundalini as a fiery serpent lies coiled and ready to rise. In the West, this is often confused with the Hara center in the abdomen where Chi (Chinese) or Ki (Japanese) energy is created. In Tibetan Buddhism, the three lowest chakras are grouped together as one chakra with sixty-four petals. From this combined chakra, energy arises.

Just as a type of calcium can form in the pineal gland that causes a lack of energy or even death, so too in the lowest chakras the energy can be turned in the wrong direction to cause harm and destruction to the spiritual aspirant who uses it for personal gain. Misdirected foundational energy can lead to selfish expressions of the human ego. Sexual energy can turn the greatest human power into the grossest, and misdirected chi energy can digress into many forms of violence. If an aspirant has not learned to curb lower desires, then this center will not produce enough energy to fire the heart into 'cooking' sense impressions into spiritual insight, wisdom, and nourishment for the gods.

A Cup of Golden Light

As to how these three lower chakras work together; they represent the past stages of evolution. While, on the other hand, the wholesome modern paths of initiation begin with the development of the three chakras above the abdomen: brow (two-petalled), throat (sixteen-petalled) and heart (twelve-petalled). Working on these upper chakras develops the fiery moral forces of the lower chakras; which, in-turn, feed the fire in the heart so that it may begin to 'rarify' sense perceptions and the environmental elements that humans consume as nourishment. Once the heart has aligned its moral force with those of the throat, brow, and crown chakras, the spiritual world lights up the plasma generator in the brain and creates endless energy for all of the nerves, or chakras.

Here is how it works

Particle Stream. A continuous stream of heated etherized particles rises from the heart, through the throat chakra, the brow chakra, and then to the crown chakra. These particles feed the plasma generator in the head.

Refinement. Etherized particles of carbon, oxygen, nitrogen, hydrogen, calcium, and silica become ionized and rarified in a specialized breathing process that tempers them into more refined elements.

Brain Sand. The elements feed the pineal gland the material needed to transform calcium into calcium carbonate crystals, which are then deposited in the pineal gland as brain sand.

Piezoelectrical Potential. Once the calcium carbonate crystals of brain sand are available in the pineal gland, it may become highly charged with piezoelectrical potential.

Torus Field. In the region from the fourth ventricle of the brain, where the pineal is located, to the third ventricle, exists a space the ancients call the 'Grail,' or 'cup of golden light.' Filled with fluid, the third ventricle sits in the middle of the brain, surrounded by the lateral ventricles (first and second) above and around the limbic system. Bio-electromagnetic fields of energy from the brain stem surround it, creating a magnetic field required for a plasma generator.

Electrification. As the bio-electrical and magnetic potential of the pineal gland discharges through the middle of the third ventricle, and then onto the pituitary gland, a direct current electrifies the torus field in the head. The bio-electrical potential for this low-temperature plasma generator is sparked from the pineal gland's silica-based positive potential to the pituitary's calcium-based negative potential. The calcium carbonate crystals inside of the pineal, so to speak,'reach out' to connect with the calcium potential of the pituitary and a circuit is closed, creating the stream of electrostatic and bio-electromagnetic energy needed to drive this toroidal field of energy.

Golden Light. The ancients described this phenomenon as a spark of lightning jumping across the cup of golden light, thereby creating the nourishment of warmth, light, sound, and life—a type of Holy Grail.

Nerve Honey. Golden light feeds the nervous system via the posterior half of the pituitary through excretions called nerve honey, or heavenly dew (pituitary hormones). This heavenly dew was also called the waters of life, nerve fluid, manna, and the comforter. This super-charged golden light also feeds the front half of the pituitary, which then sends the heavenly dew into the blood stream, causing a harmonizing effect.

The ancients believed that the human head was the most perfect and finished aspect of the body and that great mysteries and secrets lie hidden in the brain. Nourishment from the brain is one aspect of the mechanism, while nourishment from the heart is another aspect. For the full potential of the human to shine forth, the two torus fields of heart and head must be harmonious and synchronized. This type of heart-mind matrix can bring the feeling of the heart into the brain—bathing the higher centers within the head with radiant heart warmth—which then nourishes the blood and nerves through the processes described above. The lower chakras work as the foundational elements for the higher and are instrumental to the process.

The challenge with the threefold system of energy created by the human is that it is easy to produce; but not as easy to synchronize and cohere, as it requires a proper mood-of-soul. The correct alignment and use of these three fields of forces constitutes a key factor in human spiritual evolution. The more consciousness we bring to the process, the more energy we can produce.

Plasma Generators in the Human Body

Modern technologies of energy production, called magneto-hydrodynamic generators, can provide a functional example of how the earthly and cosmic nutrition streams and the etherization of the blood occur within the human body, and, consequently in one's own spiritual development. Plasma generators are some of the most powerful direct current generators in use today. To produce direct current, the generators stream a heavy-metal impregnated gas/plasma (a conductor) across an open magnetic gap. In a closed system these generators will keep going, once started, and continue as long as the magnetic field holds, and the gas/plasma keeps passing over the gap in the magnetic field.

Magneto-hydrodynamic (MHD) generators are capable of transforming thermal energy and kinetic energy directly into electricity. Likewise, the magnetic energy of larger systems, such as the Earth and Sun, are said to be generated in a similar fashion.

The circulation of the blood throughout the body by the beating heart produces enough kinetic energy to establish a field of magnetic force in and around the heart and torso. As the blood stream passes through the heat of the lung/blood exchange, the presence of iron and other metals establishes the metallic fluid necessary to create this MHD dynamo. Blood also acts like a gas.

Near the heart is a flame about the size of a human thumb. Like a small furnace stoked by the breathing process. The little flame arises from the interaction of the lung passing the warmth of oxygen to the heart. When the heat from the lungs creates this flame between the lung and heart, the metal-laden gas of the blood flows through this gap. Here, direct electrical current is established. Both electrostatic and electromagnetic forces create a torus of energy in a coherent field of bio-electromagnetic energy.

The energy created by this human MHD generator is far beyond the previous attempts to explain bioenergetics as a simple transfer of cellular energy. The human heart creates a field of magnetism that extends up to fifteen feet. This energy field is basically the center of three fields of force: one in the heart, one in the brain, and one that extends from the combined three lower chakras.

These centers of energy production in the brain, heart, and lower abdomen relate to soul capacities that also find their centers of activity in these three areas. Thinking finds its home in the brain, feeling in the heart, and willing in the three lowest chakras.

It only takes modern science to examine the three centers of vital forces (thinking, feeling, and willing) to reveal a wealth of information about the resonant fields of morphic energy that are created by these plasma generators. Still little understood by science, the three centers generate a tremendous amount of energy. Although scientists may use instruments to determine accurate measurements of this energy, they still have not yet discovered its source and nature.

Interestingly, these fields of force have been found to resemble the Van Allen belts of the Earth that create and maintain the magnetic fields of the globe. These donut-shaped fields of force are called toroidal fields; which are key mechanisms for thinking, feeling, and willing. When activated by consciousness through practices such as yoga, meditation, prayer, or contemplation, these forces evolve to become the spiritual forces of Moral Imagination, Moral Inspiration, and Moral Intuition.

Here is the key: the processes whereby these toroidal fields of force come into being, and are sustained, are directly connected to the earthly and cosmic nutrition streams. They constitute the manifested energy that arises through the expansion of consciousness. When nourished properly, both physically and spiritually, these force fields are potentially unlimited, giving the aspirant the ability to attain virtually unlimited spiritual power.

Great Thoughts About the Heart

In researching the human heart, we encountered many great minds who have concerned themselves with the mysteries of the heart and brought forward their best perspective on the central importance of the cardiovascular system for health and spiritual development. One could extract a summary of these ideas to share the content; but we felt it was important to present these diverse opinions in the original words of the author so as to not lose the poetic quality of their insight. Each author shares their own penultimate expression of wisdom concerning the heart in words that cannot easily be abbreviated or condensed. Therefore, we have chosen to present these concepts in somewhat long quotations that give the flavor and emphasis of the original. Much of the content is also to be found within the quotations of Dr. Rudolf Steiner found herein; but in a different form. Each of these authors build their view of the human heart upon Steiner's indications and try to take that content further through their expression of spiritual scientific facts that are part of their own understanding and interpretation.

***The Heart*, Sue Pegler**

"The heart is a dance hall and a meeting place where opposites meet, and polarities exist side by side: where opposing spirals twirl without interrupting each other. It is a place with an immense richness of nerve endings, a second brain of sorts. The heart is a space that is the inside-out in time, the fourth dimension of inner space and time. It is a place where etheric or life force streams come in from the world through nourishment and the senses. These streams are mediated in the heart through the interplay of pulse and breath. It is a place where the soul or emotional life builds pictures of the world and expresses them through speech and movement. The translation of inner intention to external deeds happens in the heart. It is the seat of conscience and morality. Through the experience of another's heart space or love, new links to the world are forged.

"The heart is the organ of self-realization and self-consciousness. It is the central organ of reflection and integration and can respond flexibly to the demands of the whole organism. It is an organ of love that practices the gesture of giving and receiving but does not act out of power.

"The volume of blood that leaves the heart at any time is regulated not only by the venous return, but also by the hunger of the organs for oxygen and food. The heart is formed by the spiraling flow of blood. The spiral tendency arises when time enters space and develops towards a center. As the blood moves through the heart, spiraling in vortices, it reaches a still point. In each heartbeat there is a brief moment where the blood stops—a moment of death, a moment of eternity. Finding this still point means finding the harmony of inner coherence between heart and brain. From this inner coherence, one can begin to work towards harmony and coherence with the environment."

The Art of Perceiving from the Heart, by Paul Salkovskis

"Perceiving is not just hearing, seeing, and listening. Perceiving from the heart goes further than that. It is feeling, sensing, knowing how to listen without judging. It's having no prejudices, savoring life with all its flavors and touching reality with all its textures. We now know that the art of perception depends on many different factors: our motivation, our emotions, culture, intuition, past experiences, and expectations. Essentially, everybody perceives the world differently.

"Perceiving from the heart has to do with sensitivity and openness. It is the ability to not only retain what our senses convey to us, but also to apply resolve, feeling, empathy and intuition in order to get to deeper interpretations. It allows us to be more aware of things, nature, people and the world.

"Perceiving from the heart is also one of the highest abilities that human beings can develop. It allows us to synchronize our senses (brain) with our emotions (heart) using our experiences. We do it with objectivity and a love that invites us to see the world through the lens of respect and consideration. Let's learn to perceive our surroundings with more awareness, openness and, most of all, heart.

"The perception of spatial layout is influenced by emotions like fear, disgust, social support, and sadness that can produce changes in vision and audition—change perception. The perceptual system is highly interconnected, allowing emotional information to influence perceptions and influence cognition. Taking the adaptive significance of emotion into account allows us to make predictions about when and how emotion influences perception. Emotion influences perception and states or capabilities of the body can alter perception."

Heart Lectures, Ehrenfried Pfeiffer

"The radiation from this etheric organ of the heart is actually developing into a spiritual sense organ. A new sense organ is developing in this Etheric Heart, and this is the only organ by which man is able to sense and to recognize the Etheric Christ.

"In our time there are certain changes taking place in the heart, by which gradually a fifth chamber will develop. In this fifth chamber man will have a new organ which will allow him to control life forces in a different way than is possible at the moment.

"The heart is not a pressure pump; but an organ in which the etheric space is created so that the blood is sucked to the heart rather than pumped.

"In discussing the blood circulation and the motion of the heart, Rudolf Steiner said that with some people the heart is not quite in its proper place. He said that in the case of dancers, the heart is moved from its proper position on the left to the right side. When this happens, it makes man more perceptive in an inner way to the influence of his surroundings.

"Together with the wrong concept of the heart as a pump is connected the fact that we have a wrong social life today. A healthy social life can develop only if the old pump-concept is removed and is replaced by the proper one. He said that only when people know that it is the invisible in man which moves the heart, will it be possible to construct proper machines and to solve social problems.

"The heart is a different muscle because its fibers are laid down differently, and also it is a hollow muscle. The fact that it is a hollow sphere brings about an inner motion because there is empty space inside.

"Concentrate your entire God-made Cosmos to a center, and from this center radiate outward what will someday be a new Cosmos. This is what makes the heart move, the motion which radiates out from the heart.

"The etheric center of the heart draws the blood towards it and then pulses out again. Here is where substance is transformed into ether, and forms rise-up to the etheric brain and thence to the physical brain so that it can function and so that there may be harmony in the organs of the body. The organs and their functioning are regulated by what takes place between the Etheric Heart and the etheric brain. Through this heart muscle, with a hollow sphere and etheric center inside it, pulses the blood. The blood enters the heart with its four chambers. Between the second and the third chamber it goes to the lung to be regenerated, and from the fourth it goes out to the body again. There is no pulse in the main vein which brings blood to the heart—there is no pressure—it is taken from every vein by suction.

"In the lung, with its oxygen, the blood is touched by the outer world. The old, poisoned, used up blood goes back from the lung as regenerated blood. There is really a constant dying and regeneration. New blood is really born. The heart is the only muscle that only gets tired once (except if diseased) and that is in the moment of death. This shows the eternal youth force in the Etheric Heart; the heart lives entirely in cosmic rhythms.

"Changes in the heart take place with everything we eat. The secret of digestion is that we do not take foreign matter into our system; but all foods are broken down and their forms are changed. Indigestion takes place when this process has not been carried out. This imposes action on the heart. The heart has the task of regulating everything and the blood mirrors everything that happens in our body. The kidney in a healthy person is able to filter out sugar from the blood. Then at another point, in the glomeruli, the blood reabsorbs the sugar. It is necessary that the sugar be out while the blood is being purified in the kidneys, then it is returned. Through the lung the blood is regenerated, through the kidney the blood is purified, and the heart cooperates in both these processes.

"At the moment when a person becomes spiritually active, at that moment the composition of the blood changes again.

"With every pulse of the heart a certain amount of substance is absorbed, is taken away as physical pressure and added to the etheric substance. This then begins to radiate outward. A clairvoyant can see the amount of radiation that goes up from the heart to the brain. The radiation from this etheric organ of the heart is actually developing into a spiritual sense organ. A new sense organ is developing in this Etheric Heart, and this is the only organ by which man is able to sense and to recognize the Etheric Christ. 'Not I, but Christ in me' has to work through the Etheric Heart, transforming substance into pure ether, pure radiance.

"If you become aware of the heart as a spiritual organ, you begin to develop the power to see the Etheric Christ. You do this by realizing that the force in the heart is the same as the force in the Sun, physically as well as spiritually.

"It is a peculiarity of the heart that it is the only bodily organ which is self-maintaining. This is because the blood going through the heart also nourishes the heart. The coronary vessels around the heart are like hands holding it. These coronary vessels nourish the heart and take away the used-up substance. The etheric is not able to take up the impact of physical things on the heart. So, it becomes stiff or clogged. We can then suffer a sudden end. Modern scientists also know that fear or despair bring about an increase of these diseases. These diseases come because the heart does not get proper spiritual nourishment."

***Clairvoyance and Consciousness: The Tao Impulse in Evolution*, by T. H. Myer**

"The present-day sense organs were laid down during the time of Old Saturn. The heart, on the other hand, has only developed during the Earth evolution. The senses, therefore, have a very ancient past. By comparison the heart is only at the beginning of its evolution; this is demonstrated by a peculiarity of its anatomical structure; it possesses striated muscles which are otherwise only found where muscles can be activated voluntarily. The heart is therefore predisposed to become a voluntary muscle and will reach perfection (even if not in a physically material form) during the future evolutionary phase of the Planet Vulcan.

"It is evident that such 'time-secrets of the physical body' were known about in Hibernia by the 'Great Initiate of the Secrets of the Physical Body,' Scythianos."

The Arcana of the Grail Angel, by John Barnwell, *On the Human Heart and its Mission*

"Just as love is felt as a heart-force; so, conscience is the action of this heart-force resonating in harmony with the life of thought. This is the 'still small voice' spoken of in the *Gospel of John*—a golden seed planted from above—that must be nurtured. And so, the acts of will that freely arise through this heart-force—or negate it—will determine the totality of your character; and, as a result, your future life and being.

"For if you lack conscience, you are not yet truly human, not yet truly living; but only sleeping within an illusory dream of life. Within this dream you are but merely a shadow of life—waiting for humanness to arise—needlessly creating more pain and suffering for oneself and others.

"There are those that may never find this; be kind to them so that they may find a way through their self-created cold world of darkness to the heart-force of warmth and light of which I speak. I have pondered this my whole life, and I am convinced this is really all one needs to know in order to find a sure path to wholeness as a truly human being."

Matthew **(6:19-21)**

"Lay not up for yourselves treasures upon Earth, where moth and rust doth corrupt, and where thieves break through and steal: but lay up for yourselves treasures in Heaven, where neither moth nor rust doth corrupt, and where thieves do not break through nor steal: for where your treasure is, there will your heart be also.

Matthew **(6:22-23)**

"The light of the body is the eye: if therefore thine eye be single, thy whole body shall be full of light. But if thine eye be evil, thy whole body shall be full of darkness. If therefore the light that is in thee be darkness, how great is that darkness!"

Matthew **(6:24-25)**

"No man can serve two masters: for either he will hate the one and love the other; or else he will hold to the one and despise the other. Ye cannot serve God and mammon. Therefore, I say unto you, Take no thought for your life, what ye shall eat, or what ye shall drink; nor yet for your body, what ye shall put on. Is not the life more than meat, and the body than raiment?"

***The Heart as an Organ of Perception*, by Charles B. Parselle**

"Dr. Harvey made the discovery in London that the heart functions as a pump for blood. Until then, the teachings of the Roman physician known to us as Galen, who taught that the blood moved with a kind of pulse or wave motion, had been treated as the established orthodoxy for more than fourteen hundred years. Modern research tells us that the heart is simply incapable of pumping blood through the 60,000 miles of blood vessels in a human body, and that Galen was partially right. Certainly, the heart muscle functions as a powerful pump, capable of throwing a jet of water vertically ten feet into the air, but to pump two gallons of blood per minute through 60,000 miles of blood vessels would require a pump capable of throwing a 100-pound weight a mile into the air.

"Today we know that the heart emits powerful bio-electromagnetic impulses with every heartbeat and is by far the most powerful such transmitter in the human body. Shortly after conception, the collection of cells that make up the beginnings of an embryo begin to pulsate, and those pulsations are electromagnetic.

"The developing embryo perceives nothing but the steady heartbeat of its mother. The embryonic heart develops long before the embryonic ear, which hears first only the rush of blood, but the developing embryo starts to interpret the mother's heartbeats, and those electromagnetic transmissions are interpreted as emotions. The four principal emotions are sad, mad, glad and scared, just as the four basic tastes are sweet, sour, bitter and salt, but from these simple bases we combine and interpret an enormous range of information. The heart is a transmitter and interpreter of emotional states.

"Although our science has been slow to recognize the heart as an organ of feeling and perception, our language is in no doubt. Consider the plethora of heart-based expressions in English usage: heartfelt, from the bottom of my heart, I wish with all my heart, with heart and soul, heart-stricken, heartsick, heart-rending decision, heavy-hearted, lighthearted, with an innocent heart, a black-hearted villain, the heart has its reasons that reason cannot comprehend, our hearts are joined as one, I heartily agree, and so on. As a culture, our hearts are uneasy, which is why diseases of the heart are the commonest cause of death."

The Harmony of the Human Body, by Armin Husemann

"Two opposing streams interpenetrate in the human being—a sculptural generative stream in the physical vehicle of the arterial blood and a musical stream which is embodied in the venous blood as the vehicle of degenerative processes. The 'I' uses the sculptural stream when we move and act, the musical stream when we sing, speak, and think."

The Heart-Mind Matrix, by Joseph Chilton Pearce

"'There is only one heart,' Baba explained, 'the one beating in my chest is essentially the same as the one in you. Billions of egos in heads up there, but only one heart.' He further claimed that in the center or 'cave' of the heart, there is a point from which the entire universe arises and radiates outwardly. Meditate on the heart long enough and you will begin to sense the presence of these waveforms enveloping you like a warm cocoon of love and power. As Earth's magnetic fields stream out into space, so the heart's electromagnetic field streams out beyond our body. These magnetic waves of heat and Earth fuse or merge in varying ways, depending on the coherence of our heart's field. Coherent heart-fields merge into Earth's radiating fields, which, in turn merge with those of the Sun. Thus, we are incorporated into and reciprocally interact, directly and indirectly, with this whole solar system, to the extent our heart-fields are coherent."

***The Mystery of the Blood*, by James Dyson**

"The blood is that organ through which all these substance processes are inter-connected, mediated, held in a condition of openness to influences of temperature, pressure, hormonal variations and much else of a more subtle, ever cosmic nature.

"Red blood cells have essentially sacrificed their life, yet they carry on functioning. They are the only cells in the body which have died and are not excreted or metabolized. They remain in a state of suspended animation for about 120 days. They carry hemoglobin and combine with the oxygen in the lungs as one of the main gases involved in the processes of cellular respiration.

"Within each of these red cells the iron prevents a death process which then allows the entire organism to continue to live through carrying the process of oxygen into the depth of the organism. White blood cells digest and sacrifice themselves in the process of dealing with foreigners in order to protect the integrity of the inner space of human immunity; they maintain physiological integrity and separateness from the outside world. They conceal some of the deepest mysteries of human existence and they guard the very foundations of our earthly life and destiny. Steiner connects the red blood cells to the phosphorus 'substance process.' Phosphorus exists in a bound form in which its energy remains hidden in the realm of potential and in a free form after the energy has been released. Red blood cells are a kind of organ of breathing, in their own right, holding the balance between the free and the bound phosphorus, between energy that is realized through a spiritualized process of combustion and energy which is held back as potential."

***The Dynamic Heart and Circulation*, by Craig Holdrege**

"We cannot understand the heart's activity unless we consider the blood, peripheral circulation, and the metabolic activity of the other organs. The heart is continually adapting its activity to the needs and state of the body and person as a whole. Changes in the blood's pressure, viscosity, warmth, and biochemical composition are communicated to the heart. This communication is mediated by the nervous system, hormones, and heart and blood vessels sensory receptors. The heart therefore exists as a perceptive center for the body via circulation. The heart is a sense organ for the organism, enabling it to perceive what transpires in the upper and lower poles of the body. The heart does not just perceive what comes to it via the blood. It also alters its activity based upon its perceptions. The heart secretes a hormone in response to the changing consistency of blood. If the blood is too viscous, it secretes a hormone named natriuretic peptide into the blood, and the hormone stimulates the kidneys to secrete more water into the blood. The heart muscle itself is a source of warmth for the blood, while the peripheral circulation can expand and contract to give off or contain warmth."

***Enlivening the Chakra of the Heart*, by Florin Lowndes**

"True human love is rooted in the spirit. Wherever such love is truly avowed and truly received, impulses will invariably be present which prepare the way for a real logic of the heart. The logic of thinking can lead to the greatest egotism. The logic of the heart is capable of gradually overcoming egotism and making all people part of an all-encompassing human community. The six virtues (control of thoughts, control of actions, perseverance, patience, faith, and equanimity) combine to form the six lotus petals of the heart that are being developed in our time. The other six petals have been developed in previous incarnations."

The Human Organs, by Walter Holtzapfel

"The sense-perceptible physical appearance receives life from the etheric body, is animated by the astral body and integrated by the ego. The etheric body is active in the liquid element, the astral body in the aeriform and gaseous processes and the ego in the warmth differentiations. It is the feelings of the soul which give rise to the movement of the blood; the soul drives the blood, and the heart moves because it is driven by the blood. The heart speaks with the inner voice of conscience, audible only to each individual alone.

"But what is suffered involuntarily by man today, will later, at a higher stage of evolution, be in his own power. Later on, he will drive his blood by his own volition, and cause the movement of his heart as today he moves the muscles of his hand. The heart with its peculiar structure is a crux, a riddle for modern science. It has diagonally striped fibers, which are otherwise only to be found in voluntary muscles. Why? Because the heart has not yet reached the end of its evolution, but is an organ of the future, because it will in the future be a voluntary muscle. Thus, it already shows the rudiments of this in its structure.

"Four organs characterize the predominance of one of the four elements, the lung by the predominance of the earth element, the liver by that of the watery element, the kidney by the predominance of the element of air, and the heart by the predominance of the warmth element. In the warmth there lives the ego. The warmth is the true element of the human ego."

Warmth and the Heart: The Human Ego Organization, Heinz-Hartmut Vogel

"The heart is actually a universal organ which develops a unique and simple polarity in its anatomy and function by uniting center and periphery. In rhythmical alternation the periphery becomes center, and the center becomes periphery. The individual self is carried out into the environment and the outer world is brought into one's inner world. We call this balancing force the 'I' or Ego. We actively identify ourselves with our 'I' in the confrontation and harmonizing of our being with the surrounding world.

"The heart and circulation together form the central organ of the Ego organization. The Ego organization, working by means of the 'connective tissue foundation system' and intermediate metabolism, maintains rhythmical order in the physical organism. In the heart, the polar streams of venous and arterial blood come into direct contact. The right venous heart is subject to an endothermic warmth process, the left arterial heart to an exothermic warmth process. In the interstitium between the right and left heart and capillary systems, the regenerative metabolic process and form-giving nerve-sense process are harmonized. The silica process serves the balance-creating Ego organization in the heart.

"Ego activity and Ego organization (individualized warmth or Ego warmth and the silica process) largely coincide in the blood, which is the organ of the Ego. Silica, as a substance, is found in the blood only in the minutest quantities. Consequently, the Ego is active in the blood almost exclusively as warmth of will, and only to a limited extent in its sense perceptive nature. From this point of view, the heart is clearly more of a sense organ than the blood system.

"The Ego in the physical body lives in warmth. The Ego organization makes use of the silica process in order to work in the physical; but only in such a way that it continually overcomes silica as substance and is freed from it. Through warmth activity, the Ego organization dissolves physical form. The substances taken up in nutrition are first destroyed and then new substances are formed.

"In their anatomical construction and their energetic function, the right and left heart repeat the polar formative principles of the venous liver process and the arterial kidney process.

"Myocardial infarction stems from a failure of the balance-creating warmth/silica organization which is the physical carrier of the Ego organization. Following this, the upper nerve-sense man and lower metabolic man become dissociated. These processes strike directly against one another in the left heart. Here the arterial blood process is most strongly exposed to the influence of the catabolic sense-nerve process. Thus, it is the left heart that failure of the Ego organization and silica process takes place. Therapeutic indications have been given by Steiner for this situation."

The Bleeding Wound of King Amfortas, Karal Jan Tusenius

"As the largest and least formed organ of the body, the blood is par excellence the bearer of the field of tension between physical substance and the working of processes. In the periphery, where the blood flows through capillaries, and to a certain extent leaves even these smallest of blood vessels, the blood is much less substantial and not, or hardly, subject to gravity. Thus, there arises in these areas the possibility for the activity of non-physical influences. The rhythmic alteration between concentrating and diluting, between major and minor circulation, between the large vessels, the heart, and the periphery, thus represents the interaction between the congesting and the sucking activities of the heart and the peripheral tissues. In this, the heart plays a sensing (nerve-sense) and an impelling (metabolic) role.

"The blood is a suspension of cells in plasma, a solution of protein and salts. The principal component of the blood plasma is water containing dissolved ions and three classes of proteins; carrier proteins, coagulation proteins, and immunoproteins. Blood cells consist of red blood cells (erythrocytes), platelets and white blood cells (leukocytes). The main function of the red blood cells is to carry oxygen to the tissues and to return to the lungs carrying carbon dioxide.

"Platelets work with coagulation proteins to defend the circulatory system in the event of laceration or rupture.

"The normal function of white blood cells is to defend the organism against infection. So, both in the plasma proteins and in the blood cells there is an interesting tripartite division consisting of, first:

Salt principle: carrier proteins and carrying, hardly vital, red blood cells

Mercury principle: coagulation proteins working together with the half-vital platelets in the field of maintaining a balance between structuring and dissolving processes

Sulphur principle: immunoproteins and vital white blood cells, being the most autonomous and active part of the blood in the defense mechanism

"Leucocytes, white blood cells, are described as the expression of a process of self-consciousness, the I, an ego activity. Leucocytes, which at the present time are still fulfilling their task in secret, are described as the seeds of future consciousness. The immune process of the blood seems to display to a high degree aspects of the preservation of the identity and of personality, which is characteristic of ego function. The human ego enhances the fluidity of the blood."

***Polarity of Center and Periphery in the Circulatory System*, by Heinrich Brettschneider**

"The arterial system, is a biological system that slows down blood flow, increases the pressure wave amplitude and transposes pressure pulsations into a higher octave by breaking each pressure curve into two peaks. In other words, it is both a biological flow resistor and a biological pressure amplifier, that is, a pressure wave resonator. Approxi-mately 85% of the body's blood encounters almost no resistance to its flow, that is, it flows without being under pressure. The so-called low-pressure system includes the capillaries, the venous system, the right side of the heart, pulmonary circulation, and the left atrium. This low-pressure system is the polar opposite of the high-pressure system in that it relaxes in response to increased pressure and contracts in response to a drop in pressure. It is also capable of counteracting pressure without recourse to central nerve activity. Flow is inversely related to pressure. When the flow increases, pressure readings fall.

"Physiological blood flow in the capillaries is highly independent of anything correlated with the movements of the heart since there is absolutely no relationship between the cardiac cycle and the flow velocity of the blood in the capillaries themselves. Oxygen consumption in the tissues is the only measurable factor that has been shown to increase consistently in proportion to the flow of blood. Blood production by the tissues expands the vascular system, thus producing the pressure that fills the heart with blood.

"The function of the heart, with regard to the blood returning in the veins, is to regulate resistance. Human blood is two-thirds venous by volume and only one-third arterial. The blood always flows faster when the venous return increases and the total resistance to inflow exerted by the heart and vessels decreases."

Human Heart Cosmic Heart, by Thomas Cowan

"Blood actually stops moving in the capillaries, which is necessary for the efficient exchange of gases, nutrients, and waste products. After the blood stops moving, it oscillates slightly, and then begins to flow again as it enters the veins. The capillary system is massive; if it were spread out, it would cover at least one entire football field.

"Water exists in not three but four 'phases.' The fourth phase is an intermediary between liquid, or bulk, water, and the solid phase of ice. There have been many names given to this fourth phase. Pollack calls it the exclusion phase, gel phase, or structured water. He describes in his book, *The Fourth Phase of Water*, how structured water forms. Any time you have a hydrophilic surface such as gelatin or nafion (a plastic) and you put it in water, a zone of structured water will form. This zone is sometimes referred to as the exclusion zone (EZ) because it excludes toxins, solutes, and other substances. The thickness depends on the charge on the surface of the hydrophilic substance and some other factors. This fourth phase of water forms best at certain temperatures (around 4 degrees C [39.2 F]), and it highly structures the bulk water near it.

"The ability of highly hydrophilic substances, especially proteins, to structure water is central to biological life. The majority of the water in biological systems, including cells, is in the form of structured water. The cytoplasm in our cells is in a gel-like state because of the network of hydrophilic proteins that make up the interior framework of the cell.

"As water becomes structured, the electrical charges separate. The structured water becomes negatively charged while the bulk water is positively charged. There are many interesting properties of the structured water that forms right next to these hydrophilic surfaces. These include having an increased viscosity compared to bulk water near it. The structured water layer is also negatively charged as a result of having an abundance of free electrons. The presence of these free electrons is an intrinsic part of the structuring process of water. As the water becomes structured, it also becomes negatively charged. The pH of the structured water zone is different from that of the bulk water. The molecular configuration of the structured water zone is more dense than that of bulk water simply as a result of a hydrophilic surface being placed in bulk water, with essentially no outside inputs, a layer of structured water forms next to the hydrophilic surface that has a different chemical pH, electrical voltage, and molecular configuration (density) than bulk water.

"If you take the hydrophilic surface and roll it up into a tube, you produce a hydrophilic tube with a layer of structured water lining the inside of the tube. As a result of the separation of the electrical charges—the natural and inevitable consequence of the interaction of a hydrophilic tube and water—the bulk water will begin to flow from one end of the tube to the other and then out. This flow will be indefinite, unless acted upon by a force that stops it. All you need to do to get water to flow, and for mechanical work to be done, and for it to be done indefinitely, it to put a hydrophilic tube in a pot of water. This creates a 'perpetual motion machine!'

"There are four phases of water, but for biological life two are most important: The structured water phase creates the electrical charge that does the work, and the juxtaposed bulk phase simply flows. There are many sources of natural energy that drive this flow, but the most important is Sunlight. Sunlight charges the hydrophilic tubes and creates the electrically charged structured water, causing the bulk water within the tube to flow indefinitely, as if life were just a big, blissful, abundant dance.

"Knowing this, it is easier now to imagine how blood flows in our arteries and veins. Start at the precise place and moment where the blood in the vast network of capillaries has stopped, the gases and nutrients have been exchanged, and the waste products have been picked up. The blood needs to flow upward, coalescing into larger and larger vessels until the venous blood reaches its destination of the heart. The small venules are very narrow hydrophilic tubes; they are exposed to Sunlight that pick up the Earth's electromagnetic field, and hopefully they experience the warmth and touch of another human being or animal. As a result, they, too, form a tubular layer of structured water on the inside of the venules. At the center of this layer of structured water is the positively charged bulk water with squeezed protons repelling each other. The blood begins to move upward. It goes faster and faster as the large 'field' coalesces in a raging central river. There are, of course, contributions to this upward movement from the squeezing of the muscles of the legs and arms, but they are mostly helpful to maintain the spiral movement that supports the flows. There are also valves that keep the blood from succumbing to gravity if there are weak moments in the flow. The bulk water carries the waste and nutrients, and the structured layer creates the voltage or energy that runs the systems. Life in all living systems, we are powered by the Earth and Sun.

"Pollack refers to the thick, viscous structured layer lining the vessel as the exclusion zone because it excludes toxins, solutes, and other substances. This layer protects the vessel from inflammatory damage. When the structured, protective gel layer is not formed properly, the vessel walls become damaged and inflamed. They protect themselves from the high pressure by forming plaque.

"Viktor Schauberger observed that for a stream or river to be healthy, first the flow pattern of the water must be in a vortex or spiral flow pattern. The second is that the temperature of the water, particularly at night, must be very close to or exactly 4 degrees C [39.2 degrees F]—the temperature that water is most likely to exist in the fourth, or structured, phase of water. When water is healthy, according to Schauberger, it results in a balance of the forces of gravity with the forces of levity. He was even able to observe in a waterfall a channel of light within the streaming water. This light was the force of levity that flows upward in vortices in the river. This force of levity allows for the effortless flow of water and is dependent upon certain conditions of temperature and flow dynamics (spiraling or vortex-based patterns). This is the natural state of structured water. Schauberger's natural state of structured water is also the basis for the flow of blood in our circulatory system.

"In nature, fluid motion often chooses to spiral rather than stream linearly. A beating heart, with its helical myofiber architecture and twisting-untwisting motion, also reveals spiraling streams of blood flow. This mechanism is highly conserved in vertebrates. Why does nature choose to move blood in a helical manner, and how does that make normal cardiac function efficient? These are important but complex questions that are just being answered."

Healing Sounds: Fundamentals of Chirophonetics, by Dr. Alfred Baur

"Rudolf Steiner has often pointed out that in many respects we should regard the heart as a sense organ. It perceives the nature of the blood passing through it, therefore, we can justifiably compare what takes place in the heart with a sort of taste perception. The rhythmical movement is probably the fundamental basis of its sensory activity. The activity of the heart implies a center, which looks into and actively perceives a wisdom-filled moving and living environment.

"In the vortex process within the heart, we can find that sensitive chaos which can sense how the blood flows. From the movement of the blood, it can sense how the fluids are mixed.

"The blood pulsates in accordance with the predominating temperament of the moment. The 'mixture of blood' is equivalent to the pulse which skips, thumps, creeps, or drags. How a person deals with life depends on the nature and mixture of this 'special fluid.' The will to act is based on the metabolic processes of the blood.

"The heart is the result of the circulation of the blood, and not the reverse, because the blood already circulates long before the heart of the embryo is formed. The heart just listens, experiencing the quality of our deeds through their influence on the movement of the blood. Then another mighty transformation of the heart occurs: the content which has been absorbed while listening is poured out into the world.

"The contents of the inverted experiences which were absorbed in one incarnation are now poured into the external world and thus karma can express itself. Now one can perceive what the inverted heart of the past incarnations are poured outward, and from outside our destiny comes toward us. It is the contents of our heart from a past incarnation which have been thrust out that now obstruct our path.

"We must seek the source and origin of our ability to speak within the human heart. For the etheric forces of the heart overflow, and this surplus of life-force creates the necessary preconditions for articulation in the mouth. If the heart retained its abundance, the result would be an excess of vitality, and man would possess the physical strength of a lion. In this overflow, however, the activity of the heart is transformed into the activity of articulation. The same etheric forces which pulsatingly structure the blood-flow in the heart are now raised to a new level, and they sub-divide the breath.

"*The Heart Perceives:* The sensory activity of the heart is based on the perception of the blood's movement. This varies according to the qualitative consistency of the blood. The heart perceives the temperament of the blood.

"*The Language of the Heart:* The heart is not a pump. The blood is set into movement through hunger for breath or nourishment. The heart articulates the flow of the blood as the tongue articulates the breath. Articulation is a metamorphosed event of the heart.

"*The Heart as a Tongue:* The heart listens to our deeds. It stores the moral value of our deeds within itself. Its contents flow into the world in the following earthly life. Then the contents of the heart from the past incarnation speak as the language of destiny."

Functional Morphology: The Dynamic Wholeness of the Human Organism, by Dr. Johannes Rohen

"The sinus node is one of the major elements in the cardiac conduction system, the system that controls the heart rate. This stunningly designed system generates electrical impulses and conducts them throughout the muscle of the heart, stimulating the heart to contract and pump blood. The sinus node is the heart's natural pacemaker. It consists of a cluster of cells that are situated in the upper part of the wall of the right atrium. The electrical impulses are generated there.

"The electrical signal generated by the sinus node moves from cell to cell down through the heart until it reaches the atrioventricular node (AV node), a cluster of cells situated in the center of the heart between the atria and ventricles. The AV node serves as a gate that slows the electrical current before the signal is permitted to pass down through to the ventricles. This delay ensures that the atria have a chance to fully contract before the ventricles are stimulated. After passing the AV node, the electrical current travels to the ventricles along special fibers embedded in the walls of the lower part of the heart.

"The autonomic nervous system, the same part of the nervous system as controls the blood pressure, controls the firing of the sinus node to trigger the start of the cardiac cycle. The autonomic nervous system can transmit a message quickly to the sinus node so it in turn can increase the heart rate to twice normal within only 3 to 5 seconds. This quick response is important during exercise when the heart has to increase its beating speed to keep up with the body's increased demand for oxygen."

Life Processes in the Blood Organization, **Hemsworth Brüder von Laue**

"The gradual refinement of matter in the human being is always happening in the blood. With the aid of the blood, food units are taken hold of in the intestines and metamorphosed into living body substance sustaining the soul principle and responding to the I. This ascending metamorphosis is matched by descending, eliminatory activity producing excretions. Blood is thus the key organ for separation, holding the middle position among the life processes. It provides tools for acting outwards against the foreign nature of the environment and, on the other hand, tools for acting inwards in building up the body. It 'potentizes' substances in the human being, taking them from their ponderable state to live quality, a state where they become vehicles for soul and spirit.

"Considering the blood against this background, it is immediately apparent that the life processes active in the different blood functions are vastly different.

1. Breathing (taking in)
2. Warming (adapting)
3. Nutrition (repelling, analyzing, destroying)
4. Separation (separating)
5. Maintenance (maintaining)
6. Growth (growing)
7. Reproduction (renewing)

"Let us take the transport/inhibitory function. The blood takes up substances in infinitely many sites. In the lung it is most open to the environment, taking in air. In the organism it takes up substances everywhere. This intake is only possible because all the different substances are immediately wrapped up, so that they will not react according to their inherent nature, which only comes into play again when the blood lets go of the substances, separating them out—oxygen in the tissues, transferrin iron in the bone marrow, carbohydrates in the liver, etc. The maintenance and growth function of the blood takes effect in liver and bone marrow, not in the blood itself. Nor do we find adaptation and repulsion processes in the blood that might affect the blood itself. The inhibitory/transport function involves only the first (intake) and fourth (separation) life processes.

"The coagulation system serves to maintain the surface areas of the organism to keep inner and outer worlds apart. The system is activated when an injury has occurred. The adaptation process comes into play as viscosity changes, with fibrin hardened. It does not go against the environment but lets the vitality of the blood be frozen to a point where maintenance of the whole is assured. This, the second process, is activated so that the fifth (maintenance) may come into action.

"The system of nonspecific inflammation in the organism becomes active when foreign life has entered into the organism or tissues and been destroyed. Pathogens enter without active involvement of the organism. As local inflammation develops, the blood slows down and grows denser, changing its pH (adaptation), granulocytes migrate to the site and provide tools for chemical destruction of the pathogens. Apart from the adaptation process, this also involves repulsion. The goal of the inflammatory process is once again maintenance of the organism's integrity. No new ability (growth) is gained. The organism uses the second and third life processes (adaptation and repulsion) to safeguard the fifth (maintenance).

"The physiological composition of the blood changes when one goes through inner schooling (macrocosmic or microcosmic). Steiner emphasized that the blood has a dual relationship to the environment. On one hand, the blood only enters into relationship with the outside world in such a way that anything it receives from it has been stripped of its own inherent laws; on the other hand, it enters into a relationship that enables it to approach the outside world directly. This happens when the blood flows through the lung and comes in contact with the outside air. It is then quickened by the oxygen from the outside air and configured in such a way that nothing comes up against this configuration to weaken it; the oxygen from the air does indeed approach the instrument of the human I in a way wholly in accord with the essential nature of the I.

"Substances brought to the blood from below, through nutrition, must be carefully filtered so that nothing of their outside world character takes effect in the blood. In the lung, however, air from outside the human being comes to the blood directly (intake). The foreign nature of the air is only adapted to the organism by actively changing its humidity and temperature (adaptation). The foreign character of foods is changed in the upper gastrointestinal tract to remove all inherent laws from proteins, fats and carbohydrates. The inherent nature of metals needs to be specifically inhibited and covered over in the blood. The two ways of relating to the environment—openness to the environment in the Salt pole of the blood (red blood cells) and the shrouding of substance processes in the Sulfur pole (blue blood cells)—are polar opposites in the transport system of the blood, like positive and negative electricity.

"If we ask ourselves in which area of the blood this process takes place, attention focuses on substances such as calcium and magnesium which are partly ionized and in solution and partly withdrawn from specific ionic function, which has outside world qualities, by being hidden in albumin or other inhibitory proteins. A specific amount of free calcium ions must be present in the serum to make normal consciousness possible. We cannot, of course, expect complete crystallization in the blood, but the ionic state is the precondition for and, hence, the first step towards crystallization. The free blood salts do, however, come closest to the process of crystallizing out in the blood."

In the same Steiner lecture (GA 128), substantial changes in the blood are also described for feeling:

"The thinking process involves solid, salt-like principles being withdrawn from a fluid principle and being deposited. Feeling has to do with some particles in the blood changing from a more fluid to a denser state. The substance itself assume a denser condition due to coagulation."

"The process of thinking is like a process of depositing salts due to an activity of the blood and, in turn, causing irritation of the nervous system; an organic process, therefore, that occurs on the border of the blood and of the nervous system. We know now that everything we have called conscious thinking activity, brought about by the I (human ego), comes to expression in a kind of extremely subtle salt deposition in the blood."

"A kind of blood coagulation is given as an image for feeling, characterizing the processes at the substantial level. A bit later Steiner compared the effect feeling has on the blood with the coagulation of liquid protein. We are not in the habit of considering feeling in conjunction with the coagulation system, with the different viscosity of protein in the blood. It is remarkable that the coagulation system follows on from the inhibitor /transport system just as feeling follows thinking in the order of soul processes. Sentience (feeling) prior to birth is also a process of coagulation: blood coagulates into the mobile muscle. Will impulses as courage to act, courage before action is taken, create temperature differentiations and hence the form and configuration of internal organs. The will that performs the action reveals itself in temperature differentiations in bodily development that are connected with the functions of organs. The crystallizing and coagulating processes run parallel to thinking and feeling respectively—in organ development before birth (bone and muscle) and in the way the soul uses the body (crystallizing and coagulation in the blood)."

In *Occult Physiology* (March 27, 1911), the influence of the will on the body is described in a uniform way:

"The process connected with the will impulse expresses itself in a warmth process, an inner warming process, so to speak. Processes of combustion, the formation of combinations which we call inner processes of oxidation, occur throughout our entire organization; and, in so far as these go on below the threshold of consciousness and have nothing to do with the conscious life, will-impulses and the like, they belong to that other part of our organization which is shut off by the corresponding organs and is susceptible to influence from the subconscious life.

"The human being is thus protected inwardly on one side by a part of his organism in which these processes take their course much as they do outwardly in the macrocosm; and on the other side his protection is such that these processes are connected with his soul-processes, and are of a finer kind as has been explained. And so these physiological processes take place in our organism, salt-forming, liquefying, and warmth producing processes, which are the result of our conscious life; and others which take place outside our conscious life, in such a way that they furnish the basis for what prepares itself beforehand in the human organism in order that the processes adapted to the conscious life may take place…

Reflecting on Rudolf Steiner's work we see that, in the ordering system for blood proteins, thinking may be reflected in the forming of salts (Salt), feeling in the coagulation of proteins (Mercury), and will impulses in differentiated temperature processes (Sulphur). The balances created between shrouding and release of salts (Thinking), coagulation and fibrinolysis (Feeling), activators and inhibitors of inflammation (Willing) create the conditions under which the I can come to realization in thinking, feeling and taking action.

Steiner spoke of soul processes in *Occult Physiology* (March 27, 1911) in the following words:

"Now we have also pointed out that what we look upon as a conscious activity of the ego is after all only one part of man's being; and that, below the threshold of what enters in this manner within the horizon of our consciousness there are processes which occur in the subconsciousness, and which are held back from our consciousness, by means of the sympathetic nervous system. We have been able to indicate from various points of view that these processes which take place below the level of consciousness have also a certain kind of connection with our ego. We have said, with regard to the most unconscious part of us, our bony system, that it is organized throughout in such a way as to be able to give to the instrument of the conscious ego the basis for an ego. Thus, out of the unconscious, an ego-organization arises to meet the conscious ego-organization. Man is thus divided, as it were, into two parts: from one direction the conscious ego-organization works into the organism, and from the other there flows into man the unconscious ego-organization. We have seen that the blood-system and the bony system really form a certain antithesis; they act like opposite poles. The blood in its inner activity responds to and follows, as an instrument, the activity of the ego; on the contrary, that part which is organized as the other pole of the ego so that the ego is able to express itself in the blood, namely the bony system, withdraws itself from the quickened inner life of the ego to such an extent that the ego has no consciousness of anything that goes on within this bony system, and the processes here take their course below the surface of what goes on in the actually conscious ego-life. These are processes, therefore, which correspond to our ego-activity yet at the same time are as truly dead as our blood-processes are living; and they are, as a matter of fact, only one portion of those processes which remain unconscious to the ego, and which only gradually rise more and more up into the conscious."

These unconscious soul processes, which also act on the blood, are not accessible to our intentions but depend on the macrocosm and are mainly active prior to birth.

"Thus we have, here again, two opposite poles. Man is a thinking being, and it is the thought-process that makes him inwardly a stable being (for, in a certain sense, our thought-system is our inner bony system; we have definite, sharply-outlined thoughts; and though our feelings are more or less indefinite, wavering, and different in each one of us, the thought-systems are inserted in stable form in the feeling system). Now whereas these stable insertions of thought in the conscious life manifest themselves through a sort of animated, mobile process of salt-depositing, that which prepares the way for these in the bony system, giving them the right support, expresses itself in the fact that the macrocosm out of its own formative processes so builds up our bony system that a part of its nature consists of deposited salts. These deposited salts of the bony system are the quiescent element in us: they are the opposite pole to those inner vital activities which are at play in the process of salt-depositing corresponding to the principle of thought. Thus we are made capable of thought through influences acting from two sides upon our organization: from one side unconsciously through the fact that our bony system is built up within us; from the other side consciously in that we ourselves bring about, after the model of our bone-building process, conscious processes which manifest themselves as of like nature in our organism, and of which we may say that they are inwardly active processes. For the salt that is here formed must again at once be dissolved by sleep, must be got rid of, for otherwise it would induce destructive processes, causing dissolution. Thus we have processes that begin with salt-depositings and then are followed by destructive processes, constituting a sort of reactionary process. In the re-dissolving of the deposits, beneficent sleep acts upon us in the way we need, to the end that we may ever anew develop conscious thought in our fully awake life of day."

***Life Processes in the Blood Organization*,**
Hemsworth Brüder von Lau

"For conscious thinking, we use the kind of salt production processes that have their model in the release of calcium from albumin and are always reversible. Steiner relates salt deposition in the skeleton to the cosmic thinking in us of which we are not conscious. This greater polarity between blood and bone is reflected within the blood in the lesser polarity between inhibitory/transport proteins and red blood cells. The latter represent the Salt process in the blood just as the bones do in the greater system. Permanent deposition of salts in the bones metamorphoses into deposition of hemoglobin in the red cells. These cells are much more advanced towards death than bones are. Their shape is also a purer reflection of the spherical form of the macrocosm. The unconscious, macrocosmic thinking process, the world thinking in us, comes to expression in bone salts, and in metamorphosed form in the red blood cells."

"The effect of a conscious inner life that is open to the surrounding world is reflected in the protein or Sulfur side of the blood. The action of the unconscious macrocosm's soul processes, which are also called thinking, feeling and will, is in bodily terms reflected on the cellular, the Salt side. The side where the blood is open and alive to the environment is closed to the conscious soul processes and vice versa."

"If we consider the blood, it will indeed be full of significance for us, presenting as a very special fluid for, on one hand, the blood shows its essential nature as turning to the lowest, humblest realm below us, showing itself to be a form of matter capable of external chemical processes (O2 uptake) so that it may be an instrument for the I. On the other hand, blood is the substance that is more protected, to enable it to achieve inward processes that cannot be achieved anywhere else for all other organ processes are necessary for this. The most subtle processes of the highest order that are stimulated from the depth of our organism combine in the blood with physical and chemical processes of the kind we see all around us in the world. In no other substance does the physical, material world we perceive through the senses come together so directly, demanding the presence, the activity of systems of forces that lie outside the sense-perceptible world—but only in our blood substance."

"The cellular aspect opens the blood to the (unconscious) environment and is the instrument for an unconscious, macrocosmic inner life. The serum aspect shuts itself off from the processes of the material environment, enveloping the imponderables connected with the environment, which makes it the instrument for an independent, conscious inner life. At first sight, it may seem surprising to speak of the higher, conscious inner activity that uses the body as related to the lower blood processes which are open to metabolism and, conversely, see the body-creating, sleeping inner activity as the basis of the aspect in the blood that is open to the environment. It reflects the polarity of life processes and soul processes, a polarity we find again and again. We perceive the archetype of the I organization in the organism—processes going in opposite directions are held in balance, thus creating the conditions for further development. In the blood organ, we see this embryonic life in the immune system, which is capable of development, remaining open to future organic development with its learning capacity."

"Blood's function lies in its ability to flow, its buffering quality, and the ability to take up substances and release them. The coagulation system of the blood with its surface-preserving function and its sequential processes may thus be seen as a reflection of the ether body in the blood."

"The function of the nonspecific inflammatory system is to kill foreign life in the organism and remove it through pus. Increased mobility, phagocytosis, and elimination of inorganic and organic poisons point to activities under the control of the human astral body. This, then, is where the astral body is reflected in the blood."

"In the coagulation system the tools for activation and inhibition are clearly distinct. In the concerted effort of immunization there are no separate 'helper' and 'suppressor' cells, but every individual process is both at the same time. Every new infection results in a new imprint, new immunization. This learning process is based in the embryonic part of the blood. Our I organization brings order into the concerted effort."

"We thus discover the threefold order of the blood, which reveals the Salt-Mercury-Sulfur forces with their configuring and process-ordering activities. The twofold order of the blood between the more embryonic, live lymph system and the image organs which develop through a sequence of metamorphoses, shows the relationship to past and future. There is also the sevenfold activity of life processes in the blood. The unbelievably differentiated nature of the blood, which as a whole is an organ of the I, is remarkable."

We hear further about this profound mystery in the following article, that was translated by Monica Gold, and is so comprehensive and valuable that it is printed in its entirety; and therefore, it doesn't have added quotation marks:

The Study of the Formation of a New Etheric Heart Organ in the Light of the Present Michaelic Mystery Culture,

by Ruth Haertl

Michaelmas, 2000

The full title of this article is '*The Study of the Formation of a New Etheric Heart Organ in the Light of the Present Michaelic Mystery Culture as Rudolf Steiner Required it for our Age in his Lectures Die Sendung Michaels und Die Offenbarung der eigentlichen Geheimnisse des Menschenwesens*.'

To begin with I will give a brief summary of the development of the etheric heart. Rudolf Steiner described the process in great detail [1] when he discussed the formation of the etheric heart in children.

Before birth etheric forces are drawn together to create the individual etheric body. These ether forces harbor substances which are taken from the entire Cosmos.

Figure 1.

In a drawing of the etheric heart [Figure 1.] Rudolf Steiner shows the periphery of the stars, the heart amid Sun and Moon, while further down the earthly is indicated. "It is important to know that when we descend into the earthly world, we draw into ourselves a kind of image from the Cosmos." This first etheric heart configuration Rudolf Steiner regards as provisional or as inherited. It remains with the child only until he loses his teeth. At age seven it falls away. Rudolf Steiner even says: "it decays." It is cast off just as the teeth are discarded at age seven. The wonderful cosmic configuration of the starry images fades more and more as the seventh birthday approaches. This happens at the time when the child's own etheric body is born.

Rays of ether configurations begin to form anew and strive from the periphery to the center. Here they accumulate around the physical heart and as they grow together, the new second etheric heart is born. It is the individualized etheric heart of the growing young person who matures from age seven to fourteen.

It happens through a process whereby bit by bit the new Etheric Heart replaces whatever dies off from the inherited heart. The new heart is condensed from the entire world sphere.

In another of Steiner's lectures we read that at puberty the astral body is restructured in a new configuration. In the same area of the body in which the second etheric heart was formed as a reflection of the stars, sun and moon, the forces of the astral body establish an additional central organ. These two organs weave in and out of each other as one central organ and in it are inscribed all deeds, all moral motivations, human intentions and ideas.

In one of his lectures Rudolf Steiner speaks of a small box in which everything concerning our life is recorded. As students on the path of initiation we are meant gradually to become able to read and interpret our past karmic deeds, we are supposed to grow towards an understanding of all that which is inscribed into the etheric heart It was the 27 of February, 1925 on his sixty-third birthday that Rudolf Steiner gave the following related meditation to Dr. Ita Wegman.

Hearts interpret Karma
When hearts learn to read
The Word,
Which creates in
Human Life;

When hearts learn to
Speak the Word
Which creates in
The Human Being

In the above-mentioned restructured astral body is a picture of all that which man has experienced in the spiritual world between death and rebirth. Great secrets are being inscribed into the astral body at that time. During man's youth they merge bit by bit with the physical and etheric organs, which harbour now deepest cosmic secrets as if imprisoned. Out of the Ego which sympathetically connects with our astral body, these secrets as positive and less positive intentions and motivations are being engraved into the etheric heart organ, the small box that was spoken of. For this reason, Rudolf Steiner can say that a joining together takes place of the Ego with the etheric and the astral hearts. This means complete adjustment of individual Karma with universal cosmic laws.

In this way we can visualize an inner dynamic process, actively shaping the human physical through the creative working of the Logos. We can say man is born out of deepest cosmic wisdom. Creative forces work through the strength of the Word into man's sheaths. The Logos in the human heart becomes an organ of destiny creatively working in harmony with the etheric and astral sheaths as well as with the ego of man. It is the creation of our awe-inspiring heart organ as it was introduced after puberty. Now a further miracle of the creation of humanity follows.

A continuous process takes place in which humanity becomes co-creator. Through the search for spirit and active work the individual human being becomes co-creator of his own destiny to an ever-higher degree. He is no longer passive; the Logos is no longer creating the human physical body alone. The fact is that the quality of becoming depends on the purposeful striving and strongest unfolding of forces of will in each human being. We ourselves can see to it that this may take place in the proper way.

We may stand in awe and wonder when we fully realize the extent of the possibilities that are laid into our own hands. In complete freedom we can work on the structural configuration of our own etheric heart; the new heart which began a process of separating from the physical heart in 1721 (See drawing). The important fact is, however, that the perfection of this new creation depends on a strictly self-directed goal orientation, as well as the most strongly activated unfolding of will forces. It must arise out of a "physiology of freedom" given by the Logos for the transformation of our own being. The phrase "Physiology of Freedom" was coined by Dr. Peter Selg, a young physician who wrote the book *Vom Logos Menschlicher Physis.* [2]

Peter Selg's deeply spiritual, yet strictly natural scientific way of thought, his unusual knowledge as a modern medical doctor, allows him to look at the physical body in a new way. He found that within the structure of the physical body created by the Logos there exists "free space" and this prompted him to coin the phrase "Physiology of Freedom." In his book *Vom Logos Menschlicher Physis* he looks at those parts of the body which point to such a "free space."

The following drawing was taken from GA 190 April 5th, 1919. (Figure 2.) It points to the physical heart as it swims in the sac of the surrounding separated etheric heart. If we consider these ideas carefully there arises before our inner eye Rudolf Steiner's *Philosophy of Freedom* (*Philosophy of Spiritual Activity*) (chapter 9). There he talks about the emergence of ego consciousness through the physical body and the possibility for this ego consciousness to evolve because the Ego takes part in all spiritualised thinking. Further it says in the ninth chapter that the physical organisation has no part in the essence of thought, that instead, indeed, the physical withdraws and creates a space for thought. Man's thought is free! The will, however, is as yet only accessible through the physical body. It can be freed if the activity of thinking can be so strengthened that the ego is released slowly from the depth of the will. The reader can see how the majestic process of creating in freedom is deeply connected with the miraculous and creative work of the individual human being as he frees himself from that which hinders the rightful unfolding of the etheric heart. We are talking about the etheric heart as an organ for future lives, an organ with an eye for karmic cognition.

Figure 2.

This has truly been placed into man's hands because, according to Rudolf Steiner, in the year 2100 this process is destined to slowly reach a conclusion.

Although on one hand that which was described is part of a normal evolutionary process, there is another side to it, a prerequisite that may not be overlooked. According to Rudolf Steiner, it is important that mankind creates a spiritual compensation, a counterweight to the past, when the heart was a God-given, a God-protected organ. Human beings must connect the separated Etheric Heart to the spiritual world through a transformed thinking and feeling life. In our age they need to find a new Michaelic path on which they search for the truth, then they will find the right way to this cosmically created third Etheric Heart. This new spiritual and dynamic path gives man the possibility to structure his Etheric Heart organ as a sense organ ever more in the greatest possible diversity. As the third heart is created by the Logos in Michaelic freedom in conjunction with man, it grows in size as large as the entire blood organism. It is an invisible sense organ, an inner cognitive eye of the heart revealing the karmic chain of events throughout incarnations.

Rudolf Steiner has indicated how the spirit-pupil can learn to think with such a spiritual heart and how he can protect and care for such knowledge. When Michaelic thinking has truly been activated, spirit knowledge is gathered through the separated heart, not through the noble head which disregards the subjective as well as man's feelings; yes, Michael will open the path of thought from the head to the heart, and hearts not heads begin to have thoughts. All of this follows naturally the great revelation of the creation of the third heart after the loosening of the newly formed Etheric Heart.

It is Michael's intention that in the future, intelligence will stream through the hearts of human beings and that it will be connected to the same divine spiritual forces that helped to create man in the beginning of time.

With regard to the fifth heart chamber I was led to Ehrenfried Pfeiffer's autobiography. [3] He touches briefly on this deep occult secret but points to no further references by Steiner. He merely indicates the point/circle meditation, given by Rudolf Steiner in the curative course.

In summarizing we can say that through the separation of the etheric heart and its further expansion over the entire blood circulation an opposing pole has been set into motion.

It has become possible for souls connected to Michael to be engaged in a goal-oriented schooling for initiation, and thus to enter into closer connection with the spiritual hierarchies and the etheric Christ, who reveals Himself today as an Angel. It is Michael's aim that spiritual schooling will lead to heart-knowledge and that the etheric eye of the heart will become an organ of cognition.

We read the following in Rudolf Steiner's *Michael-Letters*:

> "The Christ-force imprints human imaginations into the cosmic ether."

> "That which man experiences as strength of conscious imagination becomes world content."

"Hearts begin to have thoughts, that is the new way of thinking with the heart."

"The newly developed heart-organ slowly transforms into an eye or better a sensing-heart-eye-organ."

"Everyone who strives in the light of spiritual science and connects himself with the creative World-Logos through heartfelt thoughts, sooner or later will learn to read Karma. By doing so he adds to the substance of the etheric-youth or angel-being through which the etheric Christ reveals Himself today."

For spiritually active pupils in the Michaelic stream, the Third Etheric Heart becomes:

1. An eye for self-cognition, the realization of the true self as the eternal being of man.
2. Likewise, it becomes the eye of the Ego-sense, which perceives the other in his true being.
3. An eye of cognition for supersensible beings and for the etheric Christ Himself, protected and cherished in the Michaelic mystery-culture of will as it is destined for our epoch.
4. It will also become possible to perceive the karma of others as well as one's own karmic chain.

All this grows from the fruits of a trained will. I refer to the September verse of the *Calendar of the Soul*:

O Nature, your maternal life
I bear within the essence of my will.
And my will's fiery energy
Shall steel my spirit striving,
That sense of self springs forth from it
To hold me in myself.

When Dr. Kaelin, a medical doctor and research scientist, asked Rudolf Steiner why there was such a rapid increase in heart problems, he explained it with the fact that the Etheric Heart is loosening from the physical. This was mentioned earlier.

It can be seen from Rudolf Steiner's answer that we at the beginning of the 21st century stand at the focal point regarding the developmental process of the Etheric Heart. We may not fail to research all possible facts with the greatest clarity possible, we may not fail to practice, exercise and purify ourselves while searching for the truth. Yes, we may contribute to the right formation of the new Etheric Heart; Michael leaves us free but he expects, and he observes us. Today most people do not practice, it is their omission, a tragic loss which occurs because of lack of knowledge which damages the physical heart. All the more, we should work on unfolding our heart organ which allows us to ascend to Moral Imagination and Moral Inspiration and to forms of cognition where we may experience our own, cognitive eye of the Etheric Heart in the Sun-Logos.

The powerful rays of the Spirit-Sun live in the new etheric heart organ. (GA 212) The human being will one day be able to rise to infinite spirit heights. Many more aspects to the theme could be researched. In Basel (Oct. 1, 1911 GA 130) Rudolf Steiner spoke about the etherization of the blood, the facts are well known to students of Anthroposophy. Illnesses of the heart can predominantly be traced to a lack of spiritual activity. Moral characteristics affect the contraction and expansion of the capillary vessels, and our moral soul-life also influences the make-up of our blood.

Our blood, seen from a spiritual perspective, undergoes a constant process of etherization, creating a foundation for health and life. If enough spiritual activity is unfolded, it has a positive effect on the blood because used substance can be etherized. This ether substance has its occult source in the etherized blood of the Logos. It is the heart-blood of the crucified and subsequently risen Logos. He is united with the Sun ether. If man inwardly connects with the Christ Being, there lives in him indeed in the etherized substance of his etheric heart and in his etheric blood stream the blood stream of the crucified. If a human being cannot connect inwardly with the Christ, if he rejects Him, the etheric blood of the Christ bounces off the etheric blood stream of such a man. This is a profound occult truth, a prerequisite to the stupendous unfolding of the developmental process of the new etheric heart. (*The Etherization of the Blood*, a lecture given in Basle, October 1st, 1911, GA 130)

With each heartbeat, a certain amount of material substance is absorbed, taken away from physical pressure and added to the etheric substance. This etheric substance begins to radiate outward so that we can become aware of the process in a picture. To begin with, there is the human being on the physical cross of his body. Etheric rays stream out from the center of his heart. From the heart of the Christ, nailed to the cross of the Tree of Life, flows His blood into the dying Earth and into men's dying etheric bodies. As etheric Sunrays they stream far into the Cosmos. We too can take into ourselves these rays so that out of a small etheric Sun, in our new Etheric Heart organ, likewise streams can flow out far into the Cosmos. We harbor in our Etheric Heart a creatively active inner Sun that radiates warmth and light into the surroundings, into the far reaches of the Cosmos. It is the warmth ether that is predominantly active in the Etheric Heart.

We find important indications from Rudolf Steiner in a lecture given July 2, 1921 in GA 205 [*Therapeutic Insights: Earthly and Cosmic Laws*]:

> "When we look into the inner heart, we find that there are forces collecting from the metabolic and limb system. We know that that which is connected to the etheric heart-forces has been spiritualized, it follows that that which has to do with our outer life and our actions is also spiritualized and woven into it. That which is being prepared in the heart as forces turns into karmic predispositions and karmic tendencies. It is simply outrageous to speak of a heart pump...

> "You see, when one gets to know this organization and learns to differentiate then it all appears as a great connected whole. One needs to look at the entirety, life that reaches beyond birth and death. In this way one can look into the most intimate structure of man. We cannot speak of the head because the head is simply cast off; those forces are fulfilled with this incarnation, they were transformed from the previous incarnation. The metabolic activities which take place are not simply chemical processes which one can examine physiologically or chemically. There is another important nuance where morality plays a part. This moral nuance is indeed stored in the heart and carried over into the next incarnation. To study the total human being means to find in him the forces which reach beyond the earthly life."

In GA 205 July 2nd, 1921, page 110 Rudolf Steiner says: "You can imagine what a tremendous difference there is, between that which lives in our heart during this incarnation and the condition in which we find ourselves in a new life after having gone through a long development in the time between death and a new birth. And yet when you look into your innermost heart you can assess quite well, of course in a hidden way only, not in a fully developed imagination, what you will do in your next life. One can, you see, not only say in an abstract way, my next life is being prepared today in all karmic detail, but one can point to the 'little box' in which the karma rests, awaiting the future."

Another important lecture was held May 1, 1915 (GA 161) [in: *Meditation and Concentration: Three Kinds of Clairvoyance*] where Rudolf Steiner speaks about the Etheric Heart in relation to its new position in the back of the head outside the physical body. (Figure 3.) It is quite important that this is taken into account. It is further necessary to study and research the etheric heart and its position by looking at *Knowledge of the Higher Worlds* especially the part 'Some Results of Initiation.' The darkly shaded part at the back of the head in the picture would be the very first beginning of the new etheric heart. It arises as a mighty net of etherized blood which creates an individual thin little skin separating it from the cosmic ether. With this we have made another step in understanding the size and position of the etheric heart.

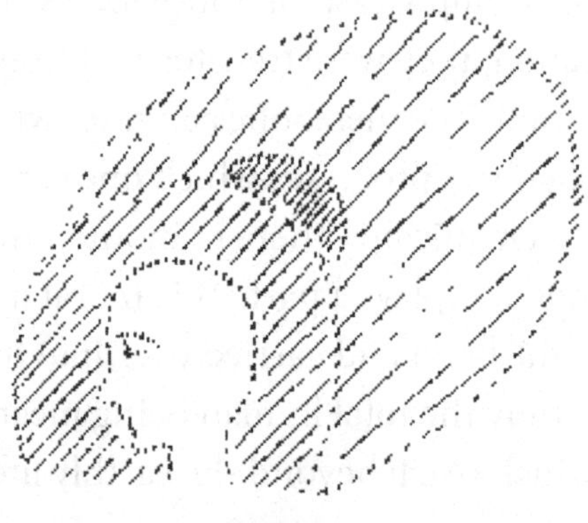

Figure 3.

Finally we might direct our glance at possibilities which this new etheric heart organ as sense organ or Sun-eye will be able to develop for the future. I have already indicated it. We hear in the lecture of the 6th of May 1922 that when we look into ourselves we can experience our etheric eye as a cognitive eye. It can become the organ for going into one's own depth. Here we experience the flaming, scorching and burning emotions, desires, passions and drives on the one hand, on the other that in us which does not connect with them, because it is our eternal being. It lives alongside of it. Therefore we can say that the new etheric organ becomes cognitive for our eternal being in the depth of the metabolism and will organization. While our head holds our soul as if buried within, we comprehend ourselves, our eternal being, in the dark depth of will purified from emotions and drives. "Now we enter the realm where the soul and spirit become one," says Rudolf Steiner in his lecture of May 6th, 1922, GA 212. "In the head or brain man is physical. That which is soul-like has been buried there, it is like a corpse. This corpse is the area to which presently all natural scientific research regarding the soul is directed. But in reality the soul is true to itself and connected to the spirit below the heart. The new and wonderful sense organ which is as large as the blood organism finds the eternal being of man next to all that which arises from the depth of will as drives and emotions."

When the pupil rises to imaginative and inspired cognition then that which arises as lower drives and instincts may not speak. There arises a sum of thoughts in mighty pictures, they reveal what man was before birth. The pupil is transported into the time before birth.

That which we see as a vision through our heart, which has become a sense organ, that is our own eternal being. We experience our own self in our eternal being. When we continue to press forward into our own being, the Sun-like quality changes. We come to a definite point where we meet inspired knowledge and where we weave with inspired cognition in a real picture-world. Now in complete consciousness through a sudden inner jolt in our spirit soul it feels as if we fuse with the Sun itself ... But at the same moment when we come to inspired cognition, when our heart-sense becomes a cognitive organ, we suddenly feel as if our very heart is being transplanted into the Sun, we feel as if we go with the Sun, the Sun is in us, belonging to us. The Sun becomes our eye, our ear as well as our warmth organ. We are jolted into the Sun-like. "We stand within the light, we touch spirit-beings with our light-organs." Here supersensible knowledge reaches another stage, a little step further. Then we not only feel ourselves within the Sun but we perceive ourselves "on the other side of the Sun" as well. We have now moved fully into the Sun, we feel part of the Sun with our innermost being and we experience the world within our being, previously it was outside of ourselves, around us. These are Rudolf Steiner's words. It is an experience which we go through unconsciously during sleep.

Now we need to reach beyond the Sun-sphere but this only happens through inspiration and later intuition. Here the physical Sun separates us from the place in which we live between death and a new birth. The physical Sun hinders us from seeing the spiritual. Through the added step, however, we now consciously experience the spirit of the Sun and we feel as if we were within the Sun wandering along world paths. We reach outside that which is Sun-like as "the Sun has a Spirit Being," a kind of Super-Sun. Just as the moon has a powerful influence on the physical of man so the Sun has a strong influence on his soul.

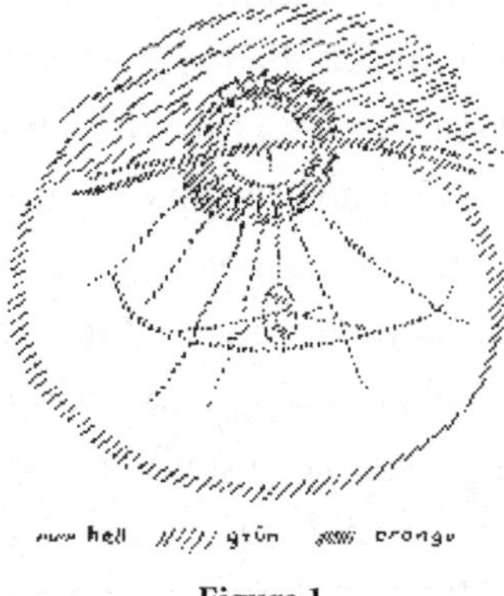

Figure 1.

Something else is said, that in the past through an instinctive clairvoyance one knew that especially the spiritually inclined people are not only what they are through Sun and Moon, but that they are what they are through the great Sun-Being. That is the reason why people in the past were painted with golden auras. It was meant to show that a person was able to reach not only into the soul realm but into the spirit and further so that the extension could become visible in the etheric. See Rudolf Steiner's drawing. No drives, passions and desires stream from that which is connected to the Super-Sun, but rather World-Soul. One experiences an inner warmth as well as an inner enthusiasm, but in pure spiritual form, not through drives and passions. There is warmth which comes from the world, from the Great Sun-Being.

All this, in summary, is the crowning of that which can one day be perceived and spiritually known by the new etheric heart organ as a Sun-eye, when the Sun as spiritual Super-Sun becomes the cognitive eye of the etheric heart.

Everything that has been mentioned here, especially the stupendous possibilities for the Etheric Heart, is of great significance because at its foundation lies a free Michaelic deed creatively taken in hand by the pupil.

It is the powerful esoteric call to each pupil of Michael, to help in the creation of a new Sun-Earth. This co-working can be undertaken when the etheric body and the etheric heart become increasingly christianized out of the new faculties of the Etheric Heart-Sun-Eye, while the heart learns to interpret karmic events by reading within the actively creating Logos.

Learning to speak the Word which structures human life requires that the awakened Michaelic culture of will forces strengthens wills. Through this mystery magic capabilities will arise for the human being of the future. Sooner or later, the new etheric heart of man will become an active organ which through karmic insight can become increasingly helpful and healing in the social sphere. To the pillar of cognition the pillar of will must be added as a column of christianized blood.

In this way the secret of the Grail lives in the magnificent occult soul spiritual unfolding of the etheric heart. The new etheric heart as cognitive spirit-eye of man's eternal being is the place where in the Grail-Cup the etheric organ lights up as the real force, as the blood of the Redeemer. Christian Morgenstern utters:

"I lift my heart to you as a true vessel of the Grail ..."

It is the experience of being totally imbued with the spirit of eternity which fills the receiving soul of the Grail youth in a cultic spirit event at the Sun-altar. Here Spirit and soul truly unite. It is the Michaelic path to the heavenly city of New Jerusalem.

Notes:

1. *The Mission of the Archangel Michael: The Revelation of the Unique Mystery of Man.* November 21–30, 1919, Dornach. Rudolf Steiner: GA 161, 190, 205, 212, 10.

2. Peter Selg, *Vom Logos der Menschlicher Physis, die Entfaltung einer anthroposophischen Humanphysiologie im Werk Rudolf Steiners.* Verlag Goetheanum August 6, 2000

3. Ehrenfried Pfeiffer, *Ein Leben fuer den Geist* [*A Life for the Spirit*] 1999, Perseus Verlag, Basel

See Also:

Heinz Herbert Schoeffler *Die Zeitgestalt des Herzens.* [*The Time Shape of the Heart*] 1974 Verlag Freies Geistesleben, Stuttgart

Ruth Haertl, *Auf der Suche nach der Wirklichkeit der Erkenntnis im Denken des Herzens aus Anthropos-Sophia im Lichte des Heiligen Gral.* [*In Search of the Reality of Knowledge in the Thinking of the Heart from Anthropos-Sophia in the Light of the Holy Grail*] Verlag Ch. Moellmann, ISBN 3-931156-84-2

Rudolf Steiner on the Human Heart

The greatest authority on the human heart, both old and new, is Rudolf Steiner. There is no end to the wisdom Steiner has shared through his Anthroposophical Society about the human heart. Everything stated in the article above is found in seed-form in the Steiner passages below. We have already presented a variety of summaries of some of Steiner's ideas above; now it is time to hear these ideas from the source. Personal commentary on Steiner's remarks have also already been presented above in the Introduction. We have highlighted certain passages to bring to the reader's attention new elements that build on the previous 'Anthroposophically Illuminated' remarks that move the narrative forward. From education to medicine, agriculture to human development, Steiner shed light on the human heart that brings forward ancient wisdom in a new form of spiritual science. We have classified the selections according to general topics for organizational purposes only.

The Heart as a Supersensible Organ of Perception

Course for Young Doctors, Rudolf Steiner, Lecture II. January 3, 1924, GA 316

"The heart is a sense organ of a different kind. … The heart is a sense organ for perceiving the inner being of man. I have often said that it is nonsense to regard the heart as a kind of pump which drives the blood through the arteries. The movement of the blood is the result of the activity of the Ego and astral body, and the heart is merely a sense organ which perceives the circulation, particularly the circulation from the lower to the upper man…. The task of the heart is to see how astral body and Ego work on the human being. Therefore, the heart is an entirely spiritual sense organ…

Rudolf Steiner, *Lectures to the First Class*, Vol. II. Lesson XIV. Dornach, May 31, 1924, GA 270

"The senses are nothing other than differentiated breathing organs. Eye, ear—all are refined breathing organs. Breathing expands to all the senses. As it lives in the lung, it lives in the eye. Except that in the lungs it combines with carbon, and in the ears with highly rarefied silica. Carbon dioxide is formed in the organism. In the senses, very fine silicic acid is formed.

"Man lives downward by converting oxygen to carbon dioxide. He lives upward into the zone of his sense-nervous system by combining oxygen with silica, forming very fine silicic acid. So, we live in a way that when breath turns to blood, it generates carbon dioxide; when breath passes around the senses it generates silicic acid—downward and outward through breath: carbon dioxide; toward the senses and back from the senses to the breathing process in very fine doses of silicic acid."

***Spiritual Science and Medicine*, Rudolf Steiner, Lecture II. March 22, 1920, GA 312**

"The heart originates as a 'damming up' organ (*Stauorgan*) between the lower activities of the organism, the intake and working up of food, and the upper activities, the lowest of which is the respiratory. A damming up organ is inserted and its action is therefore a product of the interplay between the liquefied foodstuffs and the air absorbed from the outside. All that can be observed in the heart must be looked upon as an effect, not a cause, as a mechanical effect, to begin with…

"For what is the heart after all? It is a sense organ, and even if its sensory function is not directly present in the consciousness, if its processes are subconscious, nevertheless it serves to enable the 'upper' activities to feel and perceive the 'lower.' As you perceive external colors through your eyes, so do you perceive, dimly and subconsciously through your heart, what goes on in the lower abdomen. The heart is an organ for inner perception.

"The heart is primarily that organ whose perceptible motion expresses the equilibrium between the upper and lower processes; in relation to the soul (or perhaps more accurately in the subconscious) it is the perceptive organ that mediates between these two poles of the total human organization."

The Heart is Not a Pump

***From Mammoths to Mediums*, Rudolf Steiner, Lecture III. *Blood circulation and movement of the heart*, Dornach June 6, 1923, GA 350**

"The function of the heart is not to pump blood through the body. It is a sensory organ. Through the heart's activity the head can perceive the entire blood circulation. The pulsebeat is a barometer for health or illness. But the pulsebeat is also nothing other than the movement of the blood."

Theosophy of the Rosicrucians, Rudolf Steiner, Lecture XIII. The Future of Man, Munich, June 5, 1907, GA 99

"It is the feelings of the soul which give rise to the movement of the blood; the soul drives the blood, and the heart moves because it is driven by the blood. Thus the truth is exactly the opposite of what materialistic science states. Man today, however, cannot guide his heart as he will; when he feels anxiety, it beats faster, since the feeling acts on the blood and this quickens the motion of the heart. But what is suffered involuntarily by man today, will later, at a higher stage of evolution, be in his own power. Later on he will drive his blood by his own volition, and cause the movement of his heart as today he moves the muscles of his hand. The heart with its peculiar structure is a crux, a riddle for modern science. It has diagonally striped fibers, which are otherwise only to be found in voluntary muscles. Why? Because the heart has not yet reached the end of its evolution, but is an organ of the future; because it will in the future be a voluntary muscle. Thus it already shows the rudiments of this in its structure..."

Esoteric Development, Rudolf Steiner, Lecture VII, The Great Initiates, Berlin, March 16, 1905, GA 53

"I will now speak of the twelve-petalled Lotus flower in the region of the heart. Six petals of this flower were already developed in the far-distant past, and six must be developed by all men in the future, by present-day Initiates and their pupils. In all anthroposophical handbooks you can find reference to certain virtues in the forefront of those that should be acquired by anyone aspiring to the stage of Chela, or pupil. These six virtues which you find mentioned in every anthroposophical handbook concerned with man's development are: control of thought, control of action, tolerance, steadfastness, impartiality, and equilibrium, or what Angelus Silesius calls composure. These six virtues, which one must practice consciously and attentively in conjunction with meditation, bring to unfolding the six further petals of the twelve-petalled Lotus flower. And these are not gathered blindly in the anthroposophical textbooks, nor are they stamped by haphazard or individual inner feeling, but they are spoken out of the great Initiates' deepest knowledge. Initiates know that whoever really wishes to evolve to the higher supersensible stages of development must bring about the unfolding of the twelve-petalled Lotus flower. And to this end he must today develop, through these six virtues, the six petals that were undeveloped in the past. Thus you see how the great Initiates essentially gave their directions for life out of their own deeper knowledge of the human being. I could extend these remarks to still other organs of knowledge and observation, but I only wish to give you a brief sketch of the process of initiation, and for that these indications should suffice.

"When the pupil has progressed so far that he begins to form the astral sense-organs, when he has progressed so far that he is capable of perceiving not only the physical impressions in his surroundings but also what belongs to the soul—in other words, to see what is in the aura of man himself as well as what is in the aura of animals and plants—he then begins a completely new stage of instruction. No one can see in his environment that which has to do with his soul before his Lotus flowers revolve, just as one without eyes can see no color and no light. But when the barrier is pierced, when the pupil has gone beyond the preliminary stages of knowledge so that he has insight into the soul-world, then true 'pupil-ship' first begins for him. This leads through four stages of knowledge. Now what happens in this moment, when man has passed beyond the first steps and has become a Chela? We have seen how all that we have just described related to the astral body. This is organized throughout by the human body. Whoever has undergone such a development has a totally different aura. When man out of his self-consciousness has illuminated his astral body, when he himself has become the luminous organization of his astral body, then we say that this pupil has illuminated his astral body with Manas. Manas is nothing other than an astral body dominated by self-consciousness. Manas and astral body are one and the same, but at different stages of development."

Spiritual Science and Medicine, Rudolf Steiner, Lecture VIII, March 27, 1920, GA 312

"The two processes of breathing and blood formation meet again in the human heart itself. The whole outside world (including man) appears as a duality that is dammed up in the heart, and in it strives for a kind of equilibrium.

"Thus, we come to a remarkable picture, the picture of the human heart, with its interiorising character, its synthesis of everything that works from outside into our bodies. Outside in the world there is an analysis, a scattering, of all that is gathered together in the heart. (See Diagram) You come here to an important conception that might be expressed thus: You look out into the world, face the horizon and ask:— What is in these outer surroundings? What works inwards from the periphery? Where can I find something in myself that is akin to it? If I look into my own heart, I find, as it were, the inverted heaven, the polar opposite. On the one hand you have the periphery, the point extended to infinity, on the other you have the heart, which is the infinite circle concentrated to a point. The whole world is within our heart…

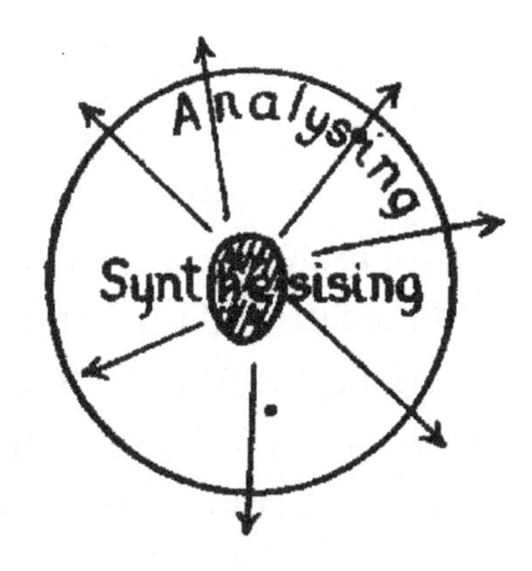

***The Human Soul in Relation to World Evolution*, Rudolf Steiner, Lecture VI, *The Formation of the Etheric and the Astral Heart*, May 26, 1922, GA 212**

"The real fact is that all that happens in the moral life, and all that happens physically in the world, are brought together precisely in the human heart. These two—the moral and the physical—which run so independently and yet side by side for modern consciousness today, are found in their real union when we learn to understand all the configurations of the human heart..

***Heart Lectures*, Ehrenfried Pfeiffer, Mercury Press, 1982**

"In our time there are certain changes taking place in the heart, by which gradually a fifth chamber will develop. In this fifth chamber man will have a new organ which will allow him to control life forces in a different way than is possible at the moment."

The Effects of Esoteric Development, Rudolf Steiner, Lecture II, The Hague, March 21, 1913, GA 145

"And here we must bring especially into prominence the fact that occult observation makes clear the experience of the relation between the physical sheath and the physical heart. The physical human heart is to the occultist an extremely interesting, an extremely important organ; for it can only be understood when we bear in mind the entire mutual relationship, including the spiritual relationship, of the Sun and the Earth. Even at the time when, after the Old Saturn period, the Old Sun period was a sort of planetary predecessor of the Earth, even then began the preparation, as it were, of the relation which now exists between these two heavenly bodies, the Sun and the Earth. And we must so bear in mind this relation between Sun and Earth that we thereby really comprehend how the Earth of today, being nourished, as it were, by the solar activities, takes in these solar activities and transmutes them. What the solid substance of the Earth takes in as solar forces, what the Earth takes up in its envelopes of air and water, in its changing conditions of heat, what it takes up in the light that encompasses the Earth, what it takes up in that part of the Earth which is now no longer physically perceptible in any way—the Earth-part of the harmony of the spheres—what the Earth receives as life-forces directly from the Sun—all this is in connection with the inner forces that work upon the human heart through the circulation of the blood. In reality all these act upon the circulation of the blood, and through this upon the heart. All external theory with respect to this process is radically wrong. External theory calls the heart a pump that pumps the blood through the body, so that one has to look upon the heart as the organ regulating the circulation of the blood. The reverse is the truth. The heart-circulation responds to the impulse given by the circulation of the blood, which is the original source of action. The blood drives the heart; not the reverse, the heart the blood. And the whole of this organism just described, which is concentrated in the activity of the heart, is none other than the human microcosmic reflection of the macrocosmic activities first received by the Earth from the Sun. The impulse received by the Earth from the Sun is reflected in that which the heart receives from the blood.

"It is different with the brain. Some details of the correspondence of the brain were given in the last lecture. The human brain has very, very little to do directly with the solar activities on the Earth. Directly, I say. Indirectly, as an organ of perception it is concerned with them; it perceives the external light and color, for instance; that, however, is only perception. But directly, in its construction, in its inner mobility, in the whole of its inward life, the brain has little, scarcely anything, to do with the effects of the Sun upon the Earth; it is much more concerned with all that streams to the Earth from outside our solar system; it is concerned with the cosmic relationship of the whole starry heavens, but not with the narrower relationships of our solar system. However, in a more limited sense, what we have to describe as the brain-substance is connected with the Moon, though only in so far as the Moon does not depend upon the Sun; but has preserved independence of it. So that what goes on in our brain corresponds to activities lying outside the forces which are imaged microcosmically in our heart. Sun dwells in the human heart; all else besides the Sun in the Cosmos dwells in the human brain.

"Thus man, as regards these two organs, is a microcosm, because through his heart he is given up to the influences exercised by the Sun on the Earth, and reflects these, as it were;

but through his brain he has an inner life directly connected with the Cosmos outside the Sun. That is a connection of extreme interest and significance. The brain is only connected with the effect of the Sun on the Earth through external perception. But just this very thing is overcome in theosophical development. Theosophical development surmounts the external sense world.

"Hence the brain is set free for an inward life so cosmic that it is unsuitable for the specialized influence of the Sun itself. When the student surrenders himself in meditation to some imagination, processes take place in his brain which have nothing at all to do with our solar system, but correspond to the processes outside it. Hence, in fact, the relationship between the heart and the brain is like that between the Sun and the starry heavens, and this manifests, in a certain respect, in the experience of the soul developing through theosophy through the fact that while this soul is devoted seriously and deeply to purely theosophical thought, the heart forms, as it were, an opposite pole, and comes in opposition to what one might call the starry-brain. This opposition is expressed in the fact that the student learns to feel that his heart and brain begin to go different ways; while previously he had no need to give attention to both separately, because they were indistinguishable, he must now begin so to do—if he is developing through Theosophy.

"It gives us an accurate idea of man's place with regard to the whole Cosmos when we thus consider the physical sheath, and bear in mind the position of man here upon the earth. Through his blood-system and heart there is within him the whole relationship between the Sun and the Earth, and when his inner powers are devoted solely to that for which on Earth he needs the brain as his instrument, then in that brain there are cosmic processes at work extending beyond our solar system. It will be evident that the pupil has an entirely new experience with respect to his heart and brain. His sensations really classify themselves, so that in the serene course of the stars displayed in the heavens at night he learns to feel the processes of his brain, and he feels the movements of the solar system in his heart. In this you see at the same time a path which becomes more important at a higher stage of initiation; you see the doors, as it were, which open from man to the Cosmos. The student who, through higher development, steps out of himself—as has been described even in exoteric lectures—and looks back at his own body, learns to recognize all the processes in his physical body; in the circulation of the blood and the activity of the heart a reflection of the hidden forces of the solar system, and in the processes of his brain, which he then sees spiritually from the outside, the secrets of the Cosmos."

***The Effect of Occult Development Upon the Self and the Sheaths of Man*, Rudolf Steiner, Lecture VI, The Hague, March 25, 1913, GA 145**

"Thus we must feel as though we were separated from our etheric body by an Abyss filled, as it were, with ether, with universal cosmic ether; as if we stood on the further shore of the etheric body, and there various processes took place. And as, in this case, all these processes take place in time, we feel like a wanderer returning to our own etheric body. In reality, we are going further and further from it, but in our clairvoyant consciousness we approach it. And in approaching this etheric body of ours we feel ourselves approaching something which thrusts us back. We come, as it were, to a spiritual rock. Then it is as if we were allowed to pass into something. At first we are outside, and then it is as though we were let into something, it seems as though we had first been outside and now were inside, but not in the manner in which we had been within it during the day. Everything depends upon being outside with the astral body and Ego, and only looking in; that is to say, we are only inside the etheric body with our consciousness. And now we can see what is going on within it.

"In a certain way, everything changes just as the physical body is transferred into Paradise; but that which goes on within the etheric body is in a still more interior connection with the everyday processes in man. Let us consider what sleep really signifies, what this 'being outside the physical body and etheric body' means. For we have assumed that the clairvoyant power is exercised at this moment through the person's suddenly becoming clairvoyant during sleep or remaining consciously clairvoyant on falling asleep. Let us consider what sleep is! That which permeates the physical and etheric body with consciousness is now outside; within the body only vegetative processes take place—everything is done to restore the forces used up during the day. And we perceive all this, we perceive how the forces of the physical, particularly those of the brain, are renewed; but we do not see the brain as the anatomist does—we see how the man of the physical world, of whom we make use for our consciousness during our waking condition, we see how this man, who has indeed been forsaken by us, but who clearly shows that he is our instrument, lies enchanted in a castle, as it were. Symbolized by the brain lying within the skull, our human nature on the Earth appears as a being under enchantment living in a castle. We see this humanity of ours as a being imprisoned and enclosed by stone walls. The symbol of this, the shrunken symbol, as it were, is our skull. We see it externally as a little skull. But when we look at the etheric forces which lie at its foundation, the earthly man actually appears to us as if he were within the skull, and imprisoned in this castle. And then from the other parts of the organism there stream up the forces which support this human being who is really within the skull as if in a mighty castle; the forces stream upwards; first the force which comes from that in the organism which is the outspread instrument of the human astral body; there streams up all that makes the human being ardent and mighty through his nerve fibers. All this streams together in the earthly brain-man; this appears as a mighty sword which the human being has forged on the Earth.

"Then stream up the forces of the blood. These, as we gradually learn to feel and recognize, appear as that which really wounds the brain-man lying in the enchanted castle of the skull. The forces which in the etheric body stream up to the earthly human being lying in the enchanted castle of the brain are like the bloody lance. And then we arrive at a unique perception. This is, that we are able to observe all that may stream up to the noblest parts of the brain. Before this we have not the slightest idea of it.

"Thus, you see that from a different standpoint I have come back again to what I have already touched upon in these lectures. No matter how much animal food a human being may eat, it is all useless for a certain part of his brain, it is merely ballast. Other organs may be nourished thereby; but in the brain there is something from which the etheric body at once thrusts back all that comes from the animal kingdom. Indeed, the etheric body even thrusts back from one part of the brain, from one small, vital part of the brain, all that comes from the plant kingdom, and allows only the mineral extract to be of value; there this mineral extract is brought into contact with the purest of what comes through the sense organs. The purest of light, the purest sound, the purest heat, here come in touch with the purest products of the mineral kingdom; for the most vital part of the human brain is nourished by the union of the purest sense impressions with the purest mineral products. The etheric body separates from this noblest part of the human brain all that comes from the plant or animal kingdoms. But all the things that the human being takes in as his food pass up also; for the brain also has less noble parts. These are nourished by all that streams up, by which the whole organism is nourished. Only the noblest part of the brain must be nourished by the most beautiful union of the sense perceptions and the highest part of the purified mineral extract. We now learn to recognize a wonderful cosmic connection between man and the whole of the rest of the Cosmos. We can now see, as it were, a part of man wherein we perceive how human thought, by means of the instrument of the nervous system which serves the astral body, prepares the sword for human strength on Earth; therein we become acquainted with all that is mingled with the blood, and to a certain extent contributes to the killing of the most precious thing in the brain. And this noblest thing in the brain is ever sustained by the union of the most delicate sense perceptions with the purest products of the mineral kingdom. And then, during sleep, when thought is not making use of the brain, there stream to the brain the products which have been formed lower down in the inner parts from the plant and animal kingdoms.

"Thus, when we penetrate into our own etheric body, it is as though we had reached an Abyss, and across it we could see what goes on in the etheric body; and all this appears in mighty pictures representing the processes of the spiritual man during sleep. The Ego and astral body—the spiritual man—descends into the castle, which is formed of that which is only seen symbolically in the skull. Here the human being lies sleeping, 'wounded' by the blood, the man of whom we see that thoughts are his strength—that which must be capable of nourishment by all that comes from the kingdom of nature, that which in its purest parts must be served by the finest, this we have described. All this symbolically represented resulted in the *Legend of the Holy Grail.* And the *Legend of the Holy Grail* tells us of that miraculous food which is prepared from the finest activities of the sense impressions and the finest activities of the mineral extracts, whose purpose it is to nourish the noblest part of man all through the life he spends on earth; for it would be killed by anything else. This heavenly food is what is contained in the Holy Grail. And that which otherwise takes place, that which presses up from the other kingdoms, we find clearly represented if we go back to the original Grail legend, where a meal is described at which a hind is first set on the table. The penetrating up into the brain where forever floats the Grail, that is, the vessel for the purest food of the human hero who lies in the castle of the brain, and who is killed by everything else—all this is represented. The best presentation of this is not that by Wolfram, 1. but it is best represented in an external exoteric way (because almost everyone can recognize, when his attention has been drawn to it, that this legend of the Grail is an occult experience which every human being can experience anew every night), it is best represented, in spite of the profanation which has even crept in there, by Chrétien de Troyes. 2. He put what he wished to say in an exoteric form, but this exoteric form hinted at what he wished to convey, for he refers to his teacher and friend who lived in Alsace, who gave him the esoteric knowledge which he put into exoteric form. This took place in an age when it was necessary to do this, on account of the transition indicated in my book, '*The Spiritual Guidance of Humanity.*' The Grail legend was made exoteric in 1180, shortly before the transition."

Notes:

1. Wolfram von Eschenbach (1170–1220), German knight, Minnesinger poet and composer, regarded as one of the greatest epic poets of medieval German literature, which he dictated in imaginative picture language to his squire as he claims he was illiterate. Therefore, we might consider him to be free of the overly intellectual trends of the medieval writers. He was referred to by Rudolf Steiner as an initiate. Author of: *Parzival*, the fragmentary *Titurel*, and the unfinished *Willehalm* ; which based on the Old French chanson de geste, *Aliscans*.
2. Chrétien de Troyes (Old French: Crestien de Troïes; flourished c. 1160–1191) French poet and trouvère known for his writing on Arthurian subjects such as Gawain, Lancelot, Perceval and the Holy Grail. Rudolf Steiner is here referring to *Perceval, the Story of the Grail* (Old French: *Perceval ou le Conte du Graal*). *Perceval* is the earliest recorded account of what was to become *the Quest for the Holy Grail*; but interestingly Chrétien describes only a 'golden grail' (a serving dish) in the central scene, and does not call it 'holy.' Chrétien also refers to a 'lance,' that appeared with the Grail, as being of equal importance. Author of: *Erec and Enide*, *Lancelot*, and *Yvain*, in addition to *Perceval.*

***From Mammoths to Mediums*, Rudolf Steiner, Lecture III, *Blood circulation and movement of the heart. Perceiving things of the spirit through the lens in the eye*, Dornach, June 6, 1923, GA 350**

"Now it is like this. When I breathe in, for example, I feed myself oxygen, as it were. When I breathe out, I give out carbon dioxide. As soon as I have given out the carbon dioxide I hunger for oxygen. I want to breathe in again. In the first place, this has nothing at all to do with my heart but with my whole body. My whole body hungers for oxygen. Because it develops this hunger for oxygen, the instinct arises to get all the blood moving, for the blood has to have oxygen. Using its astral body, the physical body sends the blood to a place where it can get oxygen.

"Or let us assume I walk, or I work. The food in me is burned up then. I have discussed this with you before. The blood then has few nutrients left. If you work, the blood always loses most of its nutrients. And what does the blood want now? It wants more food again. The blood grabs the food for itself, as it were, which the stomach and intestines have taken up. All this, the hunger for air, the hunger for food, sets the blood in motion. It is the blood which moves in the first place, and the blood takes the heart along with it. And so it is not the heart which pumps the blood through the body, but the blood moves because of its hunger for air, hunger for food, and this moves the heart. We therefore have to say that it is the invisible human being in us which moves the heart…

"Well now, gentlemen, you can see from this that even if we talk about the principle which really moves the whole human being, we find that it is something invisible. If you take the external movement of walking, you'll not at all think it is your big toe which takes a step. Instead you say to yourself: 'I am walking; it is my will which make me walk.' When the organs inside us are moving—and that is not only the heart, our intestines are also moving all the time, for instance—when the organs inside us are moving, therefore, these movements are not brought about by the physical matter in us; they are brought about by the part in us that is invisible. We therefore have to say: 'The heart is not a pump, for the heart is moved by our astral body.' So we have an astral body and this moves the heart, or rather, seeing that our I is actually also in the astral body, we also move our heart with our I, and we do so in a quite specific way

"…If I want to look outside, so that I'll know what goes on out there, I use my eyes. If I want to look inside, at the blood circulation, I use my heart. The heart does not exist to pump blood through the body; it is a sense organ which perceives everything, just as the whole of the head does. We would not be able to know anything about our blood circulation—of course, we know nothing about it directly in our brainbox, but there has to be a knowing in the head—if the head did not perceive the whole of our blood circulation through the heart.

"I have told you that the liver is an organ with sensory functions. It perceives the lower movements, for example. But the movements of the whole human being are perceived by the heart. It is this which sets the heart in motion. The movements caused by the hunger for air and the hunger for food set the heart in motion. And the movements of the heart show you if something is out of order in the body or if it is in order…

"…The pulse beat truly is a barometer for the whole state of health and sickness. The pulse beat is nothing but the movement of the blood, however. The head is all the time doing what we do when we feel the pulse of a sick person. It is continually sensing the whole blood circulation and it does so through the heart. And indeed, the head senses everything that goes on in the body, doing so through the heart…

"…We can therefore only understand what the heart really is if we know that it is in fact the inner sense organ through which the head perceives everything that is going on in the body…

"With regard to the influences on the heart, we certainly have a relationship to the movements of cosmic bodies, especially the Moon…

"…But one can get the whole body to a point where all kinds of things inside are not needed for the moment. If one does not use the heart, for instance—the circulation may continue, but you do not use the heart as a sense organ—you actually begin to perceive the whole of your blood circulation. But you'll not only perceive the blood circulation in that case. If you make your heart such that you look at your blood circulation through your body, as it were, and do not have inner sensation of the heart, nor of your pulse beat; but through them, if you learn to through yourselves—then gentlemen, you will see not just the blood circulation but you'll see the whole movement of the Moon, everything the Moon does, and you'll see how the Moon relates to the Sun. And you will then see the relationship which the heart has to Sun and Moon…

"First, we have to understand that the heart is not mechanical but takes its orientation from the human being. Then people will also find the basic principles for external machines, making them such that they take their orientation from the human being. But in a science which has so much taken the easy way that the heart is described as if the human being had just a pump there in the blood circulation, in such a science people will feel no compunction to make machines where the human being has to take his orientation from the machine. All the problems in our social situation are due to this wrong view that is taken in science. And so, one really has to understand that a proper way of thinking must first of all come upon people; for only then will it be possible to begin a proper social life. For as long as people think the heart is a pump, they will also not be able to relate to outer life in the right way. It is only when people know that the invisible human being is greater than his heart, that it is he who moves the heart, that they will also design their machines to be in accord with human nature…

***From Mammoths to Mediums*, Rudolf Steiner, Lecture IV, *Effects of light and color in earthly matter and in cosmic bodies*, Dornach, June 9, 1923, GA 350**

"Now you know that iron is also present in the human body, where it is a very important substance. Iron is in the blood and it is a very important part of human blood. If we have too little iron in the blood we are people who cannot walk properly, getting tired quickly, people who grow lethargic. If we have too much iron in the blood we get excited and smash everything to pieces. We therefore have to have just the right amount of iron in the blood, otherwise we don't do well. Well, gentlemen, people do not pay much attention to these things today, but I have mentioned this to you before: if you investigate how the human being is connected with the whole world you find that in man the blood is connected with influences that come from Mars. Mars, which always moves, of course, really always stimulates the blood activity in us. This is because of its relationship to iron. Scholars of earlier times who knew this would therefore say that Mars had the same nature as iron. So in a sense we can regard Mars as something that is like our iron. But it also has a reddish yellow shimmer, which means it is all the time growing radiant inside. Mars we thus see as a body that is all the time growing radiant inside."

***From Mammoths to Mediums*, Rudolf Steiner, Lecture XII, *Human and cosmic breathing. The Earth breathes light. Fertilization in plants and humans; fertilization of water through lightning*, Dornach, July 20, 1923, GA 350**

"You see, the things that go on in the world all depend on the interaction of opposite states or conditions. Much still has to be learned about this in modern science today. Let me tell you something about this. Imagine you have someone who is reasonably normal. If he lives to an age of about 72 years, he will have lived 25,920 days—you can work this out, I have spoken of it before. That's 72 years. People normally live that many days. And if you count the number of breaths people take, you'll find that they take exactly that number of breaths in a day. Someone who lives a normal life and whose organism is not destroyed too early—in which case he can't reach the age of 72; someone who does not live to 72 has been destroyed in some way—has as many days in his life as the number of breaths he takes in a day. That is how human beings live. Every day, from one sunrise to the next, they take 25,920 breaths, and all things being equal, they reach patriarchal age, living for 25,920 days.

"Now what does it mean that we live for 25,920 days normally, reaching patriarchal age? It means that we go 25,920 times through day and night here on Earth. We go through days and nights, an experience we may have 25,920 times. What does the Earth do when it goes through day and night? Now you see, gentlemen, the important thing—Goethe already had some idea of it, and today we can be definite about it—is that when dawn comes, the Earth draws the powers of light, powers of the Cosmos, to itself in the place where we happen to be. It is different in the other hemisphere; there it is the other way round, but it is the same process. The Earth and everything that is in the Earth thus breathes in light. It breathes out again when it is night. The Earth does within a day what we do with the air in the short time needed for breathing in and breathing out."

From Mammoths to Mediums, Rudolf Steiner, Lecture XIV, Lung knowledge and kidney knowledge, Dornach, July 28, 1923, GA 350

"Let us first look at people whose blood pressure is too low. People with low blood pressure grow extremely weak, tired, pale, and their digestion suffers severely. They grow feeble inside and do not properly manage to perform their bodily functions, and so they will go into a gradual decline. If the blood pressure is too low, therefore, people grow tired and weak and sick…

"Now let us look at people whose blood pressure is too high. There you sometimes see quite strange things. You see, if you push something like this instrument—it has to have a sharp point in front—into the skin, if you measure a blood pressure that is too high with it, you can be sure that such a person's kidneys will gradually grow useless. The kidneys start to develop their blood vessels, everything there is inside them, in a way they should not be. They calcify and grow enlarged; they degenerate, as people say. They no longer are the shape they should be. If you cut out the kidneys of such people with very high blood pressure after they have died, they look quite dilapidated.

"The question is, where does all this come from? This connection with blood pressure and kidney disease is not really understood at all by those who think in materialistic terms. We have to realize that our astral body—I have told you about this; it is an invisible body in us—lives in this pressure we have in us, in the blood pressure. It is not true at all that the astral body lives in some substance, some form of matter; it lives in a force, in our blood pressure, and the astral body is healthy when our blood pressure is right, that is, between 120 and 140 mm in mid-life. If we have the right blood pressure, our astral body enters into the physical body as we wake up and feels well in there. It can spread in all directions. So if the blood pressure is right, about 120 mm, the astral body really spreads out in our blood pressure, and it can enter into every part of the physical body when we wake up. And whilst we are awake the whole astral body spreads everywhere in us if we have this 'normal' blood pressure, as it is called.

"You see, it is the astral body which makes sure that our organs always are the right shape, the right configuration. Gentlemen, if we were to sleep all the time, so that the astral body would always be outside, the way it is when we sleep, our organs would soon grow fatty. We would not have proper organs. We need the astral body to stimulate the ether body so that we'll always have organs that are sound, having the right configuration. The astral body therefore always has to have the right blood pressure so that it may spread out…

"Let us assume the blood pressure is too high. Now if the blood pressure is too high, what will happen? You see, I once told you that if the mixture of oxygen and nitrogen in the air were different we would find it hard to live. The air contains 79 per cent of nitrogen, the rest is mainly oxygen. The amount of oxygen is small, therefore. If the air contained more oxygen we'd be old people at the age of 20. We would age rapidly. It therefore also depends on the astral body if the body ages early or late. If the blood pressure is too high, the astral body likes being in the physical body. It is really in its element in our blood pressure and will then go in really deep. And what is the consequence? The consequence is that we have the kind of kidneys at 30 that we should only have when we are 70. We live too fast when the blood pressure is high. The kidneys are sensitive organs, and so they will degenerate early. Growing old has to do with the organs growing more and more calcified. And if the blood pressure is too high, the sensitive organs will calcify too soon. The kind of kidney disease one gets with high blood pressure is really a sign that the person has aged too soon, that is, whilst still young he has made these sensitive kidneys be the way they should only be in old age.

"Now you see, gentlemen, the whole of this explanation which I have given you allows you to see that the human being does have something like a soul principle in his physical body, something I call the astral body, which goes out during the night. And so we may also say: Man lives in the forces that develop in his body. He lives in those forces, not in the physical matter."

"It is not enough to learn anthroposophical theories. If one only knows anthroposophical theories, it is merely the way people learned to read in the nineteenth century, the way they took up ideas in a superficial way. It should not be like this. The things we take in should be such that we make them our own inwardly.

"You see, gentlemen, if you have been in stale air and go out into the open air, you take pleasure in this inwardly. And in the same way you should feel pleasure inwardly, experience interest, when you leave all the stuff that is called knowledge today and come into the fresh air of the soul, being told things of the spirit once more. Inner gladness, deep interest, is what we need for the life of the mind and spirit. And when people are full of interest the blood which has grown too heavy—the blood has grown too heavy in everyone today—will grow lighter again. The kidneys are made spiritual and the result will be that things will be better in the world when people want to know something again about the things that have been taken away from them for centuries. This is something one has to say over and over again, something I have to tell you in every possible way; for it is important for us to look the truth in the face and not let ourselves be blinded by science that is not science..."

***Therapeutic Insights: Earthly and Cosmic Laws*, Rudolf Steiner, Lecture IV, *Spiritual Knowledge of the Organs*, Dornach, July 2, 1921, GA 205**

"The heart has nothing whatsoever to do with pumping the blood; rather the blood is set into activity by the entire mobility ('Regsamkeit') of the astral body, of the I, and the heart is only a reflection of these movements. The movement of the blood is an autonomous movement, and the heart only brings to expression the movement of the blood caused by these forces...

"Something is reflected from the surface of the heart that is no longer merely a matter of habit or memory; but is life that is already spiritualized when it reaches the outer surface of the heart. For what is thrown back from the heart are the pangs of conscience. This is to be considered, I would like to say, entirely from the physical aspect: the pangs of conscience that radiate into our consciousness are what is reflected by the heart from our experiences. Spiritual knowledge of the heart teaches us this.

"If we look into the inner aspect of the heart, however, we see gathered there, forces that also stem from the entire metabolic-limb organism, and because what is connected with the heart, with the heart forces, is spiritualized, within it is also spiritualized that which is connected with our outer life, with our deeds... The forces thus prepared within the heart are the karmic tendencies, they are the tendencies of karma. The heart is the organ which, through mediation of the metabolic-limb system, carries what we understand as karma into the next incarnation...

"However, if you look into the inner aspect of your hearts, you can perceive quite well—though of course only latently, not in a finished picture—what you will do in your next life. We need not confine ourselves to the general, abstract statement that what will work itself out karmically in the next life is prepared in this one, but we can point directly to the vessel in which resides the karma of the following incarnations.

"Now all these things are connected with the outer world. The lungs, as inner organs or organ system, actually contain the compressed compulsive thoughts and everything that we take up in perceiving outer objects and concentrating these in the lungs. The liver relates to the outer world in an entirely different way. Precisely because the lungs preserve, as it were, the thought material, they are structured quite differently. They are more closely connected with the earthly element, with the earth element. The liver, which conceals hallucinations, particularly the calm hallucinations, the hallucinations that merely appear, is connected with the fluid system and therefore with water. The kidney system, paradoxical as it sounds, is connected with the air element. One naturally thinks that this ought to be the case with the lungs, but the lungs as organs are connected with the earth element, though not only with it. On the other hand, the kidney system—as an organ—is connected with the air element, and the heart system as an organ is connected with the warmth element; it is formed entirely out of the warmth element. This element, therefore, which is the most spiritual, is also the one that takes up the inclination for karma into these exceptionally fine warmth structures that we have in the warmth organism."

Mysteries of the Human Heart

***Man in the Light of Occultism, Theosophy and Philosophy*, Rudolf Steiner, Lecture III, Christiana (Oslo), June 5, 1912, GA 137**

"Speaking to theosophists, I may cut the matter short and say at once that a man who has succeeded in becoming free of the instrument given him with his physical body, makes use of his etheric and astral bodies and of his ego organism. That is to say, he uses other members of his being, with which we have become familiar in theosophy.

"What now arises in the soul has a much greater inner power and is far more inwardly alive than the thoughts we are accustomed to form about external objects. It gives us moreover the feeling of being surrounded on every side by a kind of fine substantiality, which one can only describe by saying that it is like *flowing light*. You must not, however, think of the light which is communicated through the eye, that is to say, through an external bodily instrument, but imagine rather that this substance which surrounds us like a surging sea is felt and experienced inwardly It does not manifest in any sort of shining, but we experience it inwardly, and the intensity of the experience is such as to banish all feeling we might otherwise have of being in a nothingness.

"The man who actually finds himself within this element will certainly not say he is in a nothingness; for it has an astounding effect upon him, unlike anything he has ever experienced hitherto. He feels as though it would tear him to pieces and scatter him throughout space,—or we might also put it, as though he were going to melt away and be dissolved, or again as though he were losing the ground from under his feet, as though all external material support were falling from him. That is the first experience,—flowing spiritual light, without any outward manifestation at all. It is the first inward experience with which every aspirant after occultism has to become familiar.

"And now if the pupil is rather weak in nature and has not been accustomed to think much in life, he will at this point get into difficulties. Indeed, he will hardly be able to find the way further unless he has learned in life to think. This is the reason for the preparation of which we spoke yesterday, the long practice and development of a sublime intellect and power of judgment. It is not what we acquire through these in the outward sense that is of so much importance, it is the discipline we undergo in learning to think more keenly and clearly. This discipline now comes to our aid when we enter, as aspirants after occultism, into the element of flowing light; for not the thoughts themselves are effective here, but the powers we have attained for self-education by means of the thoughts. These powers go on working, and presently we have around us something more than flowing hidden light; *forms* begin to emerge,—forms of which we know that they do not come from the perception of external objects but have their origin in the element in which we ourselves are immersed.

"If we reach this point, then we do not lose ourselves in the flowing light, but experience in it forms that are far more alive than the forms seen by any dreamer or visionary. At the same time they have in them nothing whatever of the nature of external perceptions. The qualities we perceive in outward things by means of the senses are completely absent; but we do find in these forms in enhanced measure what we otherwise only experience when we make for ourselves thoughts. And yet the thoughts that come to us now are no mere thoughts, but forms that have being and are strong and secure in themselves.

"This is the first experience for the aspirant after occultism, and it continues and grows stronger and stronger in the course of his occult life. At first it is weak, at first we have to be content with a small and limited experience. Then more is given to us, gradually we learn more and more, until we come at last to experience a world that we recognize as being behind the world of the senses. A remarkable fact is brought home to us at this point. The forces that can enable us to have such an experience are not to be found anywhere within the compass of Earth life, nor are they subject to earthly laws. At the same time, we observe that our capacity for thinking about the affairs of ordinary life and about natural science, has on the other hand been developed in us by forces that do belong entirely to the Earth.

"As you know, before man attained to his present form and figure, he underwent a great many transformations. During this time of change and development, the forces of the Earth worked upon him. Gradually, little by little, the brain and the sense organs received the forms they have today. If we were to set out to explain the eye or the ear or even the brain itself, as they are today, we should have to say that at the beginning of Earth evolution all these organs were totally different. During Earth evolution the forces of the Earth have worked upon them and endowed them with the form they have today. When we think about the affairs of everyday life, as well as when we carry out investigations in the method of natural science, we use what the brain and the sense organs owe to the forces of the Earth. The activity we develop in such thinking contains nothing that has not been contributed by the forces of the Earth. The ordinary human being who sees the things around him and reflects upon them, the scientist too, who studies and works in his laboratory or observatory, make use of nothing in brain or sense organs that does not derive its origin from the forces of the Earth.

"That development, however, of our brain that enables us, by working upon it, to bring forth the higher members of our nature and to behold the flowing spiritual light, has not its source in earthly conditions but is in an inheritance from forces that worked upon man before the Earth became Earth. You will remember that before the Earth became Earth, it passed through conditions known as [Old] Moon, [Old] Sun and [Old] Saturn.

The forces which make man capable of perceiving with his senses and of permeating his perceptions with thought, do not come from those past states of the Earth. But everything that sets us free from the working of the senses and of natural scientific thinking, and makes us capable of bringing forth higher members within us, as it were straining the brain to its utmost and pressing forth the etheric and astral bodies and ego until these are able to live in the flowing light,—all this we bear in us as an inheritance from the times of Saturn, Sun and Moon; it comes to us from pre-earthly times of evolution and is nowhere to be found within the whole circumference of Earth existence.

"When science comes to the point (and it will do so, though it take a long time on the way)—comes to the point of understanding the mechanism of the senses and of the brain, it will be extraordinarily proud of the achievement. But even then it will only be able to grasp the thinking and investigating that can be accounted for out of earthly conditions and that accordingly hold good for earthly conditions alone. Man will never, so long as he restricts himself to the forces of the Earth, be able to explain the *whole* brain, nor *all* the apparatus and arrangements of the sense organs, for, in order to give a full explanation of the activities in brain and senses and of how they came to have their present forms, we must look back to what are called the [Old] Saturn, [Old] Sun and [Old] Moon conditions of the Earth. The forces that are active in man when he is not using his senses and his brain,—the forces, that is, that he inherits from [Old] Saturn, [Old] Sun and [Old] Moon—have been paralyzed and held in check by what the Earth with her forces has made of the brain and senses.

"When we enter the flowing light, we do not feel as feel as though we were *thinking* what we find there. For when we are thinking a thought we have the impression we are thinking it *now*; whereas what we experience in the flowing light does not at all give us the feeling we are thinking it now. It is most important to note this point. To the clairvoyant who enters into this condition, the forms of which I spoke do not seem like thoughts he is thinking now, but like thoughts that have been preserved in the memory, like thoughts one is able to call up into remembrance.

"You will now understand why we have to ignore our intellect and quicken and strengthen our power of memory. Out of this wide spiritual sea of light, forms emerge which are only perceptible in the way that we apprehend memories. If our memory power had not undergone a strengthening, these forms would escape us and we should perceive nothing; it would be as though there were all around us nothing but a flowing sea of inward light. That we can perceive thought-forms swimming in the sea of Inner-Light, is due to the fact that we are able to perceive not with the intellect but with a strengthened power of memory; for these forms can only be perceived by means of the faculty of memory.

"Nor is this all. What is perceived with the faculty of memory enables us to look back into long past conditions of evolution, into [Old] Moon, [Old] Sun and [Old] Saturn stages of evolution; but the forms we perceive in this way and that are like the pictures of memory, are not the only thing. In fact, they make a less powerful impression upon us than something else, something of which we could say—notwithstanding that we know quite well it is no more than a surging sea of light—that it gives us pain and pleasure that it begins even to sting and burn us, and on the other hand to fill us with bliss.

"What does the occultist discover here? In the surging sea of light he has come to perceive strange forms; these he is able now to grasp with the understanding. They do not, as at first, lay claim only to the faculty of memory; they have become so powerful that the understanding can grasp them. How do they strike him? What does he notice about them? As a matter of fact, the occultist does not notice anything particular in these forms unless he has previously interested himself in the thoughts of philosophy. Then he recognizes that the thoughts of the philosophers are in reality shadows pictures of what he is now perceiving with the eye of the spirit in the surging sea of light. Yes, the moment has come when we can at last learn what philosophy really is. All the philosophy in the world is nothing else than thoughts and ideas which are like reflections thrown up into our physical life, pictures whose origin is in the super-sensible life which the clairvoyant can perceive in the way we have described. The philosopher himself does not see what lies behind his pictures, he does not know what it is, he is thus casting up into physical consciousness. He has only the pictures. But the occultist can point to their origin, he can point to the origin of the great thoughts of all the philosophers who have ever played a part in the history of man. The philosopher sees only the shadow picture in thought, the occultist sees the real and living light that is behind. How can this be?

"The reason is that in our brain we have still something left of pre-earthly forces, forces that come from the [Old] Saturn, [Old] Sun and [Old] Moon stages of evolution. Generally speaking, these forces have to a large extent been paralyzed in us, but we have in the brain some small remnant at least of what the brain is capable of, by virtue of these forces. The forces that work in the brain of a philosopher are not earthly forces. They are a dim and weak reflection of pre-earthly forces. The philosopher is quite unconscious of the fact; but in his brain lives an inheritance from pre-earthly times, and the use he makes of his brain depends on the working of this inheritance. It would not, however, be able to work at all, had not a particular event taken place during Earth evolution, an event which the philosopher of modern times is of course quite unprepared to accept. If the Earth had been simply the re-incarnation of what had been present in [Old] Saturn, [Old] Sun and [Old] Moon, if it had been able to give man no more than the forces it had living in it from the time of [Old] Saturn, [Old] Sun and [Old] Moon, then there could never have arisen on Earth such a thing as *contemplation*, the kind of reflective thought that we find in such a marked degree in philosophy. And philosophy, you know, is really present in every single human being; everyone philosophizes a little. Philosophy is only possible on Earth because an irregularity crept in when the re-incarnation of our Earth took place. An important portion of the creative forces which brought our Earth into being was diverted; these forces did not continue to work in the same way as the rest, and they now have a spiritual influence upon man that is like the physical influence of moonlight upon the Earth.

"The effect of moonlight, as you know, is due to the fact that the Moon casts back the light of the Sun. Moonlight is reflected sunlight. Now the fact that man is able to transcend the mere memory picture of clairvoyance and, as it were, to throw something up into physical existence which makes its appearance there as philosophy, is dependent on a particular spiritual force that works plastically into the human brain, forming it and molding it. In the Mosaic books of the *Bible* this spiritual force is named Jahve or Jehovah; it is a reflected light of the Spirit, just as in a physical aspect moonlight is reflected sunlight.

"In respect of his brain, therefore, man cannot be entirely explained out of the inheritance he has brought with him from pre-earthly conditions. We can only understand the human brain when we know that just as the physical light of the Sun is thrown on to the Earth by the Moon (at a time when the sunlight itself is not shining on that part of the Earth) so man, in so far as he lives in his brain, receives spiritual light thrown back from beyond the Earth.

"Every inspiration man receives, not from his own forces, but from beyond himself, helps him to rise to a knowledge of the world which may be described as philosophical. A philosophical comprehension of the world is one that causes man to seek in all the various things of the world a single and undivided foundation. That is the characteristic of philosophy. Whether man calls this Ground of the World 'God' or 'World Spirit' is of no moment; the desire he feels to gather up everything together and relate it all to a single Ground, is due to influences of the spiritual world which are active in his brain. The moment he becomes clairvoyant and sets free his ether body, he recognizes that not only has he now succeeded in making active what he has inherited from earlier stages of evolution, but in his brain, influences are at work which may be compared with the influences of moonlight, in the sense we have already explained.

"At this point I would like to draw your attention to a fact about philosophy that will, I think, be clear to you from all we have been considering.

"As a philosopher, man does not have that which the clairvoyant perceives as a Yogic force, and which blends in with the forces inherited from earlier times. He has, however, the *thought pictures*, not knowing that behind them stand the forces which were active in pre-earthly conditions, and which are called the Jahve forces. This he does not know. He sees only the shadow pictures of thought which have been created for him by the work of his ether body upon the flowing light for as the flowing light becomes active in his brain, thought shadow-pictures are produced there and these we call 'philosophy.' The philosopher himself knows nothing of the process; he knows only that he lives in these thought pictures. I want you, however, to note—it will be useful to you later on—that as philosopher man is unconsciously clairvoyant. That is to say, he lives in shadow pictures of clairvoyant states, without himself knowing anything of clairvoyance. He lives in these shadow pictures, he achieves with them all that a philosopher can achieve and at last comes to a point where he can connect and combine the philosophical ideas and conceptions he has elaborated, relating them all to one single Being or Entity. For that is the invariable characteristic of philosophy. It is, however, not possible to find within these thought pictures the Christ Being. By working in all honesty and sincerity with the material of philosophy, we find one single 'Ground of the World,' but we never find a Christ. If you come across the idea of Christ in a philosophy, you may be quite sure it has been borrowed from tradition; it has been imported,—inconsistently, though perhaps quite unconsciously. If the philosopher remains at his philosophy, he cannot possibly find any more than the neutral God of the Worlds; he can never find a Christ. No consistent philosophy can contain the conception of Christ. It is impossible. Let us be quite clear on this point. Let anyone who has the desire and the opportunity to do so cast his eye round among the philosophers and see whether these can find the Christ in their philosophies. Take, for example, such a widely and fully developed system of philosophy as that of Hegel. You will find that Hegel cannot approach the Christ within the system of philosophy. He has as it were to bring Him in from the world outside; his philosophy does not give him the Christ.

"For the time being, we will let this suffice for a description of the first experience the aspirant for clairvoyance undergoes, an experience he learns to designate as 'unmanifest light.'

"Gently and slowly—scarcely perceptibly, to begin with—the second experience comes upon him. There are indeed many clairvoyants who have had the first experience for a long time and still hardly understand what the second experience is. The effect of its approach may be described in the following way. Whilst the flowing light is something that makes us feel we are being scattered in it, makes us feel we are, as it were, being spread abroad in space,—with the second experience, which can be called the experience of the 'unspoken word,' we have the feeling as though something were coming towards us from every direction at once.

"In the same degree to which in the first experience we feel ourselves spread out over the whole world, do we now have the impression of something coming toward us, approaching us on all sides, while we ourselves are like to dissolve away. For the man who has this experience and is not yet at home in it, the sense of melting away is accompanied by very great fear. Something bears down upon us from all around; it is as if an edge or skin of the world were approaching us. What this means for us we can express in no other way than by saying it is as though we were being addressed in a language very hard to understand, a language that is never spoken on Earth. No word that proceeds from human larynx can be compared with the speech we now experience. Only by thinking away from the spoken word everything that has to do with external sound, can we begin to form some idea of the great cosmic sounding that now bears down upon us on all sides. At first it makes but a faint impression upon us; then, as the power of occult learning and occult self-discipline increases, this perception of a spiritual world grows stronger and stronger.

"As now with clairvoyant sight we behold approaching us from all sides this vast skin of the world,—and yet not at all like an external skin; but bearing down upon us like a mighty sounding of tones—we have a strange and remarkable feeling; and the fact that we have it is a sign to us that we are on the right path. We find ourselves thinking: 'It is in very truth my own self that is approaching me; there for the first time is my own true self! Only *apparently* am I enclosed in my skin, when I live here in the physical body. In reality my being fills the world; and it is my own being that is now coming to meet me as I pass over into the occult state. It is coming toward me from all directions.' So does occult experience take its course,—first the expansion of the spiritual life, then again its concentration. And the latter we connect with a definite idea. For it comes to us like *words*,— sounding spiritually and full of deep meaning; and we form the conception of the 'unspoken word,' the 'unspoken language.'

"Now we must go a step further. For even as man has a heritage out of pre-earthly conditions that helps to form and fashion his brain, so has he also forces remaining from pre-earthly conditions which work, not in his brain, but in his heart. The heart is a very complicated organ; and as in the brain not only earthly but pre-earthly forces are active (although in external study and research we make use, as we have seen, of the earthly alone), so in the heart too we find an activity of pre-earthly forces. Whatever man needs for the obtaining—of earthly air and nourishment, whatever he needs for the care of his organism and for its maintenance in life—all this is given him in earthly forces. But for man to be able to perceive what we have termed the 'unspoken word,' not only have higher members of his being to be, as it were, pressed out of his brain, but also out of his heart.

"It can happen that for a long time a man is able to perceive as clairvoyant the spiritual light, if he has pressed forth from his brain the higher members of his body. If, however, these higher members still remain firmly united with the heart, as they are in ordinary life, then we have a clairvoyant who is able to behold the flowing light (for that he can do with the help of the soul forces that have become free from the brain); but not able to apprehend the unspoken word. For we can only begin to hear the unspoken word when the higher, super-sensible members have been freed also from the heart. The capacity of the heart to do this, so that man can unfold a soul life that is not bound to the instrument of the heart, belongs to a higher heart organism. Our ordinary soul life on the physical plane is united with the organ of the heart. When men are able to set free the higher members of their body from the physical heart, they come to experience a life of soul that is connected with a higher organism than the physical heart of blood and muscle. When the pupil learns to experience, in his soul, forces of the heart that are higher than those connected with the physical heart, then he can in very truth attain knowledge of the unspoken word; it makes itself known to him, coming towards him on every hand. Thus, whilst the perception of the super-sensible light depends on the emancipation of man's higher being from the physical brain, the perception of the unspoken word depends on the emancipation of the higher members from the physical heart.

"As there are persons who, without being themselves aware of the fact, have in them something of the pre-earthly forces that formed and fashioned the brain, so are there also persons who have in them something of the pre-earthly forces that formed and fashioned the heart. And they are much more numerous than is generally supposed. If there were not today those who not only have these ancient heritages in their being; but are moreover engaged in working upon them (we shall see later how this comes about), there would be no theosophists. You would not all of you be sitting here today! The reason why you are sitting here is simply this,—that at some moment in your life, when a theosophical book came into your hands or some truth out of theosophy was communicated to you in a lecture, immediately you became conscious of something of that ancient inheritance which you bear within you and which consists of forces that worked to form your heart before the Earth was created. The fact that what came to you through theosophy made a deep impression upon you, meant that it produced in you an experience similar to the philosopher's experience in his shadow pictures. You experienced the shadow pictures of what a *clairvoyance of the heart*, all unknown to you, was able to receive through the words that were spoken. In that moment you heard *through* the words, and what you heard was something quite wonderful; otherwise, you would not have become a theosophist. For you the external word was but an echo, coming to you from without, of what the clairvoyant heart had itself investigated by means of pre-earthly forces, an echo of what comes from the realm of occultism and had already been speaking to you in shadow pictures which you yourself could experience. Through the outer-word you heard the inner-word speaking. In the spoken word you caught the echo of the word that cannot be spoken. Through the human language you heard what is spoken from out of divine worlds in the Language of the Gods."

Color, Pt. II, Rudolf Steiner, Lecture III, _Dimension, Number and Weight_, Dornach, July 29, 1923, GA 291

"It is a fact that Art must collapse under the physical philosophy of today. Now we must put the question to ourselves: Why did Art exist in older times?

"If you go back to quite ancient times in which man still had an original clairvoyance, we find that they took less notice of dimension, number and weight in earthly things. They were not so important to them. They devoted themselves more to the colors and sounds of earthly things.

"Remember that even Chemistry calculates in terms of weight only since Lavoisier; something more than a hundred years. Weight was first use in a world-philosophy at the end of the eighteenth century. Ancient mankind simply was not conscious that everything had to be defined according to earthly measure, number and weight. Man gave his heart and mind to the colored carpet of the world, to the weaving the welling of sounds, not to the atmospheric vibrations.

"But what was the possibility that came from living in this—I might say—imponderable sensible perception? By it one had the possibility, when for instance, one approached a man, of seeing him not as we see him today; but one regarded him as a product of the whole Universe. Man was more a confluence of the Cosmos. He was more a microcosm than the thing inside his skin that stands where man stands, on this tiny spot of Earth. He thought of man more as an image of the world. Then, colors flowed together, as it were, from all sides, and gave man colors. There was world-harmony, and man in tune with it, receiving his shape from it.

"Moreover, mankind today can scarcely understand anything of the way in which ancient mystery-teachers spoke to their pupils. For when a man today wants to explain the human heart, he takes an embryo and sees how the blood-vessels expand, a utricle or bag appears and the heart is gradually formed. Well, that is not what the ancient mystery-teachers told their pupils. That would have appeared to them no more important than knitting a stocking; because after all the process looks much the same. On the contrary they emphasized something else as of paramount importance. They said: 'The human heart is a product of gold, which lives everywhere in light, and which streams in from the Universe and shapes the human heart. You have had the representation. Light quivers through the Universe, and the light carries gold. Everywhere in light there is gold. Gold lives and moves in light.' And when man lives on Earth—you know already that it changes after seven years—his heart is not composed of the cucumber and the salad and the roast veal the man has in the meantime eaten, but these old teachers knew that the heart is built of light's gold, and the cucumbers and the salad are only the stimulus for the gold weaving in the light to build up the heart out of the whole Universe."

From Crystals to Crocodiles, Rudolf Steiner, V, *The perception of thinking carried out by our inner organs*, Dornach, September 13, 1922, GA 347

"As you remember, we have seen that the human brain essentially consists of minute, star-like cells that radiate out quite far from the center and intertwine, forming the brain tissue as I described it to you. We find similar small organisms also in our blood; but our brain cells are fully alive only at night when we sleep. However, they cannot make full use of this life and move around because they are crowded together like sardines. However, the white blood corpuscles swimming in our blood can move around. They float around in the blood and move their arm-like extensions. They only come to rest and approach a deathlike condition when we sleep. In other words, sleeping and waking are connected with the activity or inactivity of the brain cells, the nerve cells in general, and the white blood cells."

***From Crystals to Crocodiles*, Rudolf Steiner, Lecture I, *On the Origin of Speech and Languages*, Dornach, August 2, 1922, GA 347**

"I have explained roughly how nutrition and breathing work in human beings. We also talked about how closely connected nutrition is with our life and that it is essentially a process of taking in substances that then become lifeless in our intestines. These substances are then revitalized by the lymph vessels, and are transmitted into the blood as living substance. There this living nourishment encounters the air's oxygen. We take in air. The blood changes. This process occurs in the chest, and it is this process that gives us our feelings.

"Thus life actually originates between the processes in the intestines and those in the blood. In turn, in the blood processes, that is, between the activities of the blood and the air our feelings come about."

***From Crystals to Crocodiles*, Rudolf Steiner, Lecture II, *On the human etheric body. Relationships between brain and thinking*, Dornach, August 5, 1922, GA 347**

"Let us think once more of that tiny organism floating in the ocean. Let's imagine that one day it eats too much. It extends its arm, takes in food here and there, and overeats. This is more than the small creature can take, and so it divides; it splits into two.

Instead of one organism there are now two. The original one has multiplied. Our white corpuscles also have the ability to multiply. There are always some dying off and others being produced in this way.

"The brain cells, which I drew for you, cannot multiply. The white blood cells are full of life, independent life, and they can reproduce. However, the intertwining brain cells cannot reproduce. One brain cell will never turn into two. As the brain grows and increases in size, new, additional cells must move into the brain from the rest of the body. They must grow into the brain. The cells in the brain never multiply there; but merely accumulate. As long as we grow, new cells must constantly move into our head from the rest of the body, so that we have a sufficiently large brain when we are grown up.

"The fact that the brain cells cannot multiply already tells us that they are almost dead. They are constantly in the process of dying. When we think about this in the right way, we discover a marvelous contrast in the human being. In the blood, we have cells, the white corpuscles that are full of life, of a desire to live. In the brain, on the other hand, we have cells that actually have a constant wish to die, that are constantly in the process of dying. Thus it is true that as far as the brain is concerned human beings are in a constant process of dying. The brain is constantly on the verge of dying.

"Well, gentlemen, I am sure you have heard of people who fainted, or perhaps you have experienced this yourselves. I know it is an embarrassing thing to experience. When people faint, they feel like they are falling. They lose consciousness.

"What has actually taken place in a person who loses consciousness this way? You know, I am sure, that very pale persons, such as anemic girls, faint very easily. Why is that so? Well, you see, they faint because in proportion to the red corpuscles, they have too many white ones. Human beings must have a certain proportion of white to red corpuscles to be properly conscious. What then does it mean to lose consciousness, for example, in fainting or in sleeping? It means that the white corpuscles are too active. When this happens, we have, as it were, too much life in us, and as a result we lose consciousness…

"…The strength required to increase brain activity when we sleep must be withdrawn from other areas of the body. It is withdrawn from some of the white blood cells. Since the white corpuscles are more at rest during the night, we should actually begin to think. We should be able to think with our bodies…"

***Therapeutic Insights: Earthly and Cosmic Laws*, Rudolf Steiner, Lecture IV, Dornach, July 2, 1921, GA 205**

"If we look into the inner aspect of the heart, however, we see gathered there forces that also stem from the entire metabolic-limb organism, and because what is connected with the heart, with the heart forces, is spiritualized, within it is also spiritualized that which is connected with our outer life, with our deeds. However strange and paradoxical it may sound to a person who is clever in the modern sense, the fact remains that the forces thus prepared within the heart are the karmic tendencies, they are the tendencies of karma. It is revoltingly foolish to speak of the heart as a mere pumping mechanism; for the heart is the organ which, through mediation of the metabolic-limb system, carries what we understand as karma into the next incarnation."

***From the Contents of Esoteric Classes,* Rudolf Steiner, No. 27, Berlin, February 26, 1908, GA 266**

"We know that [Old] Saturn existed first. Its matter wasn't even gaseous, it was a warmth matter. A man with present-day senses would not have seen [Old] Saturn; he would only have felt warmth if he was at the place where [Old] Saturn stood. A Saturn man consisted of warmth mater. The atmosphere of [Old] Saturn was fiery-bloody. Man didn't have any blood yet, but the first germ of his later blood lay in the atmosphere around him. Man's physical parts were only germinally present.

"If one looks at how after a pralaya Old Saturn changed into Old Sun with the spiritual gaze that moves over the planets one notices that [Old] Saturn's warmth atmosphere condenses into air. Man gets an etheric body on the [Old] Sun. He is a shining being. Spiritual beings work through the [Old] Sun's astral atmosphere upon the etheric body, ignite it and thereby make it shine. One calls this the sulfuric process. Something quite similar arises today in thinking. When our fiery blood runs into nerve masses there's a combustion process and things light up.

"When the [Old] Sun passes over to the [Old] Moon, air condenses to water. The [Old] Moon's body is a water body. We notice something very strange about this water body. Single water drops change their position in an extremely lively manner and race around with inner mobility. In some respects, one can compare this property of the water drops with mercury. That's why one calls this principle that's added on the [Old] Moon the mercurial principle. The parts are put together into forms by sounds, somewhat like Chladni's sound figures. First two came together, then two pairs made four, etc., just as one still finds in new plant, animal, and human forms. That's the female principle. The male principle only arose later from pure Earth forces.

"When the [Old] Moon passed over to the Earth, water condensed to Earth. The precipitating salt process took place on the Earth for the first time through the interaction of fire and water. Man arose from female and male and began to dissolve things again through thinking so that evolution could continue. Man received the erring I on Earth."

Health and Illness II, Rudolf Steiner, Lecture VII, *The Relationship Between the Breathing and the Circulation of the Blood,* Dornach, January 27, 1922, GA 348

"Now, if you consider respiration and the activity of the blood, these two processes are related in today's adult in a ratio of one breath to four pulse beats. The blood stream flows faster; after three pulsations man inhales, and after three more, he inhales again. This is how air goes through his body. The blood moves through the body: one, two, three, and with the fourth we inhale; one, two, three, and with the fourth we inhale again. This goes on throughout our body."

Philosophy, Cosmology, and Religion, Rudolf Steiner, Lecture V, *The Soul's Experiences in Sleep*, Dornach, September 10, 1922, GA 215

"... If, in daytime, we have developed a relation to the Christ, we actually meet His guiding power during this second stage of sleep. It is this guiding power of Christ through which we overcome the anxiety that oppresses the soul. Out of this anxiety there develops a cosmic relationship of the soul to the world. As a result of the development of this relationship, but in such a way that the soul experiences it as its inner life, the movements of the planetary system in our solar cosmos stand before the soul. It does not expand out into the planetary world during sleep; but an inner replica of it lives in the soul. It actually experiences the planetary cosmos in a replica. Even if what the soul experiences every night as a small, inner globe, a celestial globe, does not illuminate day consciousness, it does stream into the reality of daily life and continues on in the physical and etheric organizations in the systems of breathing and blood circulation, the whole rhythmic system, we find that these processes are accompanied by impulses and stimuli that live in the physical and the etheric body and work into waking life out of the inner planetary experience which the soul has in sleep. While we are awake, therefore, the planetary movements of our solar system pulse through our breathing and circulation as after-effects of sleep."

***Spiritual Science and Medicine*, Rudolf Steiner, Lecture II, Dornach, March 22, 1920, GA 312**

"Let us now continue our inquiry on the lines already laid down, and attempt to elucidate the nature of man by observing certain Polarities governing the human organism. Yesterday we found ourselves obliged to combine the weighing down forces found in the animal with certain vertical forces to form a parallelogram, and to consider an analogous phenomenon in the chemical reactions of the muscle. If these ideas are followed up in the study of the bone and muscular system and are supported by all the resources of practical experience, we might make Osteology and Muscular Pathology of greater value for medicine than has hitherto been the case. Special difficulties arise, however, if we try to connect the knowledge of man with the needs of medicine today, in our consideration of the heart. What in Osteology and Myology is only a slight defect becomes an evident defect in Cardiology. For, what is the common belief about the nature of the human heart? It is regarded as a kind of Pump, to send the blood into the various organs. There have been intricate mechanical analogies, in explanation of the heart's action—analogies totally at variance with embryology, be it noted!—But no one has begun to doubt the mechanical explanation, or to test it, at least in orthodox scientific circles.

"My outline of the subjects for consideration in the next few days will afford piecemeal proof of my general point-of-view. The most important fact about the heart is that its activity is not a cause but an effect. You will understand this if you consider the polarity between all the organic activities centering round nutrition, digestion, absorption into the blood, and so on: follow, passing upwards through the human frame, the process of digestion up to the interaction between the blood that has absorbed the food, and the breathing that receives air. An unbiased observation will show a certain contrast and opposition between the process of respiration and the process of digestion.

"Something is seeking for equipoise; it is as though there were an urge towards mutual saturation. Other words, of course, could be chosen for description, but we shall understand each other more and more. There is an interaction in the first place between the liquefied foodstuffs and the air absorbed into the organism by breathing. This process is intricate and worth attention. There is an interplay of forces, and each force before reaching the point of interplay accumulates in the heart. The heart originates as a 'damming up' organ (Stauorgan) between the lower activities of the organism, the intake and working up of food, and the upper activities, the lowest of which is the respiratory. A damming up organ is inserted and its action is therefore a product of the interplay between the liquefied foodstuffs and the air absorbed from the outside. All that can be observed in the heart must be looked upon as an effect, not a cause, as a mechanical effect, to begin with. The only hopeful investigations on these lines, so far, have been those of Dr. Karl Schmidt, an Austrian medical man, practicing in North Styria, who published a contribution to the *Wiener Medizinische Wochenschrift* (1892, No. 15), "The Heart Action and Curve of the Pulse." The content of this article is comparatively small, but it proves that his medical practice had enlightened the author on the fact that the heart in no way resembled the ordinary pump but rather must be considered a dam-like organ. Schmidt compares cardiac action to that of the hydraulic ram, set in motion by the currents. This is the kernel of truth in his work. But we need not stop short at the mechanical aspect if we consider the heart action as a result of these symbolic inter-penetrating currents, the watery and the airy. For what is the heart after all? It is a sense organ, and even if its sensory function is not directly present in the consciousness, if its processes are subconscious, nevertheless it serves to enable the 'upper' activities to feel and perceive the 'lower.' As you perceive external colors through your eyes, so do you perceive, dimly and subconsciously through your heart, what goes on in the lower abdomen. The heart is an organ for inner perception.

"The polarity in man is only comprehensible if we know that his structure is a dual one and that the upper portion perceives the lower. The following too must be considered: the lower functions—one pole of the whole human being—are considered through the study of nutrition and digestion in the widest sense, up to their interaction with respiration The interaction goes on in a rhythmic activity; we shall have to consider the significance of

our rhythmic system later. But linked up with and belonging to the respiratory activity there is the sensory and nervous activity, which includes all that appertains to external perception and its continuation and its being worked up in the nervous activity. Thus, respiration and sensory and nervous activity form one
Thus, respiration and sensory and nervous activity form one pole of the human organism. Nutrition, digestion, and metabolism in its usual sense, form the other pole of our organization. The heart is primarily that organ whose perceptible motion expresses the equilibrium between the upper and lower processes; in relation to the soul (or perhaps more accurately in the sub-conscious) it is the perceptive organ that mediates between these two poles of the total human organization. Anatomy, physiology, biology can all be studied in the light of this principle; and thus light is thrown, and only thus, upon the human organization. As long as you do not differentiate between these two poles, superior and inferior, and their mediator the heart, you will not be able to understand man, for there is a fundamental difference between the two groups of functional activity in man, according to whether they pertain to the upper or the lower polarity."

***Wisdom of Man, of the Soul, and of the Spirit,* Rudolf Steiner, Lecture III, *Higher Senses, Inner Force Currents, and Creative Laws in the Human Organism,* Berlin, October 26, 1909, GA 115**

"In the course of historical evolution, men did not acquire the capacity to comprehend what is universally human until they learned to recognize common factors by disregarding, as it were, the shades of sounds. Only in our life of conceptions can we begin to grasp the Christ Spirit in His true being. The spiritual beings whose task it is to proclaim Him in manifold forms—His messengers to whom He has assigned their missions and tasks—are the Folk Spirits of the various folk individualities. This thought has found very beautiful expression in Goethe's fragment, *Die Geheimnisse.* [*'The Mysteries'*]

"That will give a picture of what the sense of visualization is, bringing us to an important milestone. We have exhausted what we have in the way of ordinary senses, finally arriving at the study of the subconscious human activity that is able, through the force of the astral body, to push from consciousness even the harmonic series. It is the human astral body that pushes aside this harmonic series as though with tentacles. If we achieve this power over the harmonics, which means nothing else than the ability to ignore them, it signifies increased strength in our astral body.

"But even this does not exhaust the capacity of the astral body; it is capable of still higher achievements. In the cases we have so far discussed, the appearance of a visualization has presupposed the overcoming of an outer resistance; something external had to be pushed back. Now we find the astral body to be endowed with still more power when we learn that its astral substance enables it not only to push back what is outside, but also, when there is no outer resistance, to stretch forth, to eject, its astral substance through its own inner strength. If one is able thus to stretch forth the astral tentacles, so to speak, with no resistance present, then there appears what is called spiritual activity; the so-called spiritual organs of perception come into being. When the astral substance is pushed out from a certain part of the head and forms something like two tentacles, man develops what is called the two-petalled lotus flower. That is the *imaginative sense,* the eleventh.

"In proportion to his capacity for stretching out his astral tentacles, man develops other spiritual organs. As his ability to thrust out astral substance increases, he forms a second organ in the vicinity of the larynx, the sixteen-petal lotus flower, the *inspirational sense,* the twelfth. In the neighborhood of the heart the third organ develops, the twelve-petalled lotus flower, the thirteenth, the *intuitive sense.* These three senses, the *imaginative*, the *inspirational* and the *intuitive*, are additional, astral senses, over and above the physical senses. Beyond these there are still higher, purely spiritual senses; but let them here be merely mentioned.

"The question now arises as to whether these three astral senses are active only in more highly developed, clairvoyant people, or has the ordinary human being anything that can be called an activity of these senses? The answer is that everybody has them, but there is a difference. In clairvoyants these senses operate by stretching out like tentacles, while in ordinary people their effect is inward. At the top of the head, for instance, just where the two-petal lotus flower forms, there are tentacles of this kind that reach inward and cross in the brain. In other words, ordinary consciousness directs them inward instead of outward. All that is outside us we see, but not what is within us. Nobody has seen his own heart or brain, and it is the same with spiritual matters. Not only are these organs not seen, but they do not even enter consciousness. They therefore cannot be consciously employed, but they function nevertheless; they are active. Here consciousness makes no decisions whatever regarding reality.

"These senses, then, are active. They direct their activity inward, and this impulse directed inward is perceived. When the *imaginative sense* pours inward there arises what in ordinary life is called outer sensation, outer perception of something. We can have an outer perception only because what appears in the imaginative sense works its way into us. By means of this imaginative sense we are able to 'sense' a color, and that is not synonymous with seeing a color, or analogous to hearing a tone. When we see a color, we say, for instance, it is red. But through the activity of the imaginative sense we can also have a sensation connected with it—that color is beautiful or ugly, pleasant or unpleasant.

"The *inspirational sense* also directs its activity inward, and this produces a more complicated sensation: feeling. The entire life of feeling is an activity of the inspirational organ streaming inward.

"When the *intuitive sense* pours inward, thinking proper arises, that is, thought forming. So, the order of the processes is: We sense something, we have a feeling connected with it, and we form thoughts about it.

"Thus, we have ascended from the life of the senses to the soul life. Starting from without, from the sense world, we have seized hold on the soul of man himself in its activities of sentience, feeling and thought. Were we to continue along this path, examining the still higher senses that correspond to the other lotus flowers—they can hardly be called senses anymore—the entire higher life of the soul would be revealed to us in their interplay. When, for example, the eight- or ten-petal lotus flower directs its psychic activity inward, a still more delicate soul activity is engendered, and at the end of the scale we find the most subtle one of all which we call pure, logical thought. All this is produced by the working of the various lotus flowers into the inner man. Now, when this inward motion is transformed into an outer motion, when the astral tentacles stretch outward and crisscross, directing, as so-called lotus flowers, their activity outward, then that higher activity comes into being through which we rise from the soul to the spirit, where what normally appears as our inner life (thinking, feeling and willing) now makes its appearance in the outer world, borne by spiritual beings.

"We have arrived at an understanding of the human being by ascending from the senses by way of the soul to what is no longer in him, to spirit acting from without, which belongs equally to man and to surrounding nature, to the whole world. We have ascended to the spirit. As far as we have gone, I have described the human being as an instrument for perceiving the world, experiencing it with his soul and grasping it spiritually. I have not described something finished, but something that is active in man. The whole interplay of forces and activities of the senses, the soul, and the spirit is what shapes the human being as he stands before us on earth. How does this come about? We can give but brief intimations, but such as we find substantiated on all sides.

"What we see before us in observing a human being merely with our senses really does not exist at all; it is only an optical illusion. Spiritual-scientific observation actually perceives something quite different. Remember that sensibly we cannot perceive ourselves completely. We see but a part of our surface, never our back or the back of our head, for example. But we know, nevertheless, that we have a back, and we know it by means of the various senses, such as the sense of equilibrium or of motion. An inner consciousness tells us of the parts we cannot perceive externally. Indeed, there is a great deal of us that we cannot perceive unless the appropriate organs are developed.

"Let us further consider the portion of the human being that he himself can perceive sensibly—with the eye, for instance—and let us delimit it. Through what agency is he to perceive it? Actually, all that we can see of ourselves with our eyes we perceive through the sentient soul; the sentient body would not be able to perceive it. It is the sentient soul that really comprehends. The portion of the human being that he sees with his eyes, which the sentient soul confronts, is nothing but the image of the sentient body, the outer illusion of the sentient body. We must, of course, extend the concept a bit to cover those portions of the body we can touch though not see, but there, too, we have the image of the sentient body. Perception comes about through other activities of the sentient soul. The latter extends to every point at which outer perception occurs, and what it perceives there is not the sentient soul but the illusion of the sentient body. Could we perceive this, we would see that astrally something endeavors to approach but is pushed back.

"This image of the sentient body comes about as follows. From back to front there is co-operation of the sentient soul and the sentient body. When two currents meet, a damming up occurs, and thereby something is revealed. Imagine you see neither current, but only what results from the whirling together of the two. What shows as a result of this impact of the sentient soul thrusting outward and the sentient body pressing inward from without, is the portion of our external corporeality that the eye or other outer sense can perceive. We can actually determine the point on the skin where the meeting of the sentient soul and sentient body occurs. We see how the soul works at forming the body. We can put it this way. There is in the human being a cooperation of the current passing from back to front and the opposite one, resulting in an impact of sentient soul and sentient body.

"In addition to these two currents there are those that come from the right and from the left. From the left comes the one pertaining to the physical body; from the right, the one pertaining to the etheric body. These flow into each other and intermingle to a certain extent, and what comes into being at this point is the sensibly perceptible human being, his sensibly perceptible exterior. A perfect illusion is brought about. From the left comes the current of the physical body, from the right that of the etheric body, and these form what appears to us as the sensibly perceptible human being.

"In like manner we have in us currents running upward and downward. From below upward streams the main current of the astral body, and downward from above the main current of the ego. The characterization given of the sentient body as being bounded in front should be understood as meaning that it operates in a current upward from below, but that it is then seized by the current running forward from the rear, so that in a certain sense it is thereby bounded.

"But the astral body contains not only the one current that runs upward from below as well as forward from the rear, but also the other one running backward from the front: so that the astral body courses in two currents, one upward from below and the other backward from the front. This gives us four intermingling currents in the human being.

"What is brought about by the two vertical currents? We have one current running upward from below, and if it could discharge unobstructed, we would draw it thus as in the diagram, but this it cannot do. The same is true of the other currents. Each is held up, and in the center, where they act upon each other, they form the image of the physical body.

"Actually, it is due to the intersection and criss-crossing of the currents that the threefold organization of man comes into being. Thus, the lower portion that we ourselves can see should be designated as the sentient body in the narrower sense. Higher up lies what in the narrower meaning we can call our senses.

This portion we can no longer perceive ourselves because it is the region where the senses themselves are located. You cannot look into your eyes but only out of them, into the world. Here the sentient soul, or its image, is active. The face is formed by the sentient soul. But the two currents must be properly differentiated. The lower currents, streaming from all sides, are held down from above, and this lower part we can designate the sentient body. Below, the impulses proceed largely from without; while above, it is principally the sentient soul that makes itself felt. From above there streams the ego, and at the point where this current is strongest, where it is least pushed back by the other currents, the intellectual soul forms its organ.

"Now, in addition to this ego current we have one from left to right and one from right to left. Again, the whole activity is intersected. There is further a current running through the longitudinal axis of the body, effecting a sort of split up above. At the upper boundary a portion of the intellectual soul is split off, and this is the form of the consciousness soul. There the consciousness soul is active, extending its formative work into the innermost man. Among other things, it forms the convolutions in the grey matter of the brain.

"The nature of this spiritual being helps us to understand what exists in man as form. That is the way in which the spirit works on the form of the human body. It evokes all the organs plastically, as the artist chisels a figure out of stone. The structure of the brain can be comprehended only with the knowledge of how these separate currents interact in man; what we then see is the joint activity of the various principles of the human being.

"Now we must go into a few details in order to show how these facts can be fruitful when they will have become the common property of a true science. We have learned that up above there came into being the organs of the consciousness soul, the intellectual soul, and the sentient soul. The ego acts downward from above, the main portion of the astral body, upward from below. In their mutual damming up, a reciprocal action takes place that extends along the whole line, so to speak; it forms the longitudinal axis of the body, and the effect of this will be a different one at every point of the line. When the ego, for instance, is called upon to perform a conscious act, this can only be done at the point where the sentient soul, the intellectual soul, and the consciousness soul have developed their organs. Through the intellectual soul, for example, reasoning comes about, and a judgment must be localized in the head because it is there that the appropriate human forces find expression.

"Now let us assume that such an organ is to come into being, but one in which no reasoning takes place, in which the intellectual soul has no part, an organ independent of the work of sentient, intellectual and consciousness souls, in which only the physical, etheric and astral bodies and the ego have a part—an organ in which an impression received from the astral body is immediately followed by the reaction of the ego, without reasoning. Suppose that these four members of the human being—astral body and ego, etheric body and physical body—are to cooperate without any delicate activity such as reasoning or the like. What would be the nature of an organ in which these four currents work together? It would have to be an organ that would not reason. The reaction of the ego would follow directly, without reasoning, upon the impression received by the organ in question from the astral body. That would mean that the ego and the astral body act together. From the astral body a stimulus proceeds to the ego, the ego reacts upon the astral body.

"If this is to be a physical organ it must be built up by the etheric body. From the left would come the current of the physical body, from the right, that of the etheric body. They would be dammed up in the middle and a condensation would result.

"In addition, the currents of the ego and the astral body, from above and below respectively, would undergo the same process.

"If we draw a diagram of such a structure, where in one organ the currents of the physical and etheric bodies are dammed up against those of the ego and astral body, the result is nothing less than the diagram of the human heart with its four chambers:

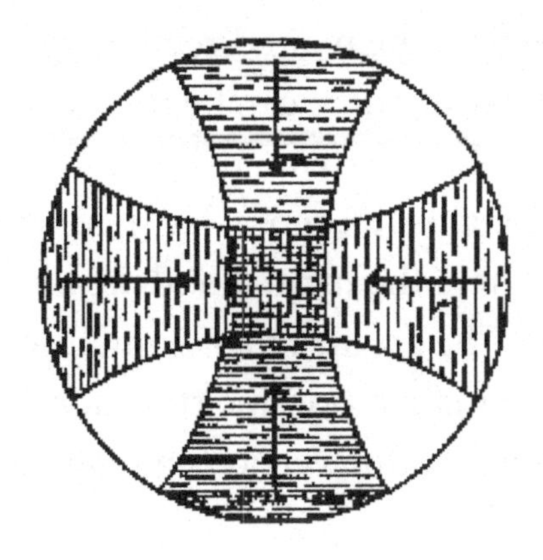

"That is the way the human heart came into being. When we consider all that the human heart achieves—the co-operation of the physical, etheric and astral bodies and the ego—it will be borne in upon us that the spirit had to build the human heart in this way…

"…Now I will tell you a case that you can observe and verify in ordinary life—close at hand in one sense, though not in another. We have considered the various currents in the human being and found them to run as follows:

From left to right, the currents of the physical body.

From right to left, those of the etheric body.

From the front backward, those of the sentient body.

From the rear forward, those of the sentient soul.

From above downward, those of the ego.

From below upward, those of the astral body.

"The ego, then, acts downward from above; so how would its physical organ have to lie? The physical organ of the ego is the circulating blood; and the ego could not function downward from above without an organ running in the same direction in the human body. Where the main direction of the bloodstream is horizontal, not vertical, there can be no ego, as in men. The main direction of the bloodstream had to raise itself in man to the vertical in order to enable the ego to lay hold on the blood. No ego can intervene where the main bloodstream runs horizontally instead of vertically. The group ego of animals can find no organ in them, because the main bloodline runs horizontally. Through the erection of this line to the vertical in man, the group ego became an individual ego.

"This difference between men and the animals shows how erroneous it is to set up a relationship inferred from purely external phenomena. That act of rising from the horizontal to the vertical is an historic incident, but it could no more have taken place without an underlying will, without the co-operation of spirit, than the raising of the hammer could have done. Only when a will, a spiritual force, courses through the blood can the horizontal line pass over into the vertical, can the upright position come about and the group soul rise to become the individual soul. It would be illogical to recognize the spiritual force in one case, that of the hammer, and not in the other, in man.

"That is the third possibility, a middle way of conviction, as it were, through which we can verify all theosophic truths. The deeper we penetrate into these matters, the clearer it becomes that this middle path to conviction is universally applicable—this middle way that fructifies ordinary experience through spiritual science. External research will be stimulated by spiritual science. Comparing the results of genuine spiritual-scientific research with outer phenomena, we are forced to the conclusion that all external processes are really comprehensible only if we take into account, without prejudice, the experiences of spiritual science. Thus, to observe the world without prejudice, that is the standpoint of anthroposophy. It receives fruitful impulses from above, from theosophy, and from below, from anthropology; it observes the facts of the spiritual world and the things of this world and explains the latter by means of the former. The building of each of our organs can be explained through spiritual activity, just as we described the transformation of the brain into an eye, and the building of the heart.

"By showing how spiritual facts and earthly things are interwoven, how spiritual truths are verified in outer phenomena, anthroposophy leads to the conviction that it is senseless not to acknowledge the higher truths that spiritual science is in a position to bring us."

***From Limestone to Lucife*, Rudolf Steiner, *Answers to Questions*, Lecture XI, *On the Christ, Ahriman and Lucifer and their relationship to man*, Dornach, May 7, 1923, GA 349**

"If you now look at something else again, the blood vessels, you'll find that they are fairly delicate in the head. On the other hand, the blood vessels are particularly well developed in the heart region; and there are also thick blood vessels in the limbs. We are therefore able to say that on the one hand we have the nerve system, and on the other the blood system.

"Now the situation is that we are born again out of the blood every day and every hour. Blood always means renewal. If we only had blood in us, therefore, we would be like creatures that grow all the time, getting bigger, creatures that are fresh and new, and so on. But you see, gentlemen, if we were nothing but nerve, consisting only of nerves, we would all the time be tired and worn; we would really be dying all the time. We therefore have two opposite principles in us—the nervous system that makes us get old all the time, actually handing us over to death all the time, and the blood system which is connected with the nutrition system and lets us grow young all the time, and so on. We can take this matter, of which I have just spoken, further. As you know, some people change in old age in such a way that we have to say they are calcified. Calcification, sclerosis develops. When people's arteries get furred up, as we say, when the walls of the blood vessels calcify, people easily reach a point where they can no longer move so well. And if the calcification gets really severe, one has a stroke, as we say. One has a stroke. This stroke, which people get, simply means that their blood vessels calcify and no longer stand up to the strain.

"What has come over someone who calcifies, who grows sclerotic? You see, it is as if the walls of his blood vessels want to turn into nerves. That is the strange thing. The nerves have to die all the time. The nerves have to be in a condition throughout life, as it were, in which the blood vessels must never be. The blood vessels have to be fresh. The nerves must all the time be inclined to die off. If someone's nerves get too soft, not sufficiently calcified, if I may put it like this, he'll go mad. So you see, nerves must not be like blood vessels and blood vessels must not be like nerves.

"This really compels us to say that man has two principles in him. One is the nerve principle. It really makes him old all the time. We really get a little bit older all the time from morning to evening. During the night this freshens up again, something that comes from the blood. And that is how it goes all the time, like the pendulum swing of a clock—grow old, grow young, grow old, grow young. Of course, if we are awake from morning to evening, we'll get older; and when we sleep from evening till morning, we'll get younger again. But there's always a little bit left over. The night does improve the situation; but a little bit of every day's getting older is left over. And when the sum of this gets big enough, the person will truly die. That is the way it is. So, we have two things in the human being that work in opposite directions—growing old and growing young. Now we can also look at this with regard to the soul. I have so far spoken of the body. You see, if getting young grows too powerful in a person, he'll get pleurisy or pneumonia. The point is that things which are really quite good, which are excellent within their limits, become illness if they get too powerful. Sickness in human beings simply means that something which they always need is getting too powerful. A temperature develops when the getting-young process grows much too powerful in us. We cannot cope with this. We begin to be too fresh with the whole of our body. We then have a temperature, or pleurisy, or pneumonia.

"Now we can also look at this from the point-of-view of the soul. You see, people can also dry up in their souls, or else get into the kind of state which in the physical body would be a temperature. People have some character traits—we don't like to hear about them, because so many people have them today—where they become pedantic, become philistines. Philistines do exist! You get to be a pedantic philistine. And if you are a teacher, someone who should be really fresh and lively, you get to be as dry as dust. And you see, this is the same as when our blood vessels calcify and dry up. We can also dry up in our souls. And on the other hand, we may also grow soft in our souls. This means we get to be zealous, mystical—or theosophists! What is it that we want in that case? We don't want to think properly. We want to reach out to all the world with our powers of fantasy and not think properly. This is the same as the temperature you get in the body. To become a mystic, a theosophist, is to develop a temperature in your soul.

"But we must always have the two things in us. We are quite unable to have insight unless we use fantasy, and we are quite unable to somehow bring things together in our work unless we are a little bit pedantic, keeping records of all kinds of things, and so on. Too much of this, and we are pedantic, we are philistines. Getting the balance right means the soul is as it should be.

"The point is that there is always something or other that has to be at the right level in a human being. If it gets too powerful it will make us sick in body or soul.

"It is also like this with the spirit, gentlemen. We cannot sleep for ever but have to wake up occasionally. Just think of the jolt it is to wake up. Just imagine the way it is with sleep. You lie there, knowing nothing about the world around you. If you're having a good sleep, someone may even come and tickle you and you won't wake up. Now think of the difference when you wake up, seeing everything around you. That is a big difference. Now when you wake up—yes, we must have the power to wake up in us; but if it is too great, if one is always waking up, if one can't sleep at all, for example, the power to wake up is too strong in us. Now there are also people who cannot ever wake up properly. Some people are always in a dim, dreamy state of mind, wanting to sleep all the time. They cannot wake up. We need the ability to go to sleep properly; yet this ability should not be too great. Otherwise, we sleep forever and never wake up at all.

"We are thus able to say that different conditions can be seen at three levels in human beings. The first level is physical. On the one hand we have our nervous system. This shows a constant tendency to harden, to calcify. So we say:

Physically:—
Hardening Calcification

You see, you are all of you at an age—with the exception of just one who is sitting there amongst you—that you must have your nervous system a little bit calcified. For if you still had the nervous system today the way you had it when you were six months old, you would all be mad. You can't have that kind of soft nervous system anymore. People who are mad have a child-level nervous system. So, we have to have the power to harden, to calcify, in us. And on the other hand, we must have the power to soften, to grow younger. The two powers need to be in balance.

Physically:—
Hardening vs. Softening
Calcification vs. Growing Young

"If we look at the soul level, we are able to say that the soul equivalent of hardening is pedantry, being philistine, materialistic, with a dry intellect.

"All this needs to be understood. We have to be a bit of a philistine or we'd be madcaps. We have to be a bit pedantic or we would not keep our things in proper order. We'd hang our jackets in the stove or in the chimney rather than in the wardrobe. So, it's not a bad thing to be a bit of a philistine and a bit pedantic; but of course not too much of it. We also have the power of fantasy, the power to be dreamers, mystics, theosophists. If all of these get too much, these powers, we will be dreamers, we'll live in fantasies. This must not happen. But on the other hand, we also should not be completely without fantasy.

"I once knew someone who hated anything by way of fantasy. He never went to the theatre, for instance, let alone the opera, for he'd say none of it was true. He had no fantasy at all. But someone who has no fantasy at all will be very dry, sneaking through life, and not a real, proper human being. So again—*things must not go to extremes.*

In the Soul:—
Pedantry Philistinism Materialism Dry Intellect
vs.
Fantasy Dreaminess Mysticism Theosophy

If we now look at the spiritual side of things, we have the power of hardening in waking up. Waking up, we firmly take hold of the body, using our limbs. And the power which at the physical level causes softening, getting younger, we have here on going to sleep. Then we sink into dreams. We no longer have our bodies in hand.

In the Spirit:—
Waking Up vs. Going to Sleep

"We can say that human beings are constantly in danger of falling into the one extreme or the other, either becoming subjected to too much softening, or going into excessive hardening.

"If you have a magnet, you know it attracts iron. We speak of two kinds of magnetism in the magnet. And that is true. We have positive magnetism and negative magnetism. The one attracts the magnetic needle, the other repels it. They are opposites.

"You'll agree that when it comes to physical, bodily things, we are not afraid to call things by their names. We need names. I have now described something to you in body, soul and spirit which every one of you can perceive for himself, something we always see, and about which you can all be quite clear in your minds. But we need names. When we have positive magnetism, we have to understand that this is not the iron; it is something in the iron. There is something invisible in the iron.

"Someone who will not admit that there is something invisible in the piece of iron will say: 'You are daft! Iron is supposed to have a magnetism in it? This is a horseshoe. I use it to shoe my horse.' I think you'll agree that someone who'll not admit that there is something invisible in the iron and uses it just to shoe his horse is an idiot. You can also use this horseshoe for quite a different purpose if it has magnetism inside it.

"Now you see, something invisible, something we cannot perceive with the senses, is present in the hardening process. And this invisible, supersensible principle, which one can observe if one has the gift for it, is called ahrimanic. The powers that want to make the human being into a kind of corpse all the time are ahrimanic. If only the ahrimanic powers were there, we would all the time turn into corpses, we would be pedantic, human beings turned to stone. We would wake up all the time and be unable to sleep. The powers that soften us and make us younger, taking us into fantasy, are the luciferic powers. We need the luciferic powers so that we may not become living corpses. But if only luciferic powers were present, well, then we would be children for the whole of our lives. The luciferic powers are needed in the world, so that we do not become old people at three years of age. The ahrimanic powers are needed in the world, so that we do not remain children forever. These two opposing powers must be present in the human being.

"Now it is important that these two powers must be in balance. How is the balance held? Nothing of these two powers should gain the upper hand.

"You see, it is now the year 1923, as you know. This whole time from the beginning of the century until 1923 has really been such that humanity is in danger of falling prey to the ahrimanic powers. Just consider—we are educated in an ahrimanic way today, unless there is a Science of the Spirit. Just think—our children go to primary school where they have to learn things that must seem very odd to them, things that cannot possibly interest them. I have mentioned this before. They have always seen their father. He looks like this—hair, ears, eyes—and then they are supposed to learn this: father [writing on the board] is their father. It is something quite alien to them. And that is how it is with all the things children are supposed to learn initially in primary school. They are not the least bit interested. And that is, of course, the reason why we must establish sensible schools again, where children may first of all learn things that would interest them. If the teaching were to continue the way it is done at the moment, people would grow old very early, for it is ahrimanic. This makes people old. The way children are educated at school today—*it is all ahrimanic.*

The way it has been in these 1,900 years is that the whole of human evolution has gone in the ahrimanic direction. It was different before.

"If you go back to, let us say, the time from the year 8,000 BC to the turning-point of time, things were different then. People then faced the danger of not being able to grow old. They did not have schools in those early times the way we have today. Schools were only for people who had already reached a respectable age and were meant to be real scholars. They had schools for those people. There were no schools for children then. They would learn from life. They would learn the things they saw. And so, they did not have schools, nor was any kind of effort made to teach the children anything that was alien to them. The danger with this was that people might become utterly luciferic, dreamers, in short, luciferic. And they did. Much wisdom existed in those early times, as I have told you. But this luciferic principle had to be controlled, otherwise they might have gone on all day telling each other ghost stories! That was something people were particularly fond of then. We are thus able to say that in very early times, from about the year 8,000 BC to the turning-point of time, it was a luciferic age. And then came an ahrimanic age.

"Let us take a look at the luciferic age. You see, the people who were the scholars in those early times had some problems. At that time scholars would live in places that were like towers. The tower of Babylon about which the *Bible* tells us was one of those buildings. That is where the scholars lived. These scholars would say: 'Yes, of course, we are fortunate. For fantasy also wants to take over our minds. We always want to go into ghostly, luciferic things. But we have our instruments. With them we look into the stars and see how they move. This puts a rein on our fantasy.' You see, if I look at a star and want it to go a particular way, it won't do it. So then my own fantasy is reined in. The scholars therefore knew that they could use the phenomena of the world to keep a rein on their fantasy. Or they would have instruments for physics. They would know: 'If I were to think that burning a very small piece of wood will give me a huge fire, I can imagine this, but when I do it in reality the small piece of wood will only give me a small fire.'

"That was really the purpose of those ancient schools—to keep a rein on the lively powers of imagination those people had. And their problem was that they would say: 'Yes, but there are all the other people who cannot be scholars.' And so, they made their teachings public, sometimes honestly so and sometimes in a dishonest way. These are the ancient religious teachings, and they were certainly based on great knowledge. Only it would sometimes happen, of course, that the priests went astray. And the result is that the dishonest teachings—the honest ones have largely been lost—have come down to posterity. That was the way in which a rein was kept on the luciferic element.

"As to how things are in the ahrimanic way—this you know. Present-day science is going more and more ahrimanic. The whole of our science today is really designed to make us all dried up. For in this science people really only know the physical world, which is the calcified, material world. And this is the ahrimanic element in our present civilization.

"Between the two is the principle which we call Christian in the true sense. You see, gentlemen, people do not really know the truly Christian spirit today. If you take the element known as 'Christian' in this world today, this is indeed something we would have to fight, that is obvious. But the spirit of whom I also said a few things the last time we met, who was born at the turning-point of time and lived for 33 years—this individual was not the way people say he was. His true aim was to teach the whole of humanity the things that will make it possible to create a balance between the ahrimanic and luciferic elements. And to be Christian is indeed to look for the balance between the ahrimanic and luciferic elements."

Anthroposophical Approach to Medicine, Rudolf Steiner, Lecture IV, Stuttgart, October 28, 1922, GA 314

"A very profound understanding of the human organism is necessary before we can estimate the value for it of an external remedy. Let us begin with something that is always present as a remedial agent in the human organism—the *iron in the blood*. The iron in the blood unceasingly plays the role of a remedial agent, protecting man from his innate tendency to disease. I will describe it to you, to begin with, in a primitive way. You know that if the brain, with its weight of some 1,500 grams, were to rest upon its base, the cerebral blood-vessels there would obviously be crushed. The brain does not rest upon its base but swims in the cerebral fluid, and in accordance with the principle of buoyancy, loses as much of its weight as the weight of the volume of fluid displaced. Thus the brain presses on its base with a weight of only about 20 grams, instead of 1,500 grams. This is a fact of fundamental importance because it shows us that the force of gravity is not the determining factor in that which underlies the functions of the brain, in Ego-activity, for instance. This Ego-activity and also, to a great extent, conceptual activity—in so far as it is not volitional but purely conceptual, ideational activity—is not dependent on the gravity of the substance in question but on the force of buoyancy. (I am speaking here entirely of the physical correlate, namely, the brain activity.) It is dependent on the force which strives to *alienate* the substance from the earth. In our Ego and our thoughts, we do not live in the element of weight, but in the force of buoyancy.

"The same thing holds good for much else in the human organism—above all, the iron-bearing corpuscles swimming in the blood. Each of these corpuscles loses as much of its weight as the weight of the volume of fluid displaced. And now, if our soul-being lives in the force of buoyancy, just think what this possession of iron-bearing blood corpuscles must mean for the whole life of feeling and perception, indeed for the whole life of the organism. In other words: If in a given case there is irregularity in what is going on in the blood simply as a result of the buoyancy of the iron-bearing corpuscles, we know that iron in some form or other must be introduced, but in such a way, of course, that the iron will unfold a right action in the blood, and not elsewhere.

"In terms of Spiritual Science, this means that the relation of the etheric to the astral organism of man is bound up with the iron-content of the blood. The possibility, however, of promoting the corresponding balance, of enabling the organism to lead the necessary amount of foodstuff into the domain of the kidney activities, is provided by regulating the iron-content in the blood. And by imbuing the actual dynamic element in the blood either with weight or with the force of buoyancy—according to how we regulate the iron-content—we are thereby regulating the whole circulation of blood, which in turn reacts upon the kidney activities. In adding to or decreasing the iron-content we have brought about a fundamental regularization of the blood circulation: that is, of the interplay between the etheric and astral parts of man."

***Man as Symphony of the Creative Word,* Part One, Rudolf Steiner, Lecture III, *The Connection between Cosmic Conditions, Earthly Conditions, the Animal World and Man*, Dornach, October 21, 1923, GA 230**

"No other animal has the same proportion between the blood weight and the entire body weight as the cow; other animals have either less or more blood than the cow in proportion to the weight of the body. And weight has to do with gravity and the blood with egoity; not with the Ego, for this is only possessed by man, but with egoity, with separate existence. The blood also makes the animal—the higher animal at least. And I must say that the cow has solved the world problem as to the right proportion between the weight of the blood and the weight of the whole body—when there is the wish to be as thoroughly animal as possible."

"You see, it was not for nothing that the ancients called the Zodiac 'the animal circle.' The Zodiac is twelvefold; it divides its totality into twelve separate parts. Those forces, which come out of the Cosmos, from the Zodiac, take on form and shape in the animals. But the other animals do not conform to the zodiacal proportion so exactly. The cow has a twelfth part of her body weight in the weight of her blood. With the cow the blood weight is a twelfth part of the body weight; with the donkey only the twenty-third part; with the dog the tenth part. All the other animals have a different proportion. In the case of man, the blood is a thirteenth of the body weight."

"You see, the cow has seen to it that, in her weight, she is the expression of animal nature as such, that she is as thoroughly as possible the expression of what is cosmic. A fact I have mentioned repeatedly during these days—namely that one sees from the astral body of the cow that she actually manifests something lofty in physical-material substance—this comes to expression of itself through the fact that the cow maintains the partition into twelve in her own inner relationships of weight. The cosmic in her is at work. Everything to do with the cow is of such a nature that the forces of the Earth are working into spiritual substance. In the cow, Earth-heaviness is obliged to distribute itself according to zodiacal proportion. Earth-heaviness must accommodate itself to allow a twelfth part of itself to fall away into egoity. What the cow possesses as spiritual substance has necessarily to enter into earthly conditions."

"Thus, the cow, lying in the meadow, is in actual fact a spiritual substance, which Earth-matter takes up, absorbs, makes similar to itself.

"When the cow dies, this spiritual substance which the cow bears within herself can be taken up by the Earth, together with the earthly matter, for the well-being of the life of the whole Earth. And man is right when he feels regarding the cow: 'You are the true beast of sacrifice, for you continually give to the Earth what it needs, without which it could not continue to exist, without which it would harden and dry up. You continually give spiritual substance to the Earth, and renew the inner mobility, the inner living activity of the Earth.'

"When you behold on the one hand the meadow with its cattle, and on the other hand the eagle in flight, then you have their remarkable contrast: the eagle who, when he dies, carries away into the expanses of Spirit-Land that Earth-matter, which—because it is spiritualized—has become useless for the Earth; and the cow, who, when she dies, gives to the Earth heavenly matter and thus renews the Earth. The eagle takes from the Earth what it can no longer use, what must return into Spirit-Land. The cow carries into the Earth what the Earth continually needs as renewing forces from Spirit-Land."

From the Contents of Esoteric Classes I, Rudolf Steiner, No. 28, Berlin, March 14, 1908, GA 266

"During the Old Saturn period, there was only a warmth globe on which the spirits of darkness attained their human stage. The blood we had then was dark. There was a hidden fire or warmth on the planet, but no light. When Old Saturn disappeared, the Old Sun rose from the darkness, the second, air element with its oxygen made Old Saturn's glimmer burst into flames, and then there was light, as is symbolized by the alchemist's sulfur. Blood turned from black to yellow.

"During the Old Moon period the whole atmosphere was watery; but not like the water we know. It was divided into spherical drops that moved past each other with tremendous speed. One finds this condition of Old Moon substance in quicksilver; that also divides into very small spheres and is more mobile than all other substances. During the Old Moon period blood was as white as this substance, and it was given forms by the world tone. These forms are female. The whole Old Moon represents the female principle.

"The fourth, earth element appeared during the Earth period in connection with the third alchemistic substance—salt, the symbol of crystallization and dissolution. This is where the male element appears. Our present men with their red blood are shaped on the Earth. Everything that dissolves is salt.

"Thus, we have four kinds of fire in the four kinds of blood: black on Old Saturn, yellow on Old Sun, white on Old Moon, and red on Earth. The warmth that now lives in our blood is the warmth of the planet Old Saturn. All these bloods, or fires, are still in us and are instruments for spirits who work in and on us, until we will be individualized enough to do what these spirits do. Saturn spirits find a point of attack in the warmth of the blood and Ego. Some of them are very bad and dangerous…

"…The four kinds of fire refer to our four lower sheaths that are the 'children' of the I. They must be 'burned in the fire of the spirit,' so that they can become a fourfold philosophical fire in the Future Vulcan period. We must 'add fire to fire,' that is, the fiery, lower passions must be purified by uniting them with the higher, spiritual fire…

"…Blood is the I's instrument. Old Saturn spirits work in the warmth of our blood, as Christ worked in Jesus' blood from age thirty on. Before that Jesus had worked on his physical, etheric and astral bodies. Then Christ took hold of the blood and purified it during the three years. That's why blood had to flow. When we've purified our four bodies in the same way we'll then have the four-fold philosophical fire that belongs to the Future Vulcan period."

True and False Paths in Spiritual Investigation, Rudolf Steiner, Lecture III, _Form and Substantiality of the Mineral Kingdom in Relation to the Levels of Consciousness in Man_, Torquay, August 13, 1924, GA 243

"In what I am about to say I must perforce use a terminology that describes the material world; it should not be accepted in its literal meaning only. When we speak of the heart or head, the commonsense view conjures up a picture of a physical heart or head. But they are, of course, spiritual in origin. And so, when we look at man in his totality, as an entity consisting of body, soul, and spirit, we have the clear impression that his center of gravity lies in the heart. This center guards him against extremes, prevents him from being the plaything of external circumstances and lends him stability. If we retain that courageous spirit which I have just mentioned, we shall ultimately find ourselves firmly anchored in the Universe.

"When a person loses consciousness, he is not firmly anchored. If he suffers a psychic shock—for under these conditions he is more susceptible to pain than normally and after all, pain is an intensification of inner feeling—then he is not in a normal state of consciousness. Under conditions of pain normal consciousness is expelled. Between birth and death man lives in a kind of intermediate state of consciousness. This may well serve the normal purposes of daily life. But if this consciousness becomes too weak, too tenuous, he loses consciousness. If it becomes too dense, too concentrated, pain ensues. The loss of consciousness in a state of swoon, and the state of tension under the influence of pain, are polarities which illustrate the aberrations of consciousness. This describes exactly our reactions to the world of mineral crystals before we become aware of their substantiality—on the one hand, the feeling that in a state of swoon we might at any moment be dissolved in the Universe, and on the other hand that under the influence of pain we might collapse.

"Then we feel that everything that provides stability is centered in the cardiac region. And if we have developed our consciousness to the level already indicated, we then perceive that everything that sustains our ordinary waking consciousness, all that keeps it 'normal,' if I may use this somewhat crude expression, is gold, aurum, which is finely distributed over the Earth and works with greater immediacy upon the heart than upon any other organ.

"Previously we became acquainted with the formation, the crystallization of minerals. We now become aware of their substantiality, of their metallity. We realize in what manner this metallic nature works upon man himself.

"Outwardly we see the crystal formations of the metals in the mineral world. But we know inwardly that the forces of gold which are finely distributed over the Earth sustain our heart and maintain the normal consciousness of our daily life. And so we can say, gold works upon the heart center of man. On the basis of this information, we are now in a position to start our investigations. If, taking the metal gold as we know it, we concentrate upon its color, its hardness and all aspects of its composition and structure and then transform the experience into inner reality, we find that gold is related to the heart. By concentrating on other metals, on iron and its properties, for example, we discover what effect iron has upon us. Gold has a harmonizing influence; it resolves tension and conflict and man is thereby restored to a state of inner equilibrium. If, after becoming familiar with all its aspects, we concentrate intently on iron, forgetting the entire Universe and concentrating solely upon the metal itself, so that we become, as it were, inwardly merged with iron, become identified with iron, then we feel as if our consciousness were rising up from the regions of the heart. We are still fully conscious as we follow this consciousness as it ascends from the heart to the larynx. If we have carried out our spiritual exercises adequately, no harm can result; otherwise, a slight feeling of faintness overtakes us. As our consciousness ascends, we recognize this condition from the fact that we have developed an intense inner activity, a heightened consciousness. Then we gradually transpose ourselves into this ascending consciousness and contact the world where we see the group-soul of the animals. By concentrating on the metallity of iron we have now entered the astral world.

"When we become acquainted with the form of the metals, we reach the realm of the higher spiritual beings; when we become acquainted with their substantiality and metallity we enter the astral world, the world of souls. We feel our consciousness rising upward to the larynx and we emerge into a new sphere. We owe this shift of consciousness to our concentration upon iron, and we feel that we are no longer the same person as before. If we attain this state in full, clear consciousness, we are sensible of having transcended our former self; we have entered into the etheric world. The Earth has vanished, it no longer holds any interest for us. We have ascended into the planetary spheres which, as it were, have become our abode. Thus, we gradually withdraw from the body and become integrated into the Universe. The path from gold to iron is the path leading into the Universe.

"After gold and iron, we next concentrate upon tin, upon its metallity, its color and substantiality, with the result that our consciousness becomes wholly identified with tin. We feel that our consciousness is now rising to still higher levels. But if we undertake this step without adequate preparation, we suffer a near total swoon, scarcely any sign of consciousness remains. If we have prepared ourselves in advance, we can hold ourselves in this state of diminished consciousness; but we feel that our consciousness is withdrawing still further from the body and ultimately reaches the region between the eyes. Though the vast expanse of the Universe encompasses us, we are still within the realm of stars. The Earth, however, begins to appear as a distant star. And we conclude that we have left our body on Earth—*that we have ascended into the Cosmos and share the life of the stars.*

"All this is by no means as simple as it sounds. What I have described to you, what we experience when we follow the path of Initiation, namely, that consciousness is situated in the larynx, the base of the skull or the forehead, is an indication that all these various states of consciousness are permanently present in man. All of you sitting here have within you these states of consciousness, but you are not aware of it. Why is this so? Now man is a complex being. If, at the moment when you were conscious of the whole laryngeal organization, you could dispense with your brain and sense organs, you would never be free of this slight subconscious feeling of faintness. And in effect this is so; it is simply overlaid by the ordinary heart consciousness, the gold consciousness. It is common to all of you, it is part of your human make-up. *A part of you that shares this consciousness is situated in the stars and does not exist on Earth at all.*

"The tin consciousness lies further out in the Cosmos. It would be untrue to state that the Earth is your sole habitat. It is the heart that anchors your consciousness to the Earth. That which has its center in the larynx is out in the Cosmos and, situated still further out, is that which has its center in the forehead (tin). The iron consciousness embraces the Mars sphere, tin the Jupiter sphere. *Only in the gold consciousness do you belong to the Earth.* You are always interwoven with the Universe, but the heart consciousness conceals this from you.

"If you meditate on lead or some similar metal and again concentrate on its substantiality and metallity, you relinquish the body completely. You are left in no doubt that your physical body and etheric body are left behind on Earth. They appear strange and remote. They concern you as little as the stone concerns the rock on which it rests. Consciousness has left the body through the crown (the sagittal suture) of the head. Wherever we turn, a minute quantity, a tincture of lead is always to be found in the Universe. This form of consciousness reaches far out into space; with the consciousness that is centered in the cranium man always remains in a state of complete insensibility.

"Picture to yourselves the state of illusion in which man habitually lives. When he is sitting at his desk making up his accounts or writing articles he fondly imagines that he is thinking with his head. That is not the reality. It is not the head as such—but rather, it is its physical aspect that belongs to the Earth. The head consciousness extends from the larynx upwards far out into the Universe. The Universe reveals itself solely in the head center. *What determines your human condition between birth and death is the heart center*. Whether you write good or bad articles, whether your accounts may or may not be to your neighbor's disadvantage—this is determined by the heart center. It is pure illusion to imagine that man's head consciousness is confined to the Earth alone, for, in effect, it is in a permanent state of insensibility. And that is why it is also peculiarly subject to pain from which other organs are free. Let me take this point a little further. When, in our present state, we try to find the reasons for this situation we are continually threatened from the spirit with the annihilation of our intellectual consciousness, with a breakdown of the whole consciousness and a collapse into total insensibility.

"Our picture of man is then as follows: in the larynx (iron) man develops the consciousness that reaches to the archetypes of the animal kingdom. It is the consciousness that belongs to the stars; but we are unaware of it in ordinary life. Higher still, in the region of the eyes (tin) is the consciousness of the archetypes of the plant kingdom and below are their reflected images. Crowning all is the center of the lead consciousness which reaches to the Saturn sphere; our head center is oblivious of the articles we write, for they are the product of the heart center. But the head is fully aware of the happenings in cosmic space. Our description of terrestrial events and activities proceeds from the heart; the head, meanwhile, can concentrate on the manner in which a divine being manifests himself in a pyrites, in a crystal of salt or of quartz.

"When Initiate consciousness surveys the audience present here, it is evident that you are listening to what I am saying with your hearts, whilst your three higher levels of consciousness are out in the Cosmos. The Cosmos is the scene of activities of an order wholly different from those known to ordinary earthly consciousness. In the Cosmos, especially in what is enacted there and radiates far and wide, is woven for all of us the web of our destiny, our karma."

***True and False Paths in Spiritual Investigation*, Rudolf Steiner, Lecture V, *The Inner Vitalization of the Soul through the Qualities of the Metallic Nature*, Torquay, August 15, 1924, GA 243**

"The mystery behind the metallity of silver is of a very special kind. If the cosmic impulse behind copper awakens the first higher level of consciousness in the being of man, if a different cosmic force behind mercury awakens a second higher level of consciousness that is related to the world of stars and therefore to the spiritual world which we inhabit between death and rebirth, then the metallity of silver must awaken a consciousness of an entirely different order.

"When man intensifies and enhances his relationship to silver by the same process he adopted towards the metallic natures of copper and mercury, he comes into touch with a still deeper organization within him. Mercury relates him to the vascular system which, in turn, relates him to a cosmic circulation, to the spirituality of the Cosmos. The intensification of his relationship to silver brings him into direct contact with all the forces and impulses that survive from earlier incarnations.

"If a man concentrates on the peculiar properties of silver—and it is some time before the effects are registered—he concentrates within himself those forces which are responsible not only for the circulation of fluids through the vessels, but also for the circulation of warmth in the bloodstream. He then realizes that he owes his human status to the warmth circulating in his blood, in that he feels a certain inner warmth, a material, yet at the same time a spiritual element within his blood; and that in this warmth forces from former incarnations are actively working. In man's relationship to silver is expressed that which can influence the warmth-activity of the blood and also that which provides a spiritual link with earlier incarnations."

Health and Illness, Pt II. Rudolf Steiner, Lecture III, *The Effects of Alcohol on Man*, Dornach, January 8, 1922, GA 348

"Now, it is true that regarding their intellects and soul qualities, humans are in many ways alike; regarding the blood, however, there is a marked difference between man and woman. It is a difference that one is not always aware of but that is nevertheless clearly evident. This is that the influence on human beings of the red and white corpuscles that are produced within the hollows of the bone is such that the red corpuscles are more important for the woman and the white are more important for the man. This is very important: the red corpuscles are more important with the woman and the white with the man. This is because the woman, as you know, every four weeks has her menstrual period; which is actually an activity that the human body undertakes to eliminate something that must be eliminated, red corpuscles.

"After having been produced in the bone marrow, the red and white corpuscles naturally enter the blood stream. When a woman now drinks alcohol, it is the red corpuscles that are particularly affected. The red corpuscles contain iron, are somewhat heavy, and possess something of the Earth's heaviness. When a woman drinks, it affects her in such a way that there is too much heaviness in her. When a pregnant woman drinks, therefore, her developing child becomes too heavy and cannot inwardly form its organs properly. It does not develop properly inwardly, and its inner organs are not in order. In this round-about-way, gentlemen, the harmful influence of alcohol is expressed in the woman.

"In men, alcohol primarily affects the white corpuscles. If conception takes place when a man is under the influence of alcohol, or when his system is generally contaminated by the effects of alcoholism, a man's semen is ruined in a way, becoming too restless. When conception takes place, the tiny egg is released from the mother's organism. This can only be seen with a microscope. From the male, a great number of microscopic sperm are released, each one of which has something resembling a tail attached to it. The seminal fluid contains countless numbers of such sperm. This tail, which is like a fine hair, gives the sperm great restlessness. They make the most complicated movements, and naturally one sperm must reach the egg first. The one that reaches the egg first penetrates it. The sperm is much smaller than the egg. Although the egg can be perceived only with a microscope, the sperm is still smaller. As soon as the egg has received it, a membrane forms around the egg, thereby preventing penetration by the rest of the sperm cells. Generally, only one sperm can enter the egg. As soon as one has penetrated, a membrane is formed around the egg, and the others must retreat.

"You see, therefore, it is most ingeniously arranged. Now, the sperm's restlessness is greatly increased through alcohol, so that conception occurs under the influence of semen that is extraordinarily lively. If the father is a heavy drinker when conception occurs, the child's nerve-sense system will be affected. The woman's drinking harms the child's inner organs because of the heaviness that ensues. The man's drinking harms the child's nervous system. All the activities are damaged that should be present in the right way as the child grows up.

"We therefore can say that if a woman drinks, the earthly element in the human being is ruined; if a man drinks, the element of movement, the airy element that fills the Earth's surroundings and that man carries within himself, is ruined. When both parents drink, therefore, the embryo is harmed from two different sides. Naturally, this is not a proper conception; while conception is possible, however, proper growth of the embryo is not. On the one hand, the egg's tendency toward heaviness tries to prevail; on the other, everything in it is in restless motion, and one tendency contradicts the other. If both parents are alcoholics and conception occurs, the masculine element contradicts the feminine. To those who understand the entire relationship, it becomes quite clear that in the case of habitual drinkers exceedingly harmful elements actually arise in their offspring. People do not wish to believe this, because the effects of heavy drinking in men and women are not so obvious, relatively speaking. This is only because the blood is so well protected, however, being produced, after all, in the bone marrow, and because people must do a lot if they are to affect their offspring strongly. Weak effects are simply not admitted by people today."

***Health and Illness* Pt II, Rudolf Steiner, Lecture V, *The Effect of Nicotine—Vegetarian and Meat Diets—On Taking Absinthe—Twin Births*, Dornach, January 13, 1922, GA 348**

"Such a source of illness is constantly present in a person who is a heavy smoker because, without realizing it, he is always filled with a certain anxiety. Now, you know that if you suffer from anxiety, your heart pumps more quickly. This leads you to realize that the heart of a person who constantly poisons himself with nicotine continuously beats somewhat too fast. When it beats too quickly, however, the heart thickens, just as the muscle of the upper arm, the biceps, grows thicker when it is constantly strained. Under some circumstances, this is not so bad, as long as the inner tissue doesn't tear. If the heart muscle—it is also a muscle—becomes too thick from over-exertion, however, it exerts pressure on all the other organs with the result, as a rule, that beginning from the heart the blood circulation becomes disturbed. The circulation of the blood cannot be initiated by the heart, but it can be disturbed when the heart is thickened.

"The next consequence of a thickened heart is that the kidneys become ill, since it is due to the harmonious activities of heart and kidneys that the entire human bodily organization is kept functioning properly. The heart and kidneys must always work in harmony. Naturally, everything in the human being must harmonize, but the heart and kidneys are directly connected. It quickly becomes apparent that when something is amiss in the heart, the kidneys no longer function properly."

***The Evolution of the Earth and Man and the Influence of the Stars*, Rudolf Steiner, Lecture VI, Dornach, July 31, 1924, GA 354**

"But now let us think how it is when someone eats green stuff, the stems and leaves of a plant. When he eats green stuff, he is getting fats from the plants. Why is it that sometimes a stem is so hard? Because it then gives its forces to leaves that are going to be rich in carbohydrates. And if the leaves stay green—the greener they are, the more fats they have in them. So when someone eats bread, for instance, he can't take in many fats from the bread. He takes in more, for example, from watercress—that tiny plant with the very tiny leaves—more fats than when he eats bread. That's how the custom came about of putting butter on our bread, some kind of fat. It wasn't just for the taste. And why country people want bacon with their bread. There again is fat, and that also is eaten for two reasons.

"When I eat bread, the bread works upon my head because the root elements of a plant work up into the stem. The stem, even though it is stem and grows above the ground in the air, still has root forces in it. The question is not whether something is above in the air, but whether it has any root forces. Now the leaf, the green leaf, does not have root forces. No green leaf ever appears down in the earth. In late summer and autumn, when the sun forces are no longer working so strongly, the stem can mature. But the leaf needs the strongest sun forces for it to unfold; it grows toward the sun. So we can say, the green part of the plant works particularly on heart and lungs, while the root strengthens the head. The potato also is able to work into the head. When we eat greens, they give us particularly plant fats; they strengthen our heart and lungs, the middleman, the chest man.

"That, I would say, is the secret of human nutrition: that if I want to work upon my head, I have roots or stems for dinner. If I want to work upon my heart or my lungs, I make myself a green salad. And in this case, because these substances are destroyed in the intestines and only their forces proceed to work, cooking is not so necessary. That's why leaves can be eaten raw as salad.

Whatever is to work on the head cannot be eaten raw; it must be cooked. Cooked foods work particularly on the head. Lettuce and similar things work particularly on heart and lungs, building them up, nourishing them through the fats."

The Heart is the Temple of the Human Spirit

***"Freemasonry" and Ritual Work: The Misraim Service: Letters, Documents, Ritual Texts and Lectures from the History and Contents of the Cognitive-Ritual Section of the Esoteric School 1904-1914: Documents of a New Beginning after the First World War: 1921-24*, Rudolf Steiner, Explanations of the Temple Legend—Instruction III, The Human Beings Mission on Earth, N. D., GA 265 (pgs. 429-430)**

"In the temple of the human body is the Holy of Holies. Many people live in the temple without knowing anything about it. But those who have an inkling of it receive from it the power to purify themselves to such an extent that they can enter into this holiest place. Therein is the Holy Vessel that has been prepared throughout the ages as a fit container for the blood and life of Christ when the time for it arrives. When one has entered therein, one has found a way to the Holy of Holies in the great Temple of the Earth. Therein, too, many are living on Earth, without knowing anything about it; but when one discovers oneself within one's innermost sanctuary, one will be allowed to enter in and there discover the Holy Grail.

"The vessel will appear to him as though cut in wonderful shining crystal, and is formed into symbols and letters, until one gradually senses the sacred contents and it gleams in golden radiance. One enters the Mystery Center of one's own heart and a divine being emerges from this place and unites itself with the

God outside, with the Being of Christ. It lives in the spiritual light which shines into the vessel, and thereby sanctifies it."

The Festivals and their Meaning II. _Easter_, Rudolf Steiner, Lecture VIII, _Spiritual Bells of Easter_, Pt II, Cologne April 11, 1909, GA 109

"Now the outer, physical expression for the 'I' is the blood. This is a great mystery; but there have always been men who knew of it and were aware that replicas of the 'I' of Jesus of Nazareth are present in the spiritual world. There have always been men whose task it was, through the centuries since the Event of Golgotha, to ensure in secret that humanity gradually matures, so that there may be human beings who are fit to receive the replicas of the 'I' of Jesus Christ of Nazareth, just as there were persons who received replicas of his etheric body and astral body. To this end it was necessary to discover the secret of how, in the quietude of a profound mystery, this 'I' might be preserved until the appropriate moment in the evolution of the Earth and of humanity. With this aim a Brotherhood of Initiates who preserved the secret was founded: the *Brotherhood of the Holy Grail.* They were the guardians of this secret. This Fellowship has always existed. It is said that its originator took the chalice used by Christ Jesus at the Last Supper and in it caught the blood flowing from the wounds of the Redeemer on the Cross. He gathered the blood, the expression of the 'I' in this chalice—the Holy Grail. And the chalice with the blood of the Redeemer, with the secret of the replica of the 'I' of Christ-Jesus, was preserved in a holy place, in the Brotherhood of those who through their attainments and their Initiation are the Brothers of the Holy Grail.

"The time has come today when these secrets may be made known, when through a spiritual life the hearts of men can become mature enough to understand this great Mystery. If souls allow spiritual science to kindle understanding of such secrets they become fit to recognize in that Holy Chalice the Mystery of the Christ-'I,' the eternal 'I' which every human 'I' can become. The secret is a reality—only men must allow themselves to be summoned through spiritual science to understand this, in order that as they contemplate the Holy Grail, the Christ-'I' may be received into their being. To this end they must understand and accept what has come to pass as fact, *as reality*.

"But when men are better prepared to receive the Christ Ego, then it will pour in greater and greater fullness into their souls. They will then evolve to the level where stood Christ Jesus, their great Example. Then for the first time they will learn to understand the sense in which Christ Jesus is the Great Example for humanity. And having understood this, men will begin to realize in the innermost core of their being that the certainty of life's eternity springs from the corpse hanging on the wood of the Cross of Golgotha. Those who are inspired and permeated by the Christ-'I'—the Christians of future time, will understand something else as well—something that hitherto has been known only to those who reached enlightenment. They will understand, not only the Christ Who has passed through death; but the triumphant Christ of the *Apocalypse—resurrected in the spiritual fire*, the Christ Whose coming has already been predicted. The Easter festival can always be for us a symbol of the Risen One, a link reaching over from Christ on the Cross to the Christ triumphant, risen and glorified, to the One Who lifts all men with Him to the right hand of the Father.

"And so, the Easter symbol points us to the vista of the whole future of the Earth, to the future of the evolution of humanity, and is for us a guarantee that men who are Christ-inspired will be transformed from Saul-men into Paul-men and will behold with increasing clarity *a spiritual fire*. For it is indeed true that as the Christ was revealed in advance to Moses and to those who were with him, in the material fire of the thornbush and of the lightning on Sinai, so He will be revealed to us in a spiritualized fire of the future. *He is with us always, until the end of the world*, and He will appear in the spiritual fire to those who have allowed their eyes to be enlightened through the Event of Golgotha. Men will behold Him in the *spiritual fire*. They beheld Him, to begin with, in a different form; they will behold Him for the first time in His true form—*in a spiritual fire*.

"But because the Christ penetrated so deeply into Earth-existence—right into the physical bony structure—the power which built His sheaths out of the elements of the Earth so purified and hallowed this physical substance that it can never become what in their sorrow the Eastern sages feared: that the Enlightened One of the future, the Maitreya Buddha, would not find on the Earth men capable of understanding him because they had sunk so deeply into matter. Christ was led to Golgotha in order that He might lift matter again to spiritual heights, in order that the fire might not be extinguished in matter; but be spiritualized. The primal wisdom will again be intelligible to men when they themselves are spiritualized—the primal wisdom which, in the spiritual world, was the source of their being."

Rudolf Steiner from his sick bed in 1924

"Blood in the heart, striving toward the breath in the lungs, is humanity's striving for the Cosmos. The breath in the lungs, striving toward the blood in the heart, is the Cosmos forgiving humanity."

"The human being streams into the Cosmos on an ongoing basis in the flow of the blood. The Christ mystery is the revelation of the great miracle that takes place between the heart and lungs. The Cosmos becomes the human being and the human being becomes the Cosmos. The Sun carries the human being out of the Cosmos and onto Earth. The Moon carries human beings from the Earth into the Cosmos. In larger terms, what streams from the lungs to the heart is the human correlate of the descent of Christ onto the Earth; what moves from the heart to the lungs is the human correlate of the human being carried into the spirit world by the Christ impulse after death. Thus, the secret of Golgotha lives between and heart and the lungs in each human being, in a very human, organ-related sense."

***How the Spiritual World Projects into Physical Existence*, Rudolf Steiner, Lecture V, *Macrocosm and Microcosm*, Paris, May 5, 1913, GA 150**

"You have heard of the 'Golden Silence,' that refers to the fact that we have in our soul a force which creates the Word. We can grasp this force, just as we can grasp the Power of Thought; and in so doing, we overcome Time, just as through grasping of the Power of Thought we overcome Space. The memory, which in ordinary everyday life extends back to one's childhood, then extends into the pre-natal life. That is the way to get experiences of our life from the last death until the present birth and is also the way to perceive the evolution of humanity; because we then perceive those forces which guide the development of the history of man. Then we learn to know life from birth right up to death. If we but develop the force of the Silent Word, we learn to know the spiritual basis of our life on Earth. And here again it is the case that we come to an historic point, to the Mystery of Golgotha; because this is the path along which we come to the ascending and descending development of man, *the point when Christ incarnated*. We then recognize Christ as He is, in His very own forces. A special light then falls on the first lines of the *Gospel according to St. John*.

"As through the freeing of our Thought we unite ourselves with the Christ as He was on Earth, so through the freeing of the Word we unite ourselves with the Mystery of Golgotha.

"And then a third force can become independent through meditation. Meditation can not only affect the brain and the larynx; but the blood-circulation in the heart. We feel this working in a weak form in such processes as blushing and turning pale. There a psychic element affects the pulsing of the blood and reaches to the heart. Now this soul-power can be drawn away from the pulsation of the blood and be made an independent power of the soul. This happens through Meditation when the will unites itself with one's meditations. Again, we meditate: 'In the Light radiates Wisdom'; but now we form for ourselves the resolve of uniting our Will with it, so that we *Will* to accompany this radiating wisdom right through the evolution of humanity. Now if we carry out such a Meditation, we reach the point when the forces of the *All* stream into the soul.

"My dear friends, these forces can be grasped, one can draw them out of the blood, though not entirely; but they build a clairvoyant force through which we can transcend our Earth. We then learn to know the Earth as a reincarnating planet, which will incarnate anew and we human beings with it. In this way we grow through the spiritual, psychic world, right out into the Macrocosm."

***Psychoanalysis in the Light of Anthroposophy*, Rudolf Steiner, Lecture V, *Connections Between Organic Processes and the Mental Life of Man*, Dornach, July 2 1921, GA 205**

"Let us study the heart with the same idea. For spiritual-scientific research, the heart is an extraordinarily interesting organ. You know that our trivial science is inclined to treat knowledge of the heart rather lightly. It looks upon the heart as a pump which pumps the blood through the body. Nothing more absurd can be believed, for the heart has nothing to do with pumping the blood. The blood is set in motion by the full agility of the astral body and ego, and the heart's movement is only the reflex of these activities. The movement of the blood is autonomous, and the heart only brings to expression the movement caused by these forces. The heart is in fact only the organ that manifests the movement of the blood, the heart itself having no activity in relation to this blood movement. The present natural scientists become very angry if you speak of this. Many years ago, I think in 1904 or 1905, on a journey to Stockholm I explained this to a scientist, a medical man, and he was furious about the idea that the heart should not be regarded as a pump, that the blood comes into movement through its own vitality, that the heart is simply inserted in the general blood movement, participates with its beat, and so on.

"Well, something is reflected from the surface of the heart which is not a matter of memory or of habit. The life processes become spiritualized when they reach the outer surface of the heart. For what is thrown back from the heart are the pangs of conscience. That is to be taken simply, entirely as the physical aspect. The pangs of conscience which radiate into our consciousness are that ingredient in our experiences which is reflected from the heart. Spiritual cognition of the heart teaches us this.

"But if we look into its interior, we see gathered there forces which again stem from the entire metabolic and limb organism, and because everything connected with the heart forces is spiritualized that is also spiritualized within it which has to do with our outer life and deeds. And however strange and paradoxical it may sound to anyone clever in the modern sense, the fact remains that what is thus prepared within the heart are the karmic propensities, the tendencies of our karma. It is revoltingly foolish to speak of the heart as a mere pumping mechanism, for the heart is the organ which, through mediation of the limb and metabolic system, carries what we understand as karma into the next incarnation.

"You see, if we learn to know this organization we learn to differentiate and recognize its connection with the complete life extending beyond birth and death. We look then into the whole structure of the human being. We cannot speak of the head in relation to metamorphoses, for the head is simply cast off, its forces having completed their activity in the present incarnation. That which, however, exists in these four main systems, in lung, kidney, liver, and heart, after making a detour through the metabolic and limb system, passes over forming our head with all its predispositions and tendencies in the next incarnation. We must seek within the organs of our body the forces which will carry over into the next incarnation what we are now experiencing."

***Supersensible Man*, Rudolf Steiner, Lecture I, November 13, 1923, GA 231**

"In the sphere of Art, as you know, all manner of transformations are possible. When we have drawn our outline of man and then drawn within it the nervous system, we have the feeling that we have been literally painting or drawing. But now it is not so easy to paint what we hear in the realm of Cosmic Music, for it is all rhythm and melody. If we are to represent it in our picture, we must take a brush and, following the nervous system, quickly make *here* a dab of red, *there* a dab of blue, here again red, there again blue, and so on, all along the lines of the nervous system. Then at certain places we shall feel impelled to stop, we can go no further; we must now paint into the picture a definite 'form,' to express what we have heard in the spirit. We can indeed transform it into drawing, but if we want to place it within the contour-line, we find that at certain points we are obliged to go *beyond* the line and paint a new and different form, because here the rhythm blue-red, blue-red, blue-red, suddenly becomes melody. We feel we must paint in this form—and the form is what the melody sings to us! *Cosmic Rhythm—Cosmic Melody*. When we have completed the picture, we have before us Cosmic Music made perceptible in space, the Cosmic Music which becomes audible to the ear of the spirit when the picture of the planetary movements grows dim and disappears. And what we have now drawn into our picture is none other than the path along which the blood flows. When we come to an organ—to heart or lung, or to organs which take into themselves either something from the outside world or substances from within the body itself—at these points we must paint a form which attaches itself in some way to the channels of the blood. Then we get heart, lungs, liver, kidneys, stomach. From the Cosmic Music we learn how to draw these organs of secretion, and how to insert them into the blood system in our picture.

"Now we go a stage further. We pass from Inspiration to Intuition. Something new arises out of the Cosmic Music. The tones begin to blend with one another; one tone works upon another and we begin to hear *meaning* in this Cosmic Music. The Cosmic Music changes into speech—*Cosmic Speech* that is spoken forth by the Universe. At the stage of Intuition, what was known in earlier times as the Cosmic Word becomes audible. We must now draw something else into our picture of the human being. Here we must proceed just as we proceed in ordinary everyday writing, where we express something by means of words that are formed of letters. In our picture of man, we must express the meaning of the single Cosmic Words. We find that when we give expression to these Cosmic Words and bring that expression into the drawing, we have before us a picture of the *muscular* and *bony systems* in the human being, It is just as though someone were to tell us something which we then write down. Cosmic Speech tells us something—and we draw it into the picture. In what the world beyond the Earth tells us, we have thus been able to find the human being in his totality.

"But now there is another and essentially different experience that comes to us in the course of this spiritual observation. Let us return to what was said at the beginning of the lecture about the form that is inscribed in the ether by the planetary bodies. While we are engaged in this spiritual observation, knowledge of the earthly vanishes for us; it remains as a memory only. But it must be there as memory; if it were not, we should have no stability, no balance, and these are essential if we are to be knowers of the spirit. A knowledge of the spirit that excludes physical knowledge is not good. Just as in physical life we must be able to remember—for if the faculty of remembering what we do and experience is lacking, we are not in good health—so, in the realm of spiritual knowledge we must be able always to remember what is there in the physical world. In the sphere where we experience the formative activities of the planetary system, the other kind of knowledge which we had on Earth—all that is given us in the wonderful achievements of physical science—is for the moment entirely forgotten. However well and thoroughly we have known our Natural Science here on Earth, in every act of spirit-knowledge we have always again and again to remember it, we have to recall to our consciousness what we have learnt in the realm of the physical. We must say to ourselves at every turn: That is the solid ground upon which I have to stand. But it withdraws from us, it becomes no more than a memory. On the other hand, we begin now to have a new perception, which is as vivid in comparison with physical knowledge as is immediate present experience compared with remembered experience. We perceive that while we are beholding the form-giving power of the planetary sphere we are within an entirely new environment. Around us are the Beings of the Third Hierarchy: Archai [Spirits of Personality], Archangels [Spirits of Fire], Angels [Spirits of Twilight]. In this form-creating activity lives the Third Hierarchy. A new world arises before us. And now we do not merely say: From the world of the planets has come the human form in its Cosmic Archetype! Now we say: Beings of the Third Hierarchy, Archai, Archangels and Angels, are working and weaving at this cosmic archetype of the form of man!

"It is possible here in earthly existence to attain to perception of the world of the Hierarchies, by means of super-sensible knowledge. After death, every human being must necessarily experience such knowledge, and the better he has prepared himself—as he can prepare himself—during earthly existence, the easier it will be for him. On Earth, when a man wants to know what he is like in his form and figure, he can look at himself in a mirror, or he can have his photograph taken. After death no such means exist,—either for himself or in regard to his fellowmen.

After death he has to look away to the formative working and weaving of the planets. In what the planets reveal, he beholds the building up of his form. There we recognize our own human form. And working and weaving through it all are the Beings of the Third Hierarchy,—the Angels, Archangels and Archai.

"We can now progress further on our upward path. When we have recognized that the weaving life of Angels, Archangels and Archai is connected with the form of the human skin and the sense-organs that belong to it, we can advance a step further in our knowledge of man's relation with the world beyond the Earth. Only, let us first be quite clear how differently we have now to think of the human form or figure. Here on Earth we describe a man's figure, or perhaps his countenance. One man's forehead, we say, is of such and such a shape; another has a nose of a particular shape; a third has mournful eyes; a fourth laughing eyes,—and so on. But there we stop. Cosmic knowledge on the other hand reveals to us in everything that goes to make up the human form the working and weaving of the Third Hierarchy. The human form is in truth no earthly creation, The Earth merely provides the substance for the embryo. The Archai, Archangels and Angels work in from the Cosmos, building up the human form. If we now advance further and come to perceive the confluence of the planetary movements, of which confluence the nervous system and the secreting glands are an after-copy, we find, interwoven with the movements of the planets, the Beings of the Second Hierarchy: Exusiai [Spirits of Form], Kyriotetes [Spirits of Wisdom], Dynamis [Spirits of Movement]. Beings of the Second Hierarchy are active in the shaping of the cosmic archetype of the nervous and glandular systems in man. It is thus at a later period after death—that is to say, sometime after we have learned to understand the human form from its cosmic archetype—that we ascend to the world of the Second Hierarchy, and realize that the earthly human being to whom we now look back as a memory was fashioned and created in his nervous and glandular systems by the Exusiai, Kyriotetes and Dynamis. Then we no longer regard the human being as the product of forces of electricity, magnetism and the like; we take knowledge of how he as physical man has been built up by the Beings of the Second Hierarchy.

"We go still further and ascend to the sphere of Cosmic Music—Cosmic Melody and Cosmic Rhythm, where we find yet another cosmic archetype of the being of man. This time we do not move onward in the Hierarchies. It is the same Beings—the Beings of the Second Hierarchy—who are at work here too, but they are engaged in a different kind of activity. It is difficult to express in words wherein their first work—upon the nervous system—differs from their work upon the rhythmic blood-system; but we may think of it in the following way. In their work upon the nervous system, the Beings of the Second Hierarchy are looking downwards, towards Earth. In their work upon the blood system, they are looking upwards. Both the nervous system, and the blood system (as well as the organs connected therewith) are created by the same Hierarchy; but their gaze is at one time turned towards the Earth and at another upwards to the spiritual world, to the heavens.

"Finally, at the stage of Intuition where we behold how the muscular and bony system of man is woven into being by the world of the Cosmic Word, the Cosmic Speech, we come to the First Hierarchy—the Seraphim [Spirits of Love], Cherubim [Spirits of Harmony] and Thrones [Spirits of Will]. We have now reached the stage which corresponds approximately to the middle-point of the life between death and a new birth, spoken of in my Mystery Plays as the 'Midnight Hour of Existence.' Here we have to see how all those parts of man's organism which enable him to move about in the world are woven and created by the Beings of the First Hierarchy.

"Thus, when we look at the human being with super-sensible knowledge, behind every part of him we see a world of spiritual, cosmic Beings."

***Foundations of Esotericism*, Rudolf Steiner, Lecture V, Berlin, September 30, 1905, GA 93a**

"Undifferentiated space would be soundless. Space which is arithmetically organized produces sound. Here we have an example of how one can look into the Akashic Record. If one can rise to the perception of the inner arithmetic which is preserved from sound in space, then at any time one can hear again a sound which someone has spoken. For instance, one can hear what was spoken by Caesar at the crossing of the Rubicon. The inner arithmetic of sound is still present in the Akashic Record. Sound corresponds to something we call Manas. What the ear experiences as sound is the wisdom of the world. In the perception of sound, one hears the wisdom of the world. In the act of speaking, one brings forth the wisdom of the world. What is arithmetical in our speech remains in the Akashic Record. When he hears or speaks man expresses himself directly in wisdom. At the present time thinking is the form in which man can bring his will to expression in speech. Today it is only in thinking that we can unfold the will. Only later will it be possible for man, rising above the level of thought, to unfold the will in speech.

"The next step is connected with warmth. Man's activity is to be sought in what streams out from him as inner warmth. Out of what proceeds from warmth: passions, impulses, instincts, desires, wishes and so on, Karma arises. Just as the parallel organ to the ear is the organ of speech, so the parallel organ to the warmth of the heart is the pituitary gland, the Hypophysis. The heart takes up the warmth from outside, as the ear does sound. Thereby it perceives world warmth. The corresponding organ which we must have, in order to be able to produce warmth consciously, is the pituitary gland in the head, which at the present time is only at the beginning of its development. Just as one perceives with the ear and produces with the larynx, so one takes up the warmth of the world in the heart and lets it stream forth again through the pituitary gland in the brain. Once this capacity has been achieved, the heart will have become the organ it was intended to be. There is a reference to this in words from '*Light on the Path*': 'Before the soul can stand in the presence of the Masters, its feet must be washed in the blood of the heart.' Then our heart's blood streams out as today our words stream out into the world. In the future, warmth of soul will flood over mankind.

"Somewhat deeper in evolution than the warmth organ stands the organ of sight. In the course of evolution, the organs of hearing, warmth and sight, follow in sequence; the organ of sight is only at the stage of receiving, but the ear already perceives, for instance in the sound of a bell, its innermost being. Warmth must flow from the being itself. The eye has only an image, the ear has the perception of innermost reality. The perception of warmth is the receiving of something that rays outwards. There is an organ which will also become the active organ of vision. This is today germinally present in the pineal gland, the Epiphysis, the organ which will give reality to the images which today are produced by the eye. These two organs, the pineal gland and the pituitary gland as active organs, must develop into the organ of vision (eye) and the organ of warmth (heart). Today fantasy is the preliminary stage leading to a later power of creation. Now man has at most imagination. Later he will have magical power. This is the Kriya-Shakti power [Sanskrit: Kriya = Action; Shakti = Divine Feminine Power]. It develops in proportion to the physical development of the pineal gland.

"In the reciprocal relationship between ear and larynx we have a prophetic model (Vorbild). Thinking will later be interpenetrated with warmth, and still later man himself will learn to create. First, he learns to create a picture; then to create and send forth radiations; then to create beings. Freemasonry calls these three forces Wisdom, Semblance (Beauty) and Power [Strength]." (See Goethe's Fairy Tale: *The Green Snake and the Beautiful Lily.*)

***Man: Hieroglyph of the Universe,* Rudolf Steiner, Lecture XV, Dornach, May 15, 1920, GA 201**

"Consider for a moment the circulation of the blood. The blood, transmuted by the outer air, enters the left auricle, passes into the left ventricle, and from thence branches off through the aorta into the organism. We can say: Blood passes from the lungs to the heart, thence into the rest of the organism; but branching off also to the head. The blood, however, in passing through the organism takes up the nourishment. And into this is introduced all that is dependent on the Earth. All that the digestive apparatus introduces into the circulation of the blood is earthly. What is introduced through the breathing, when we bring oxygen into the blood-course, is planetary. And then we have the blood-circulation that goes to the head, which includes all that composes the head. Just as the circulatory course of the lungs with its absorption of oxygen, and giving out of carbonic acid, belongs to the planetary system; just as what is introduced through the digestive apparatus belongs to the Earth, so that part of the circulatory course that branches off above, belongs to the starry world. It is, as it were, drawn away from the aorta and then streams back and unites with the blood streaming back from the rest of the organism, so that they stream conjointly back to the heart. That which branches off above says, as it were, to the whole of the rest of the circulatory course: 'I do not share either in the oxygenating process nor in the digestive process; but I separate myself out. I invert myself upwards.' That it is that belongs to the starry world. And the nervous system might be followed up in the same way."

Macrocosm and Microcosm, Rudolf Steiner, Lecture X, _Transformation of Soul-forces and Stages in the Evolution of Physical Organs. Reading in the Akasha Chronicle,_ Vienna, March 30, 1910, GA 119

"For logic of the head we have an instrument in our physical brain. This is known to everyone through ordinary science. Admittedly we cannot say in the same sense that in our physical heart we have an instrument for the logic of the heart. For that is something far more spiritual than the logic of the head, and the heart is not to the same degree the physical organ for the thinking of the heart as is the brain for the thinking of the head. Yet the physical heart provides us with an analogy. When the thinking of the heart changes Time into Space, our whole being has to move about; we have to be involved in a perpetual circulation. Such is the definite experience of anyone who passes from ordinary memory to the higher form of memory possessed by the spiritual investigator. Whereas in an act of remembrance an ordinary man looks back to the past, the spiritual investigator has the inner experience that he is actually moving backwards in Time in the same way as he otherwise moves in Space. And this consciousness expresses itself outwardly in the experiencing of our blood, which must also be in perpetual movement if we are to go on living. In our blood we are involved all the time in the movement from the heart through the body and back, so that what really belongs to the heart is in perpetual movement. Not so what belongs to the head. The several parts of the brain remain stationary, so the brain is in very truth a physical symbol for the consciousness of Space; the flowing blood, the fluid of the heart is in its circulation an image of the mobility of spiritual consciousness. Thus, every physical phenomenon is a symbol for the corresponding spiritual reality. It is an extremely interesting fact that in our very blood we have an image of certain faculties of the spiritual investigator and also of the worlds in which he moves…

"…Reminding ourselves of what has been said about human evolution it may be affirmed that in earlier epochs man already possessed a kind of logic of the heart; at the present time he is passing through the stage of logic of the intellect; and in the future, he will regain a logic of the heart in which the logic of the intellect has been absorbed and elaborated."

Supersensible Man, Rudolf Steiner, Lecture IV, The Hague, November 17, 1923, GA 231

"The fact that we receive into ourselves in the Sun sphere the first germ of the physical heart is less important than the fact that in this germ of the heart is concentrated all that we are morally, all our qualities of soul and spirit. The spirit-germ of the heart unites with the embryonic germ of the future body because the heart in man is a spiritual being, a moral being of soul and spirit created out of the Cosmos; only later does this moral being of spirit and soul—which man now feels living within him; which man has, as it were, acquired in the course of his return journey to Earth—*unite with the embryo*. This concentration, in the germ of the heart, of his whole soul-and-spirit being is experienced by man in communion with the sublime Sun Beings—those Sun Beings who rule over the creative forces of the planetary system and therewith of earthly existence…

"…Man comes then again to the Sun. The second passage through the Sun sphere is significant in the highest degree. Since he completed his first sojourn in the Sun existence, man has passed through the spheres of Mars, Jupiter and Saturn, to the world of the Stars, and then made the return journey through Saturn, Jupiter and Mars. All this time his whole being has been given over to the Cosmos; he has become one with the Cosmos, one with the World-All. He has been living in the Cosmos; he has learned cosmic speech, he has learned to weave cosmic thoughts into his being, he has been living, not within his own life of memory—that only dawns for him later—*but within the memory of the whole planetary system*. He has felt himself one with the Beings of the higher Hierarchies in his memory of the Cosmic Thoughts and of the Cosmic Speech. Now however, when he returns once again to the Sun, he begins to shut himself off more as an individual being. Very faintly the feeling dawns that he is becoming separate from the Cosmos. This is connected with the fact that the first foundations of the heart are now being laid within him. The return journey continues. For the second time man passes through the Venus sphere and the Mercury sphere, where the spirit-germs of the other organs have to be implanted within him.

"At the moment of entrance for the second time into the Sun existence—all these happenings and processes take a very long time, and long before man enters upon earthly existence he experiences, as we shall see, what is for him a very significant turn of destiny—at the moment when, out in the Cosmos, the spirit-germ of the heart is laid within our being on the return journey to the Earth; there is, of course, not yet a physical heart. True, there is already an indication of a physical heart form; but it is surrounded and inter-woven with all that constitutes the *worth* of the human being as the outcome of his previous earthly lives. The fact that we receive into ourselves in the Sun sphere the first germ of the physical heart is less important than the fact that in this germ of the heart is concentrated all that we are morally, all our qualities of soul and spirit. Before the spirit-germ of the heart unites with the embryonic germ of the future body, the heart in man is a spiritual being, a moral being of soul and spirit out in the Cosmos; only later does this moral being of spirit and soul—which man now feels living within him; which man has, as it were, acquired in the course of his return journey to Earth—unite with the embryo. This concentration, in the germ of the heart, of his whole soul-and-spirit being is experienced by man in communion with the sublime Sun Beings—those Sun Beings who rule over the creative forces of the planetary system and therewith of earthly existence. Let me try to describe it to you in a picture. The expressions may sound strange, but they are really appropriate.

"At the time when this cosmic heart is bestowed upon man, he is living among those Spiritual Beings of the Hierarchies in whose hand lies the leadership of the whole planetary system in its connection with earthly existence. The experience is one of infinite grandeur and splendor. It is difficult to find words to describe what the human being experiences in this phase of existence. In a certain respect his feeling resembles a feeling he can have in physical existence. For just as in physical existence he feels that he is bound up with his heartbeat, with the whole activity of the heart, so, out in the Macrocosm, through his macrocosmic spiritual heart, he feels himself at one with his whole being of soul and spirit. The moral being of soul and spirit which he has become at this moment of his experience is, as it were, a spiritual heartbeat within him. His whole being seems now to be in the Cosmos, in the same way as his heartbeat is in him; he becomes aware also of a kind of circulation in connection with this heartbeat. Just as on Earth we feel in the heartbeat the blood circulation and breathing which give rise to it, so, when on the return journey through the Sun existence we begin to be aware of the beating of our spiritual, macrocosmic heart, it feels to us as though streams or currents were uniting this spiritual heart-beat with the Beings of the Second Hierarchy. Even as the blood flows to the heart from the veins in the physical organism, so into our being of spirit-and-soul pour the words of the Exusiai [Spirits of Form], Kyriotetes [Spirits of Wisdom], Dynamis [Spirits of Movement],—what they have to say concerning the World and the World's judgement upon man. The words and sounds of the spirit of the World-All are the circulation that now centers itself in this spiritual, macrocosmic heart, in this human being of soul and spirit. There, at the center, beats the spiritual heart of man. And the beat of the spiritual heart of man is the heartbeat of the world in which he is living. The bloodstream of this world is the deeds of the creative Beings of the Second Hierarchy, the forces which stream out from them. And just as the blood-stream on Earth centers itself in the heart where it is unconsciously experienced by man, so at this point of time between death and a new birth it is given to man, as a grace bestowed, to hold and cherish within him a cosmic heart—one of the organs of perception, one of the cosmic hearts, created out of the pulse-beat of the Macrocosm—*from the deeds of the Beings of the Second Hierarchy.* For let it be remembered that the physical heart is a *sense* organ, which *perceives* the movement of the blood, not a 'pump' as the physiologists imagine. The spirituality and vitality of the human being—*it is these that cause the movement of the blood.*"

Supersensible Knowledge, Rudolf Steiner, Lecture II, _Blood is a Very Special Fluid_, Berlin, October 25, 1906, GA 55

"A knowledgeable psychologist once remarked that the blood circulating through the body is not unlike a second person who, in relation to the one made of bone, muscle and nerve, constitutes a kind of outer world. And indeed, our entire being constantly takes from the blood what sustains it, and gives back what it cannot use. One could say that a person carries in his or her blood a double (*Doppelgänger*) who, as a constant companion, furnishes him or her with renewed strength and relieves a person of what is useless. It is entirely justified to refer to blood as a stream of life and compare its importance with that of fiber. What fiber is for the lower organism; blood is for the human being as a whole.

"The distinguished scientist Ernst Haeckel has probed deeply into nature's workshop, and in his popular works he quite rightly points out that blood is the last to develop in an organism. When tracing the stages of development in a human embryo, one finds rudiments of bone and muscle long before there is any indication of blood formation. Only late in embryonic development does formation of blood and blood vessels become apparent. This leads natural science to rightly conclude that blood made its appearance only late in world evolution, and that forces already in existence had first to reach a stage of development comparable to that of blood before they could accomplish what was necessary in the human organism. When as embryos human beings repeat once more the earlier stages of human evolution, they adapt to what existed before blood first made its appearance. This a person must do in order to achieve the crowning glory of evolution: the enhancement and transmutation of all that went before into that special fluid that is blood…

"Spiritual science recognizes that humans, as they appear in the sense world to physical sight, represent only a part of their true being. In fact, behind the physical body there are several more principles that are invisible to ordinary sight. Human beings have the physical body in common with the so-called surrounding lifeless mineral world. In addition, they have a life body, or ether body. What is here understood by ether is not that of which natural science speaks. The life body or ether body is not something speculative or thought out but is as concretely visible to the spiritual senses of the clairvoyant as are physical colors to physical sight.

"The ether body is the principle that calls inorganic matter into life and, in lifting it out of lifelessness, weaves it into the fabric of life. Do not for a moment imagine that the life body is something the spiritual investigator thinks into the lifeless. Natural science attempts to do that by imagining something called the 'principle of life' into what is found under the microscope, whereas the spiritual investigator points to a real definite entity. The natural scientist adopts, as it were, the attitude that whatever exists must conform to the faculties a person happens to have; therefore, what he or she cannot perceive does not exist. This is just about as clever as a blind person saying that colors are nothing but a product of fantasy. The person to pass judgment on something must be the one who has experienced it, not someone who knows nothing about it…

"Thus, the second member of a person's being is the ether body, which one has in common with the vegetable kingdom.

"A human being's third member is the astral body. This name, as well as being beautiful, is also significant; that it is justified will be shown later. Those who wish to find another name only show that they have no inkling as to why the astral body is so named. In humans and animals, the astral body bestows on living substance the ability to experience sensation. This means that not only do currents of fluid move within it, but also sensations of joy, sorrow, pleasure, and pain. This capacity constitutes the essential difference between plant and animal, although transitional stages between them do exist.

"A certain group of scientists believes that sensation should be ascribed also to plants, but that is only playing with words. Certainly, some plants do react when something approaches them, but it has nothing to do with sensation or feeling. When the latter is the case, an image arises within the creature in response to the stimulus. Even if certain plants respond to external stimuli—*that is no proof that they experience inner sensation.* The inwardly felt has its seat in the astral body. Thus, we see that creatures belonging to the animal kingdom consist of physical body, ether or life body, and astral body…

"…We can all give a name to the objects in this room. Each one of us will call the table, 'table,' the chairs, 'chairs,' but there is one word, one name that can only refer to the one who speaks it: the little word 'I.' No one can call someone else 'I.' The word 'I' must sound forth from the innermost soul to which it applies. To me, everyone else is a 'you,' and I am a 'you' to everyone else.

"Religions have recognized that the 'I' is that principle in us that makes it possible for the human soul to express its innermost divine nature. With the 'I' begins what can never enter the soul through the external senses, what must sound forth in its innermost being. It is where the monologue, the soliloquy, begins in which, if the path has been made clear for the spirit's entry, the divine Self may reveal itself.

"In religions of earlier cultural epochs, and still in the Hebrew religion, the word 'I' was called: 'The unutterable name of God.' No matter how it is interpreted according to modern philology, the ancient Hebrew name for God signifies what today is expressed by the word 'I.' A hush went through the assembly when the initiate spoke the 'Name of the Unknown God'; the people would dimly sense the meaning contained in the words that resounded through the temple: *'I Am the I Am.'*

"Thus, the human being consists of physical body, ether body, astral body and the 'I' or the essential inner being. 1. This inner being contains within itself the germ of the three further evolutionary stages that will arise out of the blood. They are: Manas or Spirit-Self, in contrast to the bodily self; Budhi or Life-Spirit; and a human's true spiritual being: Atma or Spirit-Man, which today rests within us as a tiny seed to reach perfection in a far-off future; a stage to which at present we can only look to as a far-distant ideal. Therefore, just as we have seven colors in the rainbow and seven tones in the scale, we have seven members of our being that divide into four lower and three higher.

"If we now look upon the three higher spiritual members as the 'above' and the four lower as the 'below,' let us try to get a clear picture of how the above creates a physiognomic expression in the below as it appears to physical sight. Take first what we have in common with the whole inorganic nature, that is, that which crystallized into the form of a person's physical body. When we speak of the physical body in a spiritual-scientific sense, it is not what can be seen physically that is meant, but the combination of forces behind it that constructed this form. The next member of our being is the ether body, which plants and animals also possess, and by means of which they are endowed with life. The ether body transforms physical matter into living fluids, thus raising what is merely material into living form. In animal and human the ether body is permeated by the astral body, which calls up in the circulating fluid inner participation of its movement, causing the movement to be reflected inwardly.

"We have now reached the point where the being of humans can be understood insofar as they are related to the animal kingdom. The substances, such as oxygen, nitrogen, hydrogen, sulfur, phosphorus, and so forth, out of which our physical body is composed, are to be found outside in inorganic nature. If the substances transformed by the ether body into living matter are to attain the capacity to create inner mirror images of external events, then the ether body must be permeated by the astral body. It is the astral body that gives rise to sensations and feelings, but at the animal level does so in a specific way.

"The ether body transforms inorganic substances into living fluids; the astral body transforms living substance into sensitive substance. But—and of this please take special note—a being composed of no more than the three bodies is only capable of sensing itself. It is only aware of its own life processes; its existence is confined within the boundaries of its own being. This fact is most interesting, and it is important to keep it in mind. Look for a moment at what has developed in a lower animal: inorganic matter is transformed into living substance and living mobile substance into sensitive substance. The latter is to be found only where there is at least the rudiment of what at a higher stage becomes a developed nervous system.

"Thus, we have inorganic substance, living substance, and nerve substance capable of sensation. In a crystal you see manifest certain laws of inorganic nature. (A crystal can be formed only within the whole surrounding nature.) No single entity could exist by itself separated from the rest of the cosmos. If we were to be transferred a mile or two above the Earth's surface, we would die. Just as we are conceivable only within the environment to which we belong, where the necessary forces exist that combine to form and sustain us, so too, in the case of a crystal…

"Human beings once had a clairvoyant faculty that has been superseded. However, it can still be experienced, if through certain measures the function of the higher nervous system is suspended, setting free the lower consciousness. When that happens, the world is experienced through the lower nervous system in which the environment is mirrored in a special way. Certain lower animals still have this kind of consciousness. As explained, it is extremely dull, but provides a dim awareness of a far wider aspect of the world than the tiny section perceived by humans today.

"At the time when evolution had reached the stage of the Cosmos being mirrored in the sympathetic nervous system, another event occurred in human beings. The spinal cord was added to the sympathetic nervous system. The system of brain and spinal cord extended to the organs, through which contact was established with the outer world. Once their organisms had reached this stage, humans were no longer obliged to be merely a mirror for the primordial cosmic laws; the mirror image itself now entered into relationship with the environment. The incorporation of the higher nervous system in addition to the sympathetic nervous system denoted the transformation that had occurred in the astral body. Whereas formerly it participated dully in the life of the cosmos, it now contributed its own inner experiences.

"Through the sympathetic nervous system, a being senses what takes place outside itself; through the higher nervous system, what takes place within itself. In individuals at the present stage of their evolution, the highest form of the nervous system is developed; it enables people to obtain from the highly structured astral body what is needed to formulate mental pictures of the outer world. Therefore, a person has lost the ability to experience the environment in the original dull pictures. Instead, individuals are aware of their inner life, and build within the inner self a new world of pictures on a higher level. This world of mental pictures mirrors, it is true, a much smaller section of the outer world, but does so much more clearly and perfectly.

"Hand in hand with this transformation, another one occurred on a higher evolutionary level. The reorganization of the astral body became extended to the ether body. Just as the ether body through its reorganization became permeated with the astral body, and just as there was added to the sympathetic nervous system that of the brain and spinal cord, so what was set free from the ether body—after it had called into being the circulation of living fluids—now transformed these lower fluids into what we call 'blood.'

"Blood denotes an individualized ether body, just as the brain and spinal cord denote an individualized astral body. And through this individualizing comes about that which expresses itself as the 'I.'

"Having traced man's evolution up to this point, we notice that we are dealing with a gradation in five stages: First the physical body (or inner forces); second the ether body (or living fluids, to be found also in plants); third the astral body (manifesting itself in the lower or sympathetic nervous system); fourth the higher astral body emerging from the lower astrality (manifesting itself in the brain and spinal cord); and finally the principle that individualizes the ether body.

"Just as two of humanity's principles, the ether, and astral bodies, have become individualized, so will the human being's first principle, built up out of external lifeless substances, that is, the physical body, become individualized. In present day humanity there is only a faint indication of this transformation.

"We see that formless substances come together in the human body, that the ether body transforms them into living forms, that through the astral body the outer world is reflected and becomes inner sensation, and finally this inner life produces of itself pictures of the outer world.

"When the process of transformation extends to the etheric body, the result is the forming of blood. This transformation manifests itself in the system of heart and blood vessels, just as the transformation of the astral body manifests in the system of brain and spinal cord. And, as through the brain the outer world becomes inner world, so does this inner world become transformed through the blood into an outer manifestation as the human body. I shall have to speak in similes if I am to describe these complicated processes. The pictures of the external world made inward through the brain are absorbed by the blood and transformed into vital formative forces. These are the forces that build up the human body; in other words, blood is the substance that builds the body. We are dealing with a process that brings the blood into contact with the outer world; it enables it to take from it the most perfect substance, oxygen. Oxygen continually renews the blood, endowing it with new life.

"In tracing human development, we have followed a path that leads from the outer world to humanity's inner world and back to the outer world. We have seen that the origin of blood coincides with our ability to face the world as an independent being, a being able to form his or her own pictures of the external world from its reflection within the self. Unless this stage is reached, a being cannot say 'I' to itself. Blood is the principle whereby 'I-hood' is attained. An 'I' can express itself only in a being who is able independently to formulate the pictures the outer world produces within the self. A being who has attained 'I-hood' must be able to take in the outer world and recreate it within the self…

"If we possessed only a brain without a spinal cord, we would still reproduce within ourselves pictures of the outer world and be aware of them, but only as a mirror image. It is quite different when we are able to build up anew what is repeated within ourselves; for then what we thus build up is no longer merely pictures of the outer world; it is the 'I.' A being who possesses brain and spinal cord will not only mirror the outer world, as does a being with only the sympathetic nervous system, but will also experience the mirrored picture as inner life. A being who in addition possesses blood will experience inner life within the self. The blood, assisted by oxygen taken from the outer world, builds up the individual body according to the inner pictures. This is experienced as perception of the 'I.'

"The 'I' turns its vision inwards into a person's being, and its will outwards to the world. This twofold direction manifests itself in the blood, which directs its forces inwards, building up a person's being, and outwards towards the oxygen. When humans fall asleep they sink into unconsciousness because of what the consciousness experiences within the blood; whereas when they, by means of sense organs and brain, form mental pictures of the outer world, then the blood absorbs these pictures into its formative forces. Thus, the blood exists midway between an inner picture-world and an outer world of concrete forms. This becomes clearer if we look at two phenomena. One is that of genealogy, that is, the way conscious beings are related to ancestors, the other is the way we experience external events.

"We are related to ancestors through the blood. We are born within a specific configuration, within a certain race, a certain family and from a certain line of ancestors. Everything inherited comes to expression in our blood. Likewise, all the results from an individual's physical past accumulate in the blood, just as within it there is prepared a prototype of that person's future. Consequently, when the individual's normal consciousness is suppressed, for example under hypnosis or in cases of somnambulism or atavistic clairvoyance, a much deeper consciousness becomes submerged. Then, in a dreamlike fashion, the great cosmic laws are perceived. Yet this perception is nevertheless clearer than that of ordinary dreams even when lucid. In such conditions all brain activity is suppressed, and in deep somnambulism even that of the spinal cord. In this condition what the person experiences is conveyed by the sympathetic nervous system; the individual has a dull, hazy awareness of the whole Cosmos. The blood no longer conveys mental pictures produced by the inner life through the brain; it only conveys what the outer world has built including everything inherited from ancestors. Just as the shape of a person's nose stems from his or her ancestors, so does the whole bodily form. In this state of consciousness, a person senses his ancestors in the same manner that waking consciousness senses mental pictures of the outer world. A person's blood is haunted by his ancestors; he dimly participates in their existence.

"Everything in the world evolves, also human consciousness. If we go back to the time when our remote ancestors lived, we find that they possessed a different type of consciousness. Today, during waking life we perceive external objects through the senses and transform them into mental pictures that act on our blood. Everything a person experiences through the senses is working in not only his blood but also in his memory. By contrast, a person remains unconscious of everything bestowed by ancestors. We know nothing about the shape of our inner organs. In the past all this was different; at that time the blood conveyed not only what it received from outside through the senses, but also what existed in the bodily form, and as this was inherited, we could sense our ancestors within our own being.

"If you imagine such a consciousness enhanced, you will get an idea of the kind of memory that corresponded to it. When our experiences are confined to what can be perceived through the senses, then only such sense perceptible experiences are remembered. A person's consciousness comprises only his experiences since childhood.

"In the past this was different, because the inner life contained all that was brought over through heredity. A human's mental life depicted ancestors' experiences as if they were his own. A person could remember not only his own childhood, but his ancestors' lives, because they were contained in the pictures absorbed by his blood. Incredible as it may seem to the modern materialistic outlook, there was a time when human consciousness was such that an individual regarded both his and his forefathers' physical experiences as his own. When someone said: 'I have experienced... ,' he referred not only to personally known events but also to events experienced by his ancestors. It was a dim and hazy consciousness compared with modern human waking consciousness, more like a vivid dream. However, it was much more encompassing, as it included not only his own life but the lives of ancestors. A son would feel at one with his father and grandfather, as if they were sharing the same 'I.' This was also the reason he did not give himself a personal name but one that included past generations, designating what they had in common with one and the same name. Each person felt strongly that he was simply a link in a long line of generations.

"The question is how this form of consciousness came to be transformed into a different one. It happened through an event well-known to spiritual historical research. You will find that every nation the world over describes a significant moment in history when a new phase of its culture began—the moment when the old traditions begin to lose their influence, and the ancient wisdom that had flowed down the generations via the blood begins to wane, although the wisdom still finds expression in myths and sagas.

"A tribe used to be an enclosed unit; its members married among themselves. You will find this to be the case with all races and peoples. It was a significant moment in the history of mankind when this custom ceased to be upheld—the moment when a mingling of blood took place through the fact that marriage between close relations was replaced by marriage between strangers. Marriage within a tribe ensured that the same blood flowed through its members down the generations; marriage between strangers allowed new blood to be introduced into a people.

"The tribal law of intermarriage will be broken sooner or later among all peoples. It heralds the birth of the intellect, which means the ability to understand the external world, to understand what is foreign.

"The important fact to bear in mind is that in ancient times a dim clairvoyance existed out of which arose sagas and legends, and that the clairvoyant consciousness is based on unmixed blood, whereas our awakened consciousness depends on mixed blood. Surprising as it may seem, marriage between strangers has resulted in logical, intellectual thoughts. This is a fact that will increasingly be confirmed by external research, which has already made a beginning in that direction. The mingling of blood extinguishes the former clairvoyance and enables humanity to reach a higher stage of evolution. When a person today goes through esoteric training and causes clairvoyance to reappear, that person transforms it to a higher consciousness, whereas today's waking consciousness has evolved out of the ancient dim clairvoyance.

"In our time, a person's whole surrounding world in which he acted came to expression in the blood; consequently, this surrounding world formed the inner in accordance with the outer. In ancient times it was more a person's inner bodily life that came to expression in the blood. A person inherited, along with the memory of his ancestors' experiences, also their good or bad inclinations; these could be traced in his blood. This ancestral bond was severed when blood became mingled through outside marriages. The individual began to live his own personal life; he learned to govern his moral inclinations according to his own experiences. Thus, ancestral power holds sway in unmixed blood; that of personal experience in mixed blood.

"Myths and legends told of these things: 'That which has power over thy blood has power over thee.' Ancestral power over a folk came to an end when the blood, through being mingled with foreign blood, ceased to be receptive to its influence. This held good in all circumstances.

"Whatever power wishes to subjugate a person will have to exert an influence that imprints itself in his blood. Thus, if an evil power wishes dominance over an individual, it must gain dominance over his or her blood. That is the profound meaning of the quotation from *Faust*, and the reason the representative of evil says: 'Sign your name to the pact in blood; once I possess your name written in your blood, I shall have caught you by the one thing that will hold man. I shall then be able to pull you over to my side.' That which possesses a person's blood possesses that person, and possesses the human 'I.'

"When two groups of human beings confront one another, as used to be the case in colonization, then only if there is true insight into evolutionary laws is there any possibility of foreseeing if the foreign culture can be assimilated. Take the case of a people that is very much at one with its environment, a people into whose blood the environment has as it were inserted itself. No attempt to graft upon it a foreign culture will succeed. It is simply impossible and is also the reason why in certain regions the original inhabitants became extinct when colonized. One must approach such problems with insight and realize that anything and everything cannot be forced upon a people. It is useless to demand of blood more than it is able to endure."

Note:

1. 'Ich' is the German for 'I.' Ich is often translated into English as Ego which can bring to mind misunderstandings arising from the meaning

of "Ego" in contemporary psychology. Rudolf Steiner clarified the meaning in numerous places; but as to its origin he had this to say: "The first Christian initiate in Europe, Ulfilas (c. 311-383), himself embodied it in the German language, in that man found the 'Ich' within oneself. Other languages expressed this relationship through a special form of the verb, in Latin for instance the word 'amo'; but the German language adds to it the 'Ich.'" (93a) An even more profound significance is found for the word 'Ich' when one understands from the indications of Rudolf Steiner that in his Gothic translation of the *Bible*, Ulfilas derived 'Ich' from the initials for Jesus Christ (I Ch).

An Occult Physiology, Rudolf Steiner, Lecture VI, *The Blood as Manifestation and Instrument of the Human Ego*, Prague, March 26, 1911, GA 128

"In all the preceding we have seen that the whole man, in his appearance as earth-man, has in his blood-system the instrument of the ego, so that he actually is *man* by reason of the fact that he harbors within himself an *ego*, and that this ego can create an expression of itself as far as the physical system, can work with the blood as its instrument…

"We can state thus that the blood-system is the most immediate instrument of the human ego. Yet the blood system is possible only if all the other systems are first existent. The blood is not only, according to the meaning of the poet's words, 'a very special fluid" [Goethe's *Faust*]; it is also obvious that it cannot exist as it is except by finding a place for itself in the entire remaining organism; its existence must necessarily be prepared for by all the rest of the human organism. The blood, as it exists in man, cannot be found anywhere else than in the human organism. We shall refer, further on, to the relation of the human blood to the blood of the animal; and this will be a very important consideration, since external science today takes little notice of it. Today we are dealing with blood as the expression of the human ego, taking account, at the same time, of a remark which was made in the first lecture: namely, that what is here said concerning man cannot, without further thought, be applied to any other kind of earth-being whatever. We may say then that, when once the entire remaining organism of man is constructed as it is, it is then capable of receiving into itself the circulatory course of the blood, is capable, that is, of carrying the blood, of having within itself that instrument which is the tool of our ego. The whole human organism, however, must first be built up for this purpose."

The Etheric Heart and Blood

***The Mystery of the Heart: The Sacramental Physiology of the Heart in Aristotle, Thomas Aquinas, and Rudolf Steiner*, by Dr. Peter Selg, Ch. 3, *The Heart and the Fate of Humanity*, pg. 99 (note 341 references GA 212)**

"Starting at the time of sexual maturity, all human activity begins in the etheric heart, taking a detour through the astral body. The etheric heart is the organ that arose from the reflection of the stars and the cosmos. Everything begins there.

"This is an extraordinarily important occurrence because, when you observe all of this, you find the union of what the human being does on Earth with the cosmic. If you think in terms of the etheric world, you find a compact form of the cosmos in the heart. At the same time, if you think in terms of the astral world, you see in contracted form all that is undertaken by the human being. The human being and the cosmos, with all of its cosmic events, find their connection in the heart. In all of the human body, only in the area around the heart do we find such a close correspondence between the astral body and the etheric body...

"...After all, the substance of the entire cosmos is there inside, contracted into the heart, in the etheric body..."

***Pastoral Medicine*, Rudolf Steiner, Lecture VII, Dornach, September 14, 1924, GA 318**

"Cosmic warmth enters the human organism by way of breathing. But not only warmth. The warmth carries with it light, macrocosmic chemism, and macrocosmic life, vitality. Light ether, chemical ether, and life ether from macrocosm are carried by the inhalation of warmth into the human organism. The element of warmth carries light as well as the chemical and life elements, into the human being, and gives them over to the air-inhalation process. This entire process, which lies over the air-breathing process and which appears as a refined (or even metamorphosed) breathing process."

***The Reappearance of Christ in the Etheric*, Rudolf Steiner, Lecture IX, *The Etherization of the Blood*, Basle, October 1, 1911, GA 130**

"These rays of light stream from the heart to the head and flow around the pineal gland. These streamings arise because human blood, which is a physical substance, is continually dissolving itself into etheric substance. In the region of the heart there is a continual transformation of the blood into this delicate etheric substance that streams upward toward the head and flows glimmeringly around the pineal gland. This process, the etherization of the blood, can be shown in the human being throughout his waking life. It is different now, however, in the sleeping human being. When a human being sleeps, the occult observer is able to see a continual streaming from outside into the brain and also in the reverse direction, from the brain to the heart.

"These streams, however, which in sleeping man come from outside, from cosmic space, from the macrocosm, and flow into the inner constitution of the physical and etheric bodies lying in the bed, reveal something remarkable when they are investigated. These rays vary greatly in different individuals. Sleeping human beings differ greatly from one another, and if those who are a little vain only knew how badly they betray themselves to esoteric observation when they go to sleep during public gatherings, they would try their best not to let this happen!

"Moral qualities are revealed distinctly in the particular coloring of the streams that flow into human beings during sleep; in a person of lower moral principles the streams are quite different from what is observable in a person of higher principles. Endeavors to disguise one's nature by day are useless. In the face of the higher cosmic powers, no disguise is possible. In the case of a man who has only a slight inclination toward moral principles the rays streaming into him are a brownish red in color—various shades tending toward brownish red. In a man of high moral ideals the rays are lilac-violet. At the moment of waking or of going to sleep, a kind of struggle takes place in the region of the pineal gland between what streams down from above and what streams upward from below. When a man is awake, the intellectual element streams upward from below in the form of currents of light, and what is of moral-aesthetic nature streams downward from above. At the moment of waking or of going to sleep, these two currents meet, and in the man of low morality a violent struggle between the two streams takes place in the region of the pineal gland. In the man of high morality and an outstreaming intellectuality, a peaceful expansion of glimmering light appears in the region of the pineal gland. This gland is almost surrounded by a small sea of light in the moment between waking and sleeping. Moral nobility is revealed when a calm glow surrounds the pineal gland at these moments. In this way a man's moral character is reflected in him, and this calm glow of light often extends as far as the region of the heart. Two streams can therefore be perceived in man—one from the macrocosm, the other from the microcosm.

"To estimate the full significance of how these two streams meet in man, we must first consider what was said previously in a more external way about the life of the soul and how this life reveals the threefold polarity of the intellectual, the aesthetic, and the moral elements that stream downward from above, from the brain toward the heart; we must also grasp the full significance of what was said about turning our attention to the corresponding phenomenon in the macrocosm. This corresponding phenomenon can be described today as the result of the most scrupulously careful esoteric research of recent years, undertaken by individuals among the genuine Rosicrucians. These investigations have shown that something corresponding to what has been described in connection with the microcosm also takes place in the macrocosm. You will understand this more fully as time goes on.

"Just as in the region of the human heart the blood is continually being transformed into etheric substance, so a similar process takes place in the macrocosm. We understand this when we turn our eyes to the Mystery of Golgotha, to the moment when the blood flowed from the wounds of Jesus Christ. This blood must not be regarded simply as chemical substance; but by reason of all that has been described as the nature of Jesus of Nazareth, it must be recognized as something altogether unique. When it flowed from His wounds and into the Earth, a substance was imparted to our Earth which, in uniting with it, constituted an event of the greatest possible significance for all future ages of the Earth, and it could take place only once. What happened with this blood in the ages that followed? Nothing different from what otherwise takes place in the heart of man. In the course of earthly evolution, this blood passed through a process of 'etherization.' Just as our blood streams upward from the heart as ether, so, since the Mystery of Golgotha, the etherized blood of Christ Jesus has lived in the ether of the Earth. The etheric body of the Earth is permeated by what the blood that flowed on Golgotha became. This is important. If what has thus come to pass through Christ Jesus had not taken place, man's condition on the Earth could only have been as previously described. Since the Mystery of Golgotha, however, there has existed the continuous possibility for the activity of the etheric blood of Christ to flow together with the streamings from below upward, from heart to head.

"Because the etherized blood of Jesus of Nazareth is present in the etheric body of the Earth, it accompanies the etherized human blood streaming upward from the heart to the brain, so that not only do these streams that I described earlier meet in man, but the human bloodstream unites with the bloodstream of Christ Jesus. A union of these two streams can come about, however, only if man is able to unfold true understanding of what is contained in the Christ impulse. Otherwise, there can be no union; the two streams then mutually repel each other, thrust each other away. In every age of earthly evolution, we must acquire understanding in the form suitable for that epoch. At the time when Christ Jesus lived on Earth, preceding events could be rightly understood by those who came to His forerunner, John, and were baptized by him according to the rite described in the *Gospels*. They experienced baptism in order that their sin, that is to say, the karma of their previous lives, karma, that had come to an end, might be changed, and in order that they might realize that the most powerful impulse in earthly evolution was about to descend into a physical body. The evolution of humanity progresses, however, and in our present age it is important that man should learn to understand that the knowledge contained in spiritual science must be received and gradually be able so to fire the streams flowing from heart to brain that anthroposophy can be understood. If this comes to pass, individuals will be able to comprehend the event that has its beginning in the twentieth century: the appearance of the etheric Christ in contradistinction to the physical Christ of Palestine.

"We have now reached the moment in time when the etheric Christ enters into the life of the Earth and will become visible, at first to a small number of people, through a natural clairvoyance. Then in the course of the next 3,000 years, He will become visible to greater and greater numbers of people. This will inevitably come to pass; it is an event of nature. That it will come to pass is as true as were the achievements of electricity in the nineteenth century. A certain number of individuals will see the etheric Christ and will themselves experience the event that took place at Damascus. This will depend, however, upon such human beings learning to observe the moment when Christ draws near to them. In only a few decades from now it will happen, particularly to those who are young in years—already preparation is being made for this—that some person here or there has certain experiences. If only he has truly sharpened his vision through engaging himself with anthroposophy, he may become aware that suddenly someone has come near to help him, to make him alert to this or that. The truth is that Christ has come to him, although he believes that what he sees is a physical man. He will come to realize, however, that this is a super-sensible being, because it immediately vanishes. Many a human being will have this experience when sitting silently in his room, heavy-hearted and oppressed, not knowing which way to turn. The door will open, and the etheric Christ will appear and speak words of consolation to him. The Christ will become a living comforter to men. However strange it may as yet seem, it is true nevertheless that many a time when people, even in considerable numbers, are sitting together not knowing what to do and waiting, they will see the etheric Christ. He Himself will be there, will confer with them, will cast His Word into such gatherings. We are now approaching these times, and the positive, constructive element now described will take hold of the evolution of humanity.

"No word shall be said here against the great advances made by culture in our day; these achievements are essential for the welfare and the freedom of human beings. Whatever can be gained in the way of outer progress, however, in mastering the forces of nature, is something small and insignificant compared with the blessing bestowed upon the person who experiences the awakening in his soul through Christ, Who will now take hold of human culture and its concerns. What thereby awakens in human beings will be unifying, positive forces. Christ brings constructive forces into human civilization.

"If we were to look into early Post-Atlantean times, we would find that human beings built their dwelling places by methods quite different from those used today. In those days they made use of all kinds of growing things. Even when building palaces, they summoned nature to their aid by having plants and branches of trees interlace with one another, and so on. Today, human beings must build with broken fragments. We make all culture of the outer world with the products of fragmentation. In the course of the coming years, you will understand even better how much in our culture is the product of destruction.

"Light is destroying itself within our Post-Atlantean earthly processes. Until the time of Atlantis, the earthly process was a progressive process; but since then it has been a process of decay. What is light? Light decays, and the decaying light is electricity. What we know as electricity is light that is destroying itself within matter. The chemical force that undergoes a transformation within earthly evolution is magnetism. Yet a third force will become active, and if electricity seems to work wonders today, this third force will affect civilization in a still more miraculous way. The more of this force we employ, the faster the Earth will tend to become a corpse and its spiritual part prepare for Jupiter [the Future Planetary Condition]...

"We thus realize what a tremendous advance was signified by the fact that Christ necessarily lived for three years on the Earth in a specially prepared human body in order that He might be visible to physical eyes. Through what came to pass during those three years, human beings have become ripe to behold the Christ Who will move among them in an etheric body, Who will enter into earthly life as truly and effectively as did the physical Christ in Palestine. If human beings observe such happenings with undimmed senses, they will know that there is an etheric body that will move about within the physical world; but they will know that this is the only etheric body able to work in the physical world as a human physical body works. It will differ from a physical body in this respect only, that it can be in two, three, even in a hundred, a thousand places at the same time. This is possible only for an etheric, not for a physical form. What will be accomplished in humanity through this further advance is that the two poles I have mentioned, the intellectual and the moral, will more and more become one; they will merge into unity. This will come about because in the course of the next millennia human beings will learn increasingly to observe the etheric Christ in the world; more and more they will be permeated in waking life, too, by the direct working of the good from the spiritual world. Whereas now the will sleeps by day, and man is only able to influence it indirectly through thought, in the course of the next millennia, through what from our time onward is working in us under the aegis of Christ, it will come about that the deeds of human beings in waking condition, too, can be directly productive of good."

The Human Heart, Rudolf Steiner, Dornach, May 26, 1922, GA 212

"The gathered radiance that arises at the time of puberty becomes the true Etheric Heart of man. The Etheric Heart he has before this time is one that he received as a heritage through the inherent forces of the embryo. When a man gets his etheric body, and with it makes his way into the physical organism, a kind of Etheric Heart—a substitute Etheric Heart, so to speak—is drawn together by the forces of the physical body. He keeps this Etheric Heart during his childhood years, but then it gradually decays... The first Etheric Heart slowly decays, and in its stead, as it were constantly replacing that which falls out in the etheric process of decay, there comes the new, the real, Etheric Heart. This Etheric Heart is a concentration of the whole cosmic sphere we brought with us as an ether form, a faithful image of the Cosmos, when we proceeded through conception and birth into this earthly life.

"Thus we can trace, throughout the time from birth or conception until puberty, a distinct change in the whole etheric form that the human being bears within him. One may describe it by saying: *Not until puberty does the human being possess his own Etheric Heart*—that is, the Etheric Heart formed out of his own etheric body, and not supplied provisionally by external forces.

"All the etheric forces that are working in man until puberty tend to endow him with this fresh etheric heart. It is, in the etheric sphere, a process comparable to the change of teeth. For, as you know, until the change of teeth we have our inherited teeth; these are cast out, and their place is taken by the second teeth—those that are truly our own. So, likewise, the etheric heart we have until puberty is cast out, and we now receive our own. That is the point—we receive our own etheric heart...

"Precisely herein lies the key to a more intimate knowledge of the human organs; they cannot be truly understood unless we also understand the astral which man brings with him. We must know in the first place that every single organ bears within it, in a sense, an astral inheritance, even as the etheric heart is, to begin with, an inheritance. Moreover, we must know that this inherited astral becomes permeated gradually, through and through, with that which man brings with him as his own astral body, which dives down bit by bit into the physical and etheric organs.

"The heart is an exception, in a certain sense. Here, too, an astral part dives down; but in the heart not only the astral process but the etheric, too, is concentrated. Therefore, the heart is the uniquely important organ which it is for man...

"This, once again, is clearly developed at the time of puberty. At the same place where the etheric heart—our own etheric heart—has formed itself, we now have an astral structure too, which gathers together all our actions. And so, from puberty a central organ is created wherein all our doing, all our human activity, is centered. It is so indeed: in the very region where man has his heart, all his activity is centralized—centralized, in this case, neither physically nor etherically, but astrally. And the important thing is that in the time when puberty occurs (naturally, the astral events coincide only approximately with the physical) man's own etheric heart is so far formed that it can receive these forces that develop out of our activity in the outer world. Thus, we can truly say (and in so saying we mark a real event in the human inner being): from puberty onwards man's whole activity becomes inserted, via the astral body, in his etheric heart—and in that which has grown out of the pictures of the stars, out of the images of the Cosmos.

"This is a phenomenon of untold importance. For, my dear friends, we have here a joining together with the Cosmos of what man does in this world. In the heart, as far as the etheric Universe is concerned, you have a Cosmos gathered up into a center; while at the same time, as far as the astral is concerned, you have a gathering together of all that man does in the world. This is the point where the Cosmos—the cosmic process—is joined to the karma of man.

"This intimate correspondence of the astral body with the etheric body is to be found nowhere in the human organism except in the region of the heart. But there, in truth, it is. Man has brought with him through birth an image of the Universe in his etheric body, and the entire Universe, which is there within him as an essence, receives all that he does and permeates itself with it.

By this constant coming together—this mutual permeation—the opportunity is given throughout human life for human actions to be instilled into the essence of the images of the Cosmos.

"Then when man passes through the gate of death, this ethereal-astral structure—wherein the heart is floating, so to speak—contains all that man takes with him into his further life of soul and spirit, when he has laid aside the physical and the etheric forms. Now, as he expands ever more widely in the spirit, he can hand over his entire karma to the Cosmos, for the substance of the whole Cosmos is contained within him; it is drawn together in his heart, in the etheric body of his heart. It came from the Cosmos and changed into this etheric entity, then it was gathered up as an essence in the heart, and now it tends to return into the Cosmos once more. The human being expands into the Cosmos. He is received into the world of souls. He undergoes what I described in my book, *Theosophy*, as the passage through the world of souls and then through spirit land…

"…In the region of the heart there takes place a union of the Cosmos with the earthly realm, and in this way the Cosmos, with its cosmic configuration, is taken into our etheric body. There it makes ready to receive all our actions, all that we do in life. Then we go outward again, together with everything that has formed itself within us through this intimate permeation of the cosmic ethereal with our own human actions…

"…When later, the ego slips with its astral body into the organs of the physical, this is what happens: whereas, in the little child, the ego was present only outwardly along the paths of the blood, it now unites with the blood circulation more and more inwardly, intensively, until—at puberty once more—it has entered there in the fullest sense. And while you have an astral formation around the etheric and the physical heart, the ego takes a different path. It slides into the organs of the lung, and with the blood vessels that pass from the lung to the heart approaches nearer and nearer to the heart. More and more closely united with the blood circulation, it follows the paths of the blood. By way of the forces that run along the courses of the blood, the ego enters into that which has been formed from the union of the etheric and the astral heart, wherein an etheric from the Cosmos grows together with an astral from ourselves.

"As I said, this astral body comes by degrees to contain an immeasurable amount, for all our actions are written in it. And that is not all. Inasmuch as the ego has a relation of sympathy to all that the astral body does, our intentions, our ideas, too, are inscribed there—the intentions and ideas, I mean, out of which we perform our actions. Here, then, you have a complete linking up of karma with the laws of the whole Cosmos.

"All that happens in moral life, and all that happens physically in the world, are brought together precisely in the human heart. These two—the moral and the physical—which run so independently and yet side by side for modern consciousness today, are found in their real union when we learn to understand all the configurations of the human heart."

"Naturally, all that takes place in the heart is far more hidden than the event which happens openly with the change of teeth. We have our inherited teeth; then we form teeth again out of our own organism. The former fall away, the latter remain. The former have an inherent tendency to go under; nor could they ever keep themselves intact, even if they did not fall out. The permanent teeth, on the other hand, are destroyed chiefly by extraneous conditions—including, of course, those of the organism itself. Likewise at puberty: in an invisible way, our etheric heart is given over to disintegration, and we now acquire a kind of permanent ether heart.

"Only this permanent ether heart is fully adapted to receive into itself our activities. Therefore, it makes a great difference whether a human being dies before puberty or after. When he dies before puberty, he has only the tendency for what he has done on Earth to be karmically inherited later on. Even when children die before puberty, this or that can certainly be incorporated in their karma; but it is always rather vague and fleeting. The forming of karma, properly speaking, begins only at the moment when the astral heart takes hold of the etheric heart and they join together. This, indeed, is the real organism for the forming of karma. For, at death, what is gathered up and concentrated there in the human being becomes increasingly cosmic; and in our next earthly life it is incorporated in the human being once again out of the Cosmos. Everything we do, accordingly, concerns not ourselves alone. Incorporated within us is something that comes from the Cosmos and retains the tendency, after our death, to give over our deeds to the Cosmos once more. For it is from the Cosmos that the karmic laws work themselves out, fashioning our karma. So do we bear the effects of what the Cosmos makes of our deeds back again into earthly life, at the beginning of our next life on Earth."

The Balance in the World and Man, Lucifer and Ahriman, Rudolf Steiner, Lecture II, Dornach, November 21, 1914, GA 158

"Here we must refer to another fact in human evolution that has hitherto only had influence in man's conception of the Ego; but that we shall learn to know in a much fuller and wider way through Spiritual Science. A time will come in the future when men will say: 'We are told in the *Bible* of the breath of Jehovah which was breathed into man. But into what part of man was the breath breathed?'

"If you recall all that I have said in this lecture, you will be able to see that the region into which the breath was breathed is the intervening region that is in between the onsets from before and behind and from above and below—there, in the middle, where Jehovah created man, as it were in the form of a cube. There it was that he so filled man with His own being, with His own magic breath, that the influence of this magic breath was able to extend into the regions in the rest of man that belong to Lucifer and Ahriman. Here in the midst, bounded above and below and before and behind, is an intervening space where the breath of Jehovah enters directly into the spatial human being."

The Human Soul in Relation to World Evolution, Rudolf Steiner, Lecture VI, _The Formation of the Etheric and the Astral Heart_, May 26, 1922, GA 212

"All this takes place gradually throughout the period of life between the change of teeth and puberty. At puberty the process is so far advanced that these rays, having grown together at the center, form, as it were, a distinct structure. It could be said that the surrounding stars become very pale and so too the rays, though something is still discernable. By contrast, what has come together into a ball-like formation in the center becomes particularly vivid and alive. Within this structure the physical heart, with its blood vessels, is suspended by the time puberty sets in.

"Thus, we have this extraordinary situation where the star-ether body draws inwards. As with an ether body it is, of course, present throughout the body but in later life it is undifferentiated at the periphery. During the time from the change of teeth until puberty it rays intensely from without inwards. It forms a center within which the physical heart is suspended."

"You must not suppose that until then man has no Etheric Heart. He certainly has one, but one obtained differently from the way in which he acquires the Etheric Heart he now has. For what has thus rayed together into a center becomes, at the time of puberty, the Etheric Heart. The Etheric Heart he had before this time he had received as heritage through forces inherent in the embryo. When man gathers his ether body and with it approaches the physical organism a kind of Etheric Heart, a substitute Etheric Heart, so to speak, is drawn together by the forces of the physical body. But this Etheric Heart which man has in childhood slowly decays—this may not be a very nice expression; but it does fit the situation—and is replaced gradually, as the decaying processes take place, by the new Etheric Heart. The latter is formed by a raying together of the whole Universe. In reality, it is an image of the Cosmos which we bring with us as an etheric structure when, through conception and birth, we enter earthly existence. Thus, we trace, throughout the time from birth or rather conception until puberty, a distinct change in the structure of the etheric body. One can say that not until puberty is man's own Etheric Heart present—formed out of his own etheric body. Thus, he no longer has a provisional heart."

"All the ether forces active in man up until the time of puberty tend to provide him with a fresh Etheric Heart. It can really be compared with the change of teeth in the physical sphere. At the change of teeth, the inherited teeth are pushed out and replaced with our own. Likewise, the inherited Etheric Heart, which we have until puberty, is pushed out and we get our own Etheric Heart. This is what is essential: *that we get our own Etheric Heart.*"

"Parallel with this, something else occurs. When we observe man soon after his entry into the physical world, that is, when we observe a very young child, we find an extraordinary number of organs distinguishable in his astral body. As just described, man gathers together an ether body which is an image of the external Cosmos. But in his astral body he brings with him an image of the experiences he has undergone between his last death and his present birth. Much, very much is to be seen in the astral body of the young child; great secrets are inscribed there. Very much is to be seen of his experiences since his last death. This astral body is extraordinarily differentiated and individual. The strange thing is that during the time when all that I have described takes place in the etheric body, the highly differentiated astral body becomes ever more undifferentiated. Originally, it is a structure of which one must say—if one observes it with understanding—that it comes from a different world. It has entered into this world from a realm that can be neither the physical nor the etheric. Up to the time of puberty all the many individual structures living in the astral body slip into the physical organs, as it were, primarily into those which are situated above the diaphragm (that is not quite exact; but approximately so). Wonderful structures, radiantly present in the astral body in the first days of life, gradually slip into the brain and also penetrate the sense organs. Other structures slip into the organs of breathing, yet others into the heart and through the heart into the arteries. They do not slip directly into the stomach; but through the arteries they spread into the abdominal organs. Gradually, one sees the whole astral body, which man brings with him into physical existence through birth, dive down into the organs. The astral body slips, as it were, into the organs. One could express it by saying that by the time we reach adulthood our organs have imprisoned within them the individual structures of our astral body. This may sound strange to ordinary consciousness; but it corresponds absolutely to the reality. It also provides a deeper knowledge of the human organs. One cannot fully understand the human organs unless one understands the astral body that man brings with him. One must know that each individual organ, in a certain sense, harbors within it an astral inheritance, just as the first Etheric Heart is an inheritance.

"Gradually, the inherited astral is completely permeated by what man brings with him as his astral body. This astral body dives down, bit by bit, into the physical and etheric organs. The heart is, as it were, an exception. Here too, the astral dives down; but in the heart, not only the astral process; but the etheric, too, is concentrated. This is also the reason why the heart is such a uniquely important organ for man."

"The astral body becomes ever more indefinite because it sends the distinct structures it brought over from another life through birth into the physical organs in which they become confined. This causes the astral body to become, more or less, like a cloud. But the interesting thing is that while, on the one hand, the astral body becomes cloud-like, on the other, new differentiations enter in, slowly at first, but from puberty onwards quite regularly…

"The strange thing is that what is thus inscribed has a tendency to meet inwardly just as the rays in the ether body meet in the Etheric Heart. All human deeds also meet there. This coming together is due to an outside cause. As human beings we must, right from childhood, engage in some activity. All this activity expresses itself as indicated throughout the astral body; but there is a constant resistance to its being inscribed. The influence on the organism cannot always take full effect in the upper part. It meets resistance everywhere in this part and is pushed down. Whatever we do with the help of our physical organs tends to stream upwards to the head. But the human organization prevents this from happening by holding it back. This causes the influences to collect together and form a kind of astral center.

"This, again, is clearly developed at the time of puberty, so that at the same place where our own—not the inherited—Etheric Heart formed itself we have also an astral structure which centralizes all our deeds. Thus, from puberty a central organ is created wherein all our doing, all our human activity is centered. In the same region where man has his heart *the sum total of all his activity is centralized*, but in this case neither physically nor etherically, but astrally. The significant thing is that at the onset of puberty—the astral process coincides only approximately with the physical process—man's Etheric Heart is so far prepared that it can take into itself the forces which develop from our activity in the external world. Thus, to describe what actually occurs one could say: From puberty onwards, the totality of man's actions pours, via the astral body, into the Etheric Heart—i.e., into the organ which is an image of the whole Cosmos.

"This is a phenomenon of extreme significance. When you think about it you will realize that it amounts to an interconnection of man's earthly deeds with the Cosmos. You have in the heart, as far as the etheric world is concerned, a whole Cosmos drawn together, and, at the same time, as far as the astral world is concerned, the totality of man's activity drawn together. This is where the Cosmos and its processes join with man's karma. Only in the region of the heart is there such a close correspondence between the astral and etheric bodies and man's organism. The reality is that the ether body which man brings through birth is an image of the whole Cosmos; and this essence of the Cosmos within him permeates itself with all his deeds. This flowing into one another in mutual permeation provides the opportunity for human actions continually to be inserted into the essence of the cosmic images.

"When man goes through the portal of death and lays aside his physical and etheric bodies, this etheric-astral structure—within which the physical heart, as it were, swims—contains all that which man takes with him into his further soul-spiritual life. Because within the heart, in the etheric body, the substance of the whole Cosmos is drawn together, man is able, as he grows spiritually larger and larger, to hand over to the Cosmos his entire karma. The etheric structure, which is an essence of the Cosmos drawn together in the heart, now returns to the Cosmos. The human being expands into the whole Cosmos and is received into the Soul-World. He then continues his passage through what I described in my book Theosophy as the Soul-World and Spirit-Land."

"When we observe the human organization in its becoming, we have to say: *In the region of the heart the cosmic and the earthly come together*. They form a union in such a way that the configuration of the Cosmos is taken into the Etheric Heart and there it prepares to receive all our deeds. Then when we go through the gate of death and enter a new cosmic existence, we take with us the outcome of this intimate union of the etheric and our human actions."

"This is, in fact, a concrete description of how man lives his way into his physical body and how he is able to withdraw from it again through the fact that his deeds give him the force to hold together what he formed out of the essence of the Cosmos."

"The physical body is built up within the physical-earthly realm through heredity—i.e., through embryonic forces. With this unites that which man brings down from the spiritual world after having drawn together the ether body. This 'I,' which has gone through many earth-lives and has a certain development behind it, lives within that wonderful structure he has brought with him as his astral body. His 'I' has a certain sympathy for the structures that exist in the astral body. When they slip into the organs of the physical body as described, the 'I' retains this inner sympathy which now extends to the organs. The 'I' expands more and more within the organs and takes possession of them. Indeed, the 'I' has already in earliest childhood a relation to the organs; however, at that time the hereditary conditions are present, as I explained, and the relation is, in consequence, an external one."

"Gradually the 'I' and astral body slip into the organs of the physical body. This occurs as follows: To begin with the 'I' has a somewhat separate existence along the bloodstream within the child, then it begins to unite ever more closely with the blood circulation until at puberty they are fully united. Thus, while you have an astral structure surrounding the etheric and physical heart, the 'I' takes another path to the heart. Let us say the 'I' slips into the lungs—it will then, through the veins leading to the heart, gradually approach the latter. The 'I' follows the circulating blood, becoming more and more intimately united with it, so that here again, via the detour of the ego forces circling with the bloodstream, the 'I' enters the structure formed by the union of the etheric and astral heart. This structure alone makes it possible for the cosmic-etheric to grow together with a human astral. I said earlier that the astral body gradually comes to contain an extraordinary amount because all our deeds are inscribed in it. But more than that is inscribed. Through the fact that the 'I' has sympathy for everything concerning the astral body, our intentions—that is, the ideas on which we base our actions—also become inscribed. In this way human karma unites with cosmic laws.

"Of all this taking place in man's inner being, practically nothing is known nowadays. What is known are the results of man's physical actions which are judged according to laws of nature; also known are his moral actions which are judged according to laws of morality. But man's moral and physical deeds come together in the heart. Therefore, these two things, which for man today go on side by side independently of each other, are discovered to be a unity when one learns to understand the whole configuration of the human heart. That is to say, when we understand what takes place in the heart, albeit in a much more hidden way, it is comparable to what occurs openly at the change of teeth.

"We inherit our first teeth and form the second ones out of the organism. The first fall out, the second remain. The first have an inherent tendency to decay; even if they did not fall out, they would not last. The reason that the second teeth sometimes decay is due to external circumstances; to these belong the external causes within the organism itself. Hidden from sight, at the onset of puberty, our inherited Etheric Heart succumbs to forces of decay, and we acquire a kind of permanent Etheric Heart. Only the permanent Etheric Heart is fully adapted to take into itself our deeds. Therefore, it makes a great difference whether a person dies before or after puberty. When a person dies before puberty, he has only the tendency to bequeath his earthly deeds to karma. Separate earthly deeds may be incorporated in their karma when children die before puberty; but these will be indefinite and changeable. The real building up of karma only begins from the moment when the astral heart has fully penetrated the Etheric Heart, so that the two form a unity. One could say that this union constitutes, as it were, an organism for the forming of karma; what has thus united and contracted within man, becomes after death ever more cosmic. In the next earthly life, it is again incorporated into the human being. Thus, something is incorporated in us out of the Cosmos which retains the tendency to hand over our deeds after death to the Cosmos. The laws that shape our karma are effective within the Cosmos so that at the start of a next earthly life we carry into it the consequences of what the Cosmos made of our deeds."

Heart Thinking as Living Thoughts

***Macrocosm and Microcosm,* Rudolf Steiner, Lecture IX, *Organs of Spiritual Perception, Thinking of the Heart,* Vienna, March 29, 1910, GA 119**

"An activity now begins of which it is important to take account in connection with distinguishing between true and false pictures. It can only be called *thinking of the heart*. This is something that comes about in the course of the development of which we spoke yesterday. In ordinary life we have the feeling that we think with the head. That of course is a pictorial expression, for we actually think with the spiritual organs underlying the brain; but it is generally accepted that we think with the head. We have a quite different feeling about the thinking that becomes possible when we have made a little progress. The feeling then is as if what had hitherto been localized in the head were now localized in the heart. This does not mean the physical heart but the spiritual organ that develops in the neighborhood of the heart, the twelve-petalled lotus-flower. This organ becomes a kind of organ of thinking in one who achieves inner development, and this thinking of the heart is very different from ordinary thinking. In ordinary thinking everyone knows that reflection is necessary in order to arrive at a particular truth. The mind moves from one concept to another and after logical deliberation and reflection reaches what is called 'knowledge.' It is different when we want to recognize the truth in connection with genuine symbols or emblems. They are before us like objects, but the thinking we apply to them cannot be confounded with ordinary brain-thinking. Whether they are true or false is directly evident without any reflection being necessary as in the case of ordinary thinking. What there is to say about the higher worlds is directly evident. As soon as the pictures are before us, we know what we have to say about them to ourselves and to others. This is the characteristic of heart-thinking..."

"...To develop the thinking of the heart we must have the power to go out of ourselves and look back upon ourselves from outside...

"...All true presentations of the higher worlds proceed from the thinking of the heart although outwardly they often seem to be purely logical expositions. Whatever is described in Spiritual Science has been experienced with the heart and must be cast into forms of thought intelligible to reasoning people.

"That is where the thinking of the heart differs from subjective mysticism. Anyone may experience the latter for himself; but it is not communicable to another, nor does it concern anyone else. True and genuine mysticism springs from the capacity to have Imaginations, to receive impressions from the higher worlds and then to co-ordinate these impressions by means of the thinking of the heart, just as the things of the physical world are coordinated by the intellect.

"Something else is associated with this, namely that the truths imparted from the higher worlds are tinged with something like the heart's blood. However abstract they may seem to be, however completely they may be cast into forms of thought, they are tinged with the heart's blood; for they are direct experiences of the soul. From the moment a man has developed the thinking of the heart, he experiences something that seems like a vision; yet what he experiences is not a vision but the expression of a soul-and-spiritual reality…

"From the moment a man has developed the thinking of the heart, he experiences something that seems like a vision; yet what he experiences is not a vision but the expression of a soul-and-spiritual reality just as the color of the rose is its outer manifestation, the expression of its material nature. The seer directs his gaze into the Imaginative world; there he has the impression, let us say, of something blue or violet, or he hears a sound or has a feeling of warmth or cold. He knows through the thinking of the heart that the impression was not a mere vision, a figment of the mind, but that the fleeting blue or violet was the expression of a soul-spiritual reality, just as the red of the rose is the expression of a material reality. Thus do we penetrate into the realities, into the spiritual Beings themselves, and we have to unite with them. That is why all research in the spiritual world is linked in a far higher sense and to a far greater extent than is the case in other experiences, with the surrender of our own personality. We become more and more intensely involved in the experience; we are within the Beings and things themselves."

Ancient Myths, Their Meaning and Connection with Evolution, Rudolf Steiner, Lecture VI, _Duality of the Human Being, Head and Trunk_, Dornach, January 12, 1918, GA 180

"One is in this way enabled to see how a man assimilates life-wisdom, life-experience all his life through. And one can study through it the relation between what the head can provide with its short development, and what the rest of the human being can furnish with its long development in the social life. It is really true that during his young days a man takes in certain ideas and concepts that he learns; but he then only learns them. They are then head-knowledge. The rest of life that runs more slowly, is destined to transform the head-knowledge gradually into heart-knowledge—I now call the other man not the headman, I call him the heart-man—to transform head-knowledge into heart-knowledge, knowledge in which the whole man shares, not only the head.

"We need much longer to transform head-knowledge into heart-knowledge than to assimilate the head-knowledge. Even if head-knowledge is an especially clever knowledge, one needs today the time into the twenties, is it not so? Then one is a quite clever person, academically quite clever. But in order to unite this knowledge fully with the whole man, one must keep flexible one's whole life through. And one needs just as much longer to change head-knowledge into heart-knowledge as one lives longer than to the twenty-seventh or twenty-sixth year. In so far is the human being also of a twofold nature. One quickly acquires the head-knowledge and can then, in the course of life, change it into heart-knowledge...

"If one makes oneself acquainted with the speech which the human souls speak who have gone through the gate of death, who live in the spiritual world after death, one understands to some degree the speech of the dead, the so-called dead, one can then make the experience that the dead express themselves in a very special way upon many things connected with human life. The dead have a speech today that we who are living cannot yet quite understand. The comprehensions of the dead and the living lie somewhat far apart from one another today. The dead have a thorough consciousness of how man develops quickly as headman and slowly as heart-man. And if the dead wish to express what really happens when the quickly gained head-knowledge lives itself into the slower course of the heart-knowledge, they say their wisdom-knowledge is transformed through what ascends from man as heart-warmth or love. Wisdom is fructified in man by love. So say the dead.

"And that is in fact a profound and significant law of life. One can acquire head-knowledge rapidly, one can know a tremendous amount precisely in our age, for natural science—not the natural-scientist—has made very great advances in our time and has a rich content. But this content has remained head-knowledge, it has not been transformed into heart-knowledge because people no longer pay attention to what approaches in life after the twenty-seventh year, because people do not understand how to become old—or I could say, to remain young in growing old. Because men do not keep the inner livingness their heart grows cold; the heart warmth does not stream up to the head; love, which comes from the rest of the organism, does not fructify the head. The head-knowledge remains cold theory. There is no necessity for it to remain cold theory, all head-knowledge can be transformed into heart-knowledge. And that is precisely the task of the future; that head-knowledge shall gradually be transformed into heart-knowledge. A real miracle will happen if head-knowledge is transformed into heart-knowledge! One is completely right if one vigorously declaims today against the materialistic natural science, or, really, natural-philosophy—one is completely right, but all the same, something else is true. If this natural science which has remained mere head-knowledge in Haeckel, Spencer, Huxley, etc. and is therefore materialism, became heart-knowledge, if it were absorbed by the whole man, if humanity were to understand how to become old, or younger in old age as I showed yesterday, this science of today would become really spiritual, the true pursuit for the spirit and its existence. There is no better foundation than the natural science of the present day, if it is transformed into what can flow to the head from the rest of man's organism, that is to say from the spiritual part of the organism. The miracle will be accomplished when men also learn to feel the rejuvenation of their etheric body so that the materialistic natural science of today will become spirituality. It will the sooner become spirituality the greater the number of people who reproach it with its present materialism, its materialistic folly...

"If humanity knows someday that it has a twofold nature, a head-nature and a heart-nature, then it will know too that the head obeys quite other cosmic laws than the rest of the organism. Then the human being takes his place again within the whole macrocosm, then man can do no other than form concepts that lead him to say: 'I do not stand here upon Earth as merely a higher animal, to be born and to die; but I am a being formed from out the whole Universe. My head is built up for me out of the whole Universe, the Earth has attached to me the rest of my organization, and this does not follow the movements of the Cosmos as my head does.' Thus, when we do not look at man abstractly, as modern science does; but regard him as picture in his duality, as headman and heart-man in connection with the Universe, then the human being is placed again into the Cosmos. And I know, my dear friends, and others who can judge such things know it also: if man can make heart-warm concepts of the fact that when one looks at the human head it is seen to be an image of the whole star-strewn space of the world with its wonders, then there will enter the human soul all the pictures of the connection of man with the wide, wide Universe. And these pictures become forms of narrative which we have not yet gotten, and which will bring to expression, not abstractly, but linked with feeling, what we can pour into the hearts of the youngest children. Then these hearts of young children will feel: 'Here upon Earth I stand as human being; but as man I am the expression of the whole star-strewn universal space: the whole world expresses itself in me.' It will be possible to train the human being to feel himself a member of the whole Cosmos. That is the one condition."

"The other condition is the following: when we are able to arrange the whole of education and instruction so that man knows that he is an image of the Universe in his head, and in the remaining organism is withdrawn from the Universe, that with his remaining organism he must so work upon what falls down like a rain of the soul—*the whole Universe*—that it becomes independent in man here upon Earth, then this will be a particular inner experience...

"When he comes to know that from the whole Universe there flows—unconsciously into his head, stimulating its forces—the secrets of the stars; but that all this must be worked upon his whole life through by the rest of his organism, so that he may conserve it on Earth, carry it through death back again into the spiritual world—when this becomes a living experience, then man will know his twofold nature, he will know himself as head-man and heart-man. For what I am now saying means that man will learn to solve his own riddle, to say to himself: inasmuch as I become more and more heart-man, inasmuch as I remain young, I view in later years through what my heart gives me, that which in childhood and youth I learnt through my head. The heart gazes up to the head and will see there an image of the whole starry heavens. The head however will look to the heart and will find there the mysteries of the human riddle, will learn to fathom in the heart the actual being of man. The human being will feel as regards his education: To be sure, I can learn all sorts of things with my head. But as I go on living, as I live on towards death that is to bear me into the spiritual world, what I learn through the head is fructified in the future through the love ascending from the rest of the organism and becomes something quite different. There is something in me as man that is only to be found in me as man; I have to await something. Very much lies in these words and it means very much when man is so educated that he says: I have something to await. I shall be thirty, forty, fifty, sixty years old, and as I grow older from decade to decade, there comes towards me through growing older something of the mystery of man. I have something to await from the fact that I live on…

"The time has also come when modern natural science which is so fitted for spirituality must be transformed into heart-knowledge. Our natural science is either execrable, if it remains as it is, or it is something quite extraordinarily grand, if it changes into heart-knowledge. For then it becomes spiritual science. The older science which is involved in all sorts of traditions had already transformed head-science into heart-science; the modern age has had no gift for transforming into heart-science the science it has acquired up to the present, and so it has come about that head-science, especially in the social field, has performed the only real work, and has thus brought about the most one-sided product it is possible to have.

"You see, man's head can know nothing at all of the being of man. Hence when man's head ponders over the being of man and his connection with the social life, it has to bring something quite foreign into the social common life. And that is modern socialism, expressed as social-democratic theory. There is nothing that is such pure head-knowledge as the Marxist social-democracy. This is only because the rest of mankind has shirked any concern for world problems, and in the Marxist circles they have only occupied themselves with social theories. The others have only—no, I will be polite—let themselves be prompted by professorial thoughts, which are purely traditional. But head-wisdom has become a social theory. That is to say, people have tried to establish a social theory with an instrument which is least of all capable of knowing anything about the human being. This is a fundamental error of present-day mankind, which can only be fully disclosed when people know about head-knowledge and heart-knowledge. The head will never be able to refute socialism, Marxist socialism, because in our times the head's task is to think out and devise. It will only be refuted through Spiritual Science, since Spiritual Science is head wisdom transformed through the heart."

The Human Soul in Relation to World Evolution, Rudolf Steiner, Lecture IV, _The Human Soul in Relation to Moon and Stars,_ May 6, 1922, GA 212

"While we carry out exercises which lead us to knowledge of the external spiritual world, we also make progress in the inward direction. What we first discover is that, from the viewpoint of the soul, we come to value our head with its knowledge rather less. By contrast, we become very aware of that knowledge, which is more concentrated in the heart, not so much in the physical heart as in the etheric and astral heart. At this point something of the greatest significance becomes crystal-clear knowledge…

"Well, the life of thought is, in a certain sense, a distinguished world, unconcerned about subjective states. However, when man sends his subjectivity into this distinguished realm, thus making it feel closer to his human nature, then his feelings pass through his heart. Rays from the head shoot, as it were, down into the lower part of man and from there well up again. But what is it that wells up?

"From below, there arises feelings, instincts, urges, passions; everything active in man's nature bursts forth. Within all this subjectivity, which is part of man, wells up also the effect of everything that seethes in the organism itself. The effects of whatever processes that are taking place in the stomach or intestines or in any other bodily function burst forth and come up to meet him together with the instincts and passions, so that one can indeed say that there, above, a distinguished world exists. Distinguished it may be but, as it has no concern for subjectivity, it contains no soul life. Thoughts in themselves are not subjective; for them it is quite immaterial whether Smith thinks of a lion or a triangle or whether Jones thinks of them. Thoughts are not concerned about subjects. The soul aspect only becomes evident when out of man's inner being there well up feelings or instincts which saturate the thoughts. Subjectivity only enters when, for example, Smith, being a hero, thinks of a lion and there wells-up within him feelings of a kind that make him unafraid of a lion; whereas when Jones, being a coward, thinks of a lion, he immediately wants to flee. The thought 'lion' is universal; it contains no soul element, it is spiritual. Soul comes into it when it meets the instinctive element within man. That is what imbues the thought 'lion' with a soul content which in Smith's case makes him think of some instrument with which to attack the lion and defend himself, come what may; or in Jones' case makes him think of how fast he can run, and so on. In ordinary life thoughts are imbued with soul because in one way or another the soul element always rays into the spiritual.

"However, when the ascent has been made first to imaginative cognition, and then to inspired cognition, things become different. At first there is a great struggle to beat back the instincts and desires which are now all the more in evidence for being undisguised. They must not be allowed expression; they must be vanquished completely. However, something else rises towards the heart, which has now become a wonderful sense organ—a great etheric sense organ as large as the whole blood system. Towards this heart there now rise, not what lives in instincts and passions but another kind of thought complex. These thoughts come up to meet the thoughts which have their origin in the external world and have made the head their abode in such an aristocratic manner. But the thoughts now rising through the heart to meet them are mighty pictures which do not in any way express what otherwise rises up within the organism. They express what man was before birth.

"Man learns to know himself in his existence within the spiritual world before he was born (or conceived) on Earth. That is what comes up to meet him. He is transported into his existence in the spiritual world before he descends into physical embodiment. This occurs, not through what lives in his passions and desires; but through what meets him when he has attained imaginative and inspired cognition. As he learns to know his own being within the spiritual world, he also learns to distinguish himself from what, to imaginative and inspired cognition, otherwise surrounds us as an external spiritual world. In that world we learn to know elemental beings, Angels, Archangels and so on. Out of the wisdom itself we learn to know our own being, now widened beyond Earth existence.

"This also leads to a significant insight into the working of the soul. We gradually come to recognize that the soul is completely poured out within the head. It has shaped the head in its own image and organized it for the external world, so that the latter can imprint itself and become mental pictures which we retain in memory; whereas within the rest of the organism, as I indicated yesterday, the soul life does not unite so intensely with the physical—*it remains more separate*. Therefore, when the heart becomes a sense organ, we can look down into the flaming, scorching, burning emotions, desires and passions on the one hand, but also into that which lives alongside them, yet never unites with them: *our eternal being*.

"It now becomes clear that as far as the head is concerned our soul is buried within it; there the soul rests. The head is essentially an external organ, organized for reflecting the physical environment; in the head we grasp the external physical world. We grasp ourselves when we look through the heart into the depth of our being. For ordinary consciousness the waves of emotions are all that are thrust up from that depth. When we gain more insight through higher knowledge then our eternal being comes up to meet us. Then our soul learns to unite itself with that spiritual being which is our self. We are not part of the spiritual environment which we see outside. We are that which we behold through our heart when it has become sense organ. The path which otherwise led only to the experience of our soul's external side, its urges and desires, now leads us into the eternal soul within us, which is saturated with spirit. The eternal soul is as spiritual as the spiritual environment. We have come into a sphere where soul and spirit are one.

"No matter how much you seek within the brain, only what is physical is to be found there; in the head you are yourself physical. Yet the brain is the main field of research for modern psychology. It is said that psychology investigates the soul, but only the brain is investigated. This can be done because the brain is an expression of the soul which lies entombed within it. The soul rests like a corpse within the brain and this corpse is the subject of modem psychology. The soul itself is beneath the heart where it is united with the spirit. Only its external aspect unites with the instincts and desires—*the soul's inner being does not...*

"...We are, in reality, within the Sun. We are within the external physical-etheric aspect of the Sun in all that which we externally perceive because of the Sun's presence, and our senses' inner connection with what the Sun enables us to perceive."

"However, when we attain imaginative and inspired cognition—that is, when through the heart we penetrate further into our own being—then we experience the Sun differently. At a certain point, when inspired cognition begins and we are within a world of pictures which at the same time are realities, we become aware, as if through a sudden jolt of soul and spirit—*that we have arrived within the Sun.*

"This is an experience of immense significance. On Earth the Sun shines on us; as human beings we perceive things around us because they reflect the Sunlight. But the moment we ascend to inspired cognition, when for us the heart becomes a sense organ, we suddenly experience ourselves within the Sun. We no longer look up and see the Sun move in its orbit—I am taking into account only the Sun's apparent movement—rather do we feel that with our heart we are within the Sun and moving with it. For us the heart is in the Sun and the Sun becomes our eye with which we behold what begins to appear around us. The Sun now becomes our eye and our ear and our organ of warmth. We no longer feel that we are outside the Sun; rather do we feel transported into the Sun and existing within the light. Formerly we were always outside the light; but now that we have plunged with our being into the heart, we have the feeling that our relation to the world is such that we are within the light, that our being is light. Within the undulating, weaving light we touch the spiritual beings with the organs of light which we now possess. We are now, in our soul being, akin not to the world outside the Sun, but to the world within it. And I want to emphasize that our being becomes linear, so much so, that we feel we are within the Sun's linear path. When we advance just a little further in higher cognition, we feel ourselves to be not only within the Sun but also to a certain extent beyond it. Formerly we were tiny human beings there below and we looked up at the Sun. But now that we have come into the Sun, we feel we are, with our soul being, within the Sun and the world which was formerly around us is now within us."

Verse by Rudolf Steiner

Sun, thou bearer of rays,
Thy light's power over matter
Magic's life out of the Earth's
Limitless rich depths.

Heart, thou bearer of soul,
Thy light's power over spirit
Magic's life out of the human being's
Limitless deep inwardness.

If I gaze upon the Sun
Her light speaks to me in radiance
Of the Spirit, filled with grace,
Wielding through the beings of worlds.

If I feel within my heart
The Spirit speaks its own true Word
About the human being, loved by Him
Through all time and eternity.

Looking upwards, I can see
In the Sun's bright disc
The mighty heart of worlds.

Looking inwards, I can feel
In the heart's warm beat
The human Sun ensouled.

Verse for Ita Wegman February 27, 1925

Hearts interpret Karma

When hearts learn to read

The Word,

Which creates in

Human Life;

When hearts learn to

Speak the Word

Which creates in

The Human Being.

Verses and Meditations
Rudolf Steiner

In the human Heart
There lives a part of man
Which contains matter
More spiritual than in any other organ;
Also a part of man
Of which the spiritual life
Is made more manifest in matter
Than that of any other organ.

Hence, in the microcosm that is man
Sun is the Heart,
And in his Heart is man united
Most of all with the deepest fount —
The fount of his true being.

Dodecahedron Universe

As has been presented above, the human heart is nested in the mediastinum which appears as a type of cube, or box surrounding and protecting the heart itself. In our current age, the shape of that box is a six-sided cube; but in the future, the shape of this protective enclosure will develop into a twelve-sided dodecahedron. The heart's shape and size evolve over time. This mystery of the heart is little known and even less understood. Dr. Rudolf Steiner was very keen on this idea and believed that the evolution of the heart was a key factor in the overall development of humanity. The significance of this heart evolution is critical to expand human awareness and consciousness of the inside and outside world of the individual. As humans expand beyond the awareness of the inner world of the human body, a larger, more universal perspective must arise in a new form.

This new perspective takes the step to become aware of the twelve directions raying in from the surrounding cosmic shape. The human being becomes more universal, or macrocosmic, through this expansion of awareness. Steiner insinuated this new perspective by teaching what he called, the "Twelve World Views." Only when one is able to understand the world through twelve perfectly valid, but different, World Views, is the individual able to become a universal citizen of the Cosmos. Broadening and expanding human consciousness to encompass the entire world of the stars that ray in from the twelve cosmic directions, opens the heart to the new shape it will become as the heart develops into a greater and greater sense organ of the entire Universe.

The original Foundation Stone of Rudolf Steiner's first Goetheanum was a double pentagon-dodecahedron made of copper which was laid into the ground in Dornach, Switzerland. Ten years later, a tragic fire destroyed the nearly completed building. In 1923, at the Christmas Foundation meeting, Rudolf Steiner presented a 'spiritual Foundation Stone,' the 'Dodecahedron of Man,' as he called it, to the members of the newly formed General Anthroposophical Society, which was to initiate a new phase in the revelation of the Mysteries of mankind. The meditation is mantric, that is, a spiritual revelation in which sound, form, and rhythm integrate with the esoteric meaning which is found in layers of evocative multiplicity.

> "Let us here and now lay in the ground of our hearts the dodecahedral Foundation Stone of Love. Our own hearts are the proper soil in which to lay this Foundation Stone—our hearts, in good will, imbued with love, working together to carry the anthroposophical will and purpose through the world."

The Occult Significance of Blood, Rudolf Steiner, Berlin, October 25, 1906, GA 55

"Thus, the whole cosmos lives in the form of a crystal. In the same way the whole cosmos is expressed in the living substance of a single being. The fluids coursing through a being are, at the same time, a little world, and a counterpart of the great world. And when substance has become capable of sensation, what then dwells in the sensations of the most elementary creatures? Such sensations mirror the cosmic laws, so that each separate living creature perceives within itself microcosmically the entire macrocosm. The sentient life of an elementary creature is thus an image of the life of the Universe, just as the crystal is an image of its form. The consciousness of such living creatures is, of course, but dim. Yet this very vagueness of consciousness is counterbalanced by its far greater range, for the whole cosmos is felt in the dim consciousness of an elementary being. Now, in man there is only a more complicated structure of the same three bodies found in the simplest sensitive living creature."

***Toward the 21st Century – Doing the Good, The Stone of Love*, Bernard Lievegoed**

"Rudolf Steiner describes the reality of that dodecahedral love stone. He says, 'The foundation stone will light up before the eye of our soul. Even that foundation stone which receives from universal and human love its substance, from universal and human Imagination its living picture quality and form, and from universal and human thoughts its radiating light.'

"Love is its substance; Moral Imagination is its form; thoughts are its radiating light.

"It is not an earthly thing. It is a Moral Imagination living in the hearts of a society. Such words are spoken by the hierophant, the high priest of mysteries—in this case the high priest [Rudolf Steiner] of new mysteries in which human hearts are the altars, the radiating love stones on which the hierarchies may celebrate the cosmic cult of the future."

***The Universe as a Phi-Based Dodecahedron*, by Gary Meisner, May 1, 2012**

"New findings in 2003 reveal that the shape of the universe is a Dodecahedron based on Phi. In October 2001, NASA began collecting data with the Wilkinson Microwave Anisotropy Probe (WMAP) on cosmic background radiation. Like visible light from distant stars and galaxies, cosmic background radiation allows scientists to peer into the past to the time when the universe was in its infancy. Density fluctuations in this radiation can also tell scientists much about the physical nature of space.

"NASA released the first WMAP cosmic background radiation data in February of 2003. In October 2003, a team including French cosmologists and Jeffrey Weeks, a freelance mathematician and recipient of a MacArthur Fellowship used this data to develop a model for the shape of the universe.

"The study analyzed a variety of different models for the universe, including finite vs. infinite, flat, negatively curved (saddle-shaped), positively curved (spherical) space and a torus (cylindric). The study revealed that the math adds up if the universe is finite and shaped like a dodecahedron, as in the illustration below provided by Weeks.

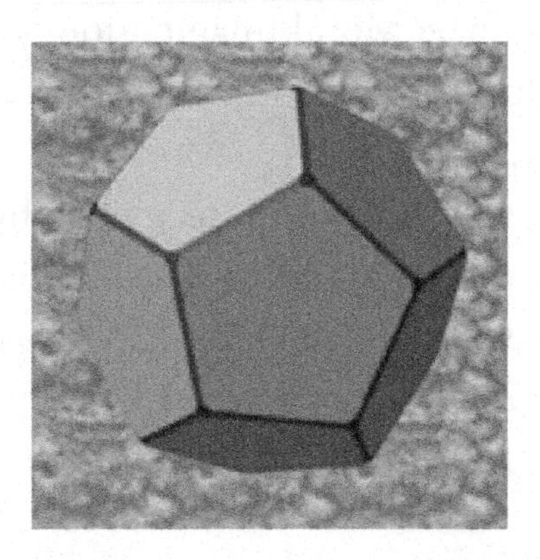

"The universe as a Dodecahedron is based on Phi, the golden ratio. The connection to Phi is found in the pentagons that form the faces of the dodecahedron. A dodecahedron consists of twelve pentagons. Take a pentagon and connect all the points to form a 5-pointed star. The ratios of the lengths of the resulting line segments are all based on phi, or 1.618. This is still a theory but supported by data that can be tested."

"This unique platonic solid (dodecahedron) incorporates the golden ratio, which is often denoted by the Greek letter phi, usually lower case: φ. When you stack a number of dodecahedra together, interesting things happen with the way the different faces and vertices rotate: they can be seen to enfold one into another, and the resulting hints of rotating helix shapes, fractals, and the spirals found in nature link not just to the broad field of sacred geometry, but to cosmological theories about the structure of our universe.

"Our universe is not really flat and infinite, but rather slightly curved, making it finite but unbounded. Curved spaces include the Poincare dodecahedral space model which lets you fly through the stacked dodecahedra that would form the surface of the 4D hypersphere our finite, but unbounded, universe resides within. Another interesting thing about a dodecahedron is that it can be constructed from five pyramids (tetrahedrons).

"Besides tutoring Eudoxos, some historians assume that Archytas also tutored Plato in mathematics at some point during the ten years that Plato spent in Sicily and Southern Italy. Plato was impressed by Archytas showing him that only five regular solid forms exist; the tetrahedron, cube, octahedron, dodecahedron, and the icosahedron. Plato develop a whole mathematical theory using these geometrical objects to associate these with the four elements the fire, earth, water, and air. And because one polyhedron was left, he introduced the 'ether' or 'quintessence.' In using triangles as building blocks for the geometric objects, he developed something like our 'quarks' as building blocks of the 'Platonic Solids.'

"Of the five solids, the tetrahedron has the smallest volume for its surface area and the icosahedron the largest; they therefore show the properties of dryness and wetness respectively and so correspond to FIRE and WATER. The cube, standing firmly on its base, corresponds to the stable EARTH, but the octahedron which rotates freely when held by two opposite vertices, corresponds to the mobile AIR. The dodecahedron corresponds to the universe because the Zodiac has 12 signs (the constellations of stars that the Sun passes through in the course of one year) corresponding to the 12 faces of the dodecahedron.

"It is clear that the very ratios of the planetary intervals from the Sun have not been taken from the regular solids alone. For the Creator, who is the very source of geometry and, as Plato wrote, 'practices eternal geometry,' does not stray from his own archetype. Thus, God, the eternal geometer must have given us the Platonic Solids on behalf of the planetary orbit structure—they were made for each other.

"Kepler was also influenced by Plato's ideas. He assigned the cube to Saturn, the tetrahedron to Jupiter, the dodecahedron to Mars, the icosahedron to Venus, and the octahedron to Mercury.

"Pacioli devotes the second part of his book, *De Divina Proportione*, published around 1509, to the Platonic Solids. He writes:

> "As God brought into being the celestial virtue, the fifth essence, and through it created the four solids . . . earth, air, water, and fire . . . so our sacred proportion gave shape to heaven itself, in assigning to it the dodecahedron . . . the solid of twelve pentagons, which cannot be constructed without our sacred proportion. As the aged Plato described in his *Timaeus*."

"The most amazing vindication of Plato has come from recent surveys of the universe that indicate that the universe may indeed be a dodecahedron, whose reflecting pentagonal faces give the illusion of an infinite universe when in fact it is finite. Plato's answer is that: 'time is an image of eternity.'

"The best candidate to fit the observed power spectrum of the universe is a well-proportioned space called the Poincare dodecahedral space. This space may be represented by a polyhedron with 12 pentagonal faces, with opposite faces being 'glued' together after a twist of 36°. This is the only consistent way to obtain a spherical (i.e., positively curved) space from a dodecahedron. The Poincare dodecahedral space is essentially a multiply connected variant of a simply connected hypersphere, although its volume is 120 times smaller.

"In the Dodecahedral Universe, a rocket leaving the dodecahedron through a given face immediately re-enters through the opposite face, and light propagates such that any observer whose line-of-sight intercepts one face has the illusion of seeing a slightly rotated copy of their own dodecahedron. This means that some photons from the cosmic microwave background, for example, would appear twice in the sky.

"The pentagon in space disperses into the number twelve and becomes the number of the transfigured spatial cube. In this way it descends into the plane becoming dodecahedron woven of triangles, squares, and hexagons—the dodecahedron in the plane. Twelve is the number of opened-up spaces, through and through transformed to the pentagon.

"In the plane, the strong qualities of three-dimensional space are preserved in it—it is revealed there. In this same way, the oldest Egyptian representations of starry space show a bow of an arch of twelve, star pentagrams. There are also ancient traditions which show that the twelve parts of the zodiac are related to the zones of the dodecahedron."

Historical Review of the Centrality of the Heart

Ancient Indian Wisdom of the Heart

Heart knowledge has evolved over time rather slowly and often has forgotten what the ancients already understood about the function and nature of the human heart. Modern science is only slightly further along in a comprehensive understanding of the cosmic significance of the human heart and its nature as a supersensible organ of perception. The ancients had the advantage of being clairvoyant and could 'see' what was actually happening in the heart. They used archaic images and descriptions of heart functions and pointed at mysteries concerning the ultimate nature of the heart. They placed the heart above all else in the grand picture of human evolution. Following this path through history is quite instructive and demonstrates that the ancients may have used poetic language to describe the heart; but their insights were just as useful now as they were then. We can learn a great deal about the evolution of the understanding of the heart by hearing historical descriptions, in the original words, concerning the truth about the heart.

In the *Vedas* and *Upanishads*, the central core of divinity possessed its true center of incarnation within the human heart. The organ itself then takes on a creating, transforming, and sculpting character. There, in the 'ether of the heart,' the divine lives in 'deepest slumber' in a 'hollow space' sheltering the Universe. It is there that the human being and the world become one. The spiritual power of the divine is divided into infinitely tiny pieces within our individual bodies, and throughout the world, generating the warmth of the heart. Out of this arises the breath, and from the breath the Aum-sound is created in the heart as the Word of Creation. It rises-up to the throat and the lungs, becoming the 'sound of the heart' and 'matrix' of the world; the voice at the center of everything, the womb of creation.

The Para-Pravesika by Ksemaraja

"That self-referential capacity of the heart is given many names in the agamas: spirit, consciousness, the ever-arising supreme word, freedom, the Supreme Self, the preeminent, sovereignty, agency, flashing vibratory throb, essence, subtle vibration and because of this, its real nature is that of the original natural egoity."

Chandogya Upanishad (8.1.1-4)

"Now, what is here in the city of brahman, is an abode, a small lotus flower. Within that is a small space. What is within that should be searched out; that, assuredly, is what one should desire to understand. As far as this world-space extends, so far extends the space within the heart. Within it, indeed, are contained both Heaven and Earth, both fire and wind, both Sun and Moon, lightning, and the stars, both what one possesses here and what one does not possess; everything here is contained within it that does not grow old with one's old age; it is not slain with one's murder. That is the real city of Brahman. In it, desires are contained. That is the soul (atman), free from evil, ageless, deathless, sorrowless, hungerless, thirstless, whose desire is the real, whose conception is the real."

Brihadaranyaka Upanishad (4.1.7)

"Brahman is the heart . . . the heart is the seat of all things. The heart is the support of all things; for in the heart alone all things are established. The highest Brahman is the heart. The heart does not leave him who, knowing this, worships it as such."

Brihadaranyaka Upanishad (5.6.1)

"This person (purusha) here in the heart is made of mind, is of the nature of light, is like a little grain of rice, is a grain of barley. This very one is ruler of everything, is lord of everything, governs this whole universe, whatsoever there is."

Svetasvatara Upanishad (4.17)

"That god, the all-worker, the great soul (Mahatman) ever seated in the heart of creatures, is framed by the heart, by the thought, by the mind. They who know that become immortal."

Katha Upanishad (6.16-17)

"There are a hundred and one channels of the heart. One of these passes up to the crown of the head. Going up by it, one goes to immortality. The others are for departing in various directions. A person of the measure of a thumb is the inner soul (Antaratman; the Inner-Atman) ever seated in the heart of creatures."

Taittiriya Upanishad (1.6.1)

"This space that is within the heart—therein is the person, consisting of mind, immortal, resplendent."

Maitri Upanishad (6.22)

"By closing the ears with the thumbs, they hear the sound of the space within the heart. Of it there is this sevenfold comparison: like rivers, a bell, a brazen vessel, a wheel, the croaking of frogs, rain, as when one speaks in a sheltered place. Passing beyond this variously characterized (sound-brahman), men disappear in the supreme, the non-sound, the unmanifested Brahman. The ether-storehouse of the heart is bliss, is the supreme abode. This is our self, our yoga too; and this, the heat of fire and Sun."

Mahanarayanopanisad Upanishad (13.6-12)

"In the middle of that (narrow space of the heart or sushumna) remains the undecaying, all-knowing, omni-faced, great fire, which has flames on every side, which enjoys the food presented before it, which remains assimilating the food consumed, (the rays of which spread scattering themselves vertically and horizontally) and which warms its own body from the insole to the crown. In the center of that fire which permeates the whole body, there abides a tongue of fire, of the color of shining gold, which is the topmost among the subtle."

Brihadaranyaka Upanisad (4.2.3)

"Indra by name is this person here in the right eye. Now that which has the form of a person in the left eye is his wife, Viraj. Their meeting-place is the space within the heart. Their food is the red lump in the heart. Their covering is the net-like work in the heart. The path that they go is that channel which goes upward from the heart. Like a hair divided a thousand-fold, so are the channels called hita [blessed; good], which are established within the heart. The person here who among the senses is made of knowledge, who is the light in the heart."

Khandogya-Upanishad

"There is this city of Brahman (the body) and in it the palace, the small lotus (the heart) and in it that small ether. Now what exists within that small ether, that is to be sought for, that is to be understood. As large as the ether of space is, so large is that ether within the heart. Both Heaven and Earth are contained within it, both fire and air, both Sun and Moon, both lightning and stars, and whatever is not, all that is contained within it. Ether does not age, and at the death of the body this ether is not spilled. It is this ether, or Brahman, that is the True Self, free from ignorance and change and partaking of the qualities of reality. The Lord of the past and of the future, should be meditated upon as a light (flame) the size of the thumb in the cavity of the heart. The spot in the heart which is the last of all to die is the seat of life, the center of all, Brahma, the first spot that lives in the fetus, and the last that dies. This spot contains potential mind, life, energy, and will. During life it radiates prismatic colors, fiery and opalescent. When the time of death arrives, the spirit withdraws its radiations from the parts and extremities of the body in the heart. The heart becomes luminous; from it the soul departs. There are a hundred and one arteries of the heart; one of them penetrates the crown of the head; moving upward; by it a human reaches the immortal. He is going to the Sun, for the Sun is the door of the world, the little door in the wall of heaven."

The Rig Veda

In the *Rig Veda*, the terms for heart (hrd and hrdaya) occur close to a hundred times. Here are some of the descriptions of the heart:

- able to see what is denied to the physical eye
- by which one comes into touch with the Gods

- enables a human being to penetrate into deep secrets and mysteries
- it is in or by the heart that visions are fashioned into words
- visions undergone in the heart are explicitly described as a purification or clarification
- the soma juices which are drunk by the officiants are believed to be in their hearts
- through the heart, the light of higher insight and contact with the transcendent one arises through the heart, one becomes all-seeing
- inspired seers pay heed to the god who is not subject to decay within their heart
- clarified butter of the word flows from the ocean in the heart
- words of the poets come to and touch the heart of a god
- the poet bears the soma in his heart
- the spiritual heart is the soul and its psychic activity
- the heart is considered the seat of feelings
- Atman, the spiritual heart, has no physical or mental dimensions
- the 12 petalled heart chakra is a level or dimension of our being and of the entire manifestation
- the spiritual heart is a spark of God
- Atman (the spiritual heart) and Brahman (the absolute) are one
- our heart—our eternal, undying self—is identical with Brahman
- the spiritual heart is a reflection of everything, the supreme consciousness

- the heart is the essence of everything, the background of existence
- we are all revealing the same heart, the same divine self, the same ultimate reality
- the heart of man and the heart of the world are a single heart
- we should surrender into the heart, into the supreme reality, into God
- the godly atom of the self is to be found in the right chamber of the heart
- the self is in the cave of this heart, here lies the dynamic, radiant spiritual heart
- the spiritual heart, is the intuition of who we are
- the limitlessness of the spiritual heart is absolute because it has no form—it can contain totality
- we should lower the mind to the heart
- the heart is the object, means, and subject of meditation
- the spiritual heart is the witness of consciousness, the profound and intimate self
- the heart becomes the knower, the instrument of knowledge, and the object of knowledge
- meditation starts from the heart and returns to the heart
- the divine reality of existence, the present, the "I Am," resides in the heart
- when we withdraw the senses and center ourselves in the heart, we can search 'the interior'

- we pass from the usual 'conquering' attitude of the mind to a receptive, contemplative disposition using surrender to attain lucidity
- the spiritual heart has a radiance of pure presence, not action of the ego
- the heart has a plenitude of the wholeness
- the attention of the heart-mind has an attitude of waiting, peace, and sacredness
- attention emanates from the heart and ends up in the heart
- real knowledge resides in the heart, in the wisdom that illuminates us with brightness
- the best way of keeping the awareness of the spiritual heart is to love
- the spiritual heart generates love, devotion, zeal, fervor, heartiness, ardor, adoration, ecstasy
- our spiritual heart (as the organ of perception) needs to be cultivated
- art and contemplation are some of the ways to cultivate our spiritual heart
- we should meditate for the revelation of the spiritual heart and love
- we should teach the sacred principles of the kingdom of the heart
- the heart produces pure love, yearning, fervor, the sacred tremor, and the aspiration for God
- complete silence of the mind is necessary before entering the secret sanctuary of the heart

- initiates of the spiritual heart are able to rise above their egos toward the supreme essence
- the heart is a subtle organ of wisdom, or transcendental intellect
- the rational mind cannot understand the reasoning of the heart
- spiritual intuition comes from the heart
- rational thinking is the reflection of the energy of the heart—reflected knowledge
- the mind knows through information—the heart knows through surrender, trust, and joy
- the knowledge of the heart is instantaneous and undivided, revelation, whole, non-dual
- the heart is named 'The circle of the Sun'
- intuition comes from the heart, is divine, and participates in universal spiritual wisdom
- the heart is the Spiritual Sun, the place of revelation, the vital center of being, and intuition
- the heart is a visible manifestation of God to humanity—a sacred symbol
- the primordial subtle energy ascends from the heart to the mind
- the mind is seen as a Moon which simply reflects the light of the heart's Sun
- in the heart, all the vain noise of the world is quieted—a sanctuary of silence
- in the 'Cave of the Heart,' the consciousness of unity is revealed—the world and man are one

- the heart should be trained to increase its purity and capacity to love, witness, and surrender
- the spiritual heart is a gateway to infinity, where the supreme self, Atman, is revealed

The Triadic Heart of Siva, by Abhinavagupta (c. 950 – 1016 AD)

"The heart (hrdaya), the resting place of all, is mantra, which, in its essence, is nothing but free consciousness, which also is simply the power of transcendental speech."

"The power which resides in the heart of consciousness is freedom itself. The purpose of its creative activity is the immortal group, the entire range of perceiving subject, perceived object, and process of perception."

"The heart is, above all, formed of an undivided self-referential consciousness."

"My heart, which is composed of the emission of the quivering flashing condition of the union of the Mother and Father, whose body is full, which generates that concealed light which has five faces, producing the great and quite new manifestation, which is the abode of the stainless manifesting energies, because of its quivering and throbbing, is the supreme immortal group. Within whom all this universe appears, appearing as the external luminous projection during the process of manifestation. Situated in the supreme, which is trembling, which is immovable, to Her I bow down, the one Goddess who is the perception of one's own self."

"The heart is called the place where there is a repose in the pure light and pure consciousness, which is not different from the parts of the body. Only the light of the heart truly exists; in creative activity it is the active agent, and this activity, when it reposes in itself, is the self-referential capacity of consciousness, whereas when it begins to spread outwards, it causes the manifestation of the universe."

"The nature of such a consciousness is its capacity for self-referral, and because of that, there always arises a spontaneous sound which is termed the supreme, the great heart. That self-consciousness in the heart in which the entire universe without remainder is dissolved, present at the beginning and at the end of perception of objects, is called in the authoritative texts 'the vibration,' and more precisely, 'the universal vibration,' and its nature is an overflowing in the self. For that vibration, which is a slight motion of a special kind, a unique vibrating light, is the wave of the ocean of consciousness, without which there is no consciousness at all. For the character of the ocean is that it is sometimes filled with waves and sometimes waveless. This consciousness is the essence of all. The insentient universe has consciousness as its essence, because its very foundation is dependent on that, and its essence is the 'great heart.'"

"When the heart is in a state of contraction, the awakened awareness of the individual self is in fact a state of ignorance. But when this contraction ceases to function, then the true nature of the self-shines forth."

"In the two conditions, the inner and the outer, there exists a vibration of consciousness whose nature is the three powers, a vibration which is both universal and particular, which is always in the process of expanding and contracting because it so wishes to appear even though in reality it is beyond all expansion and contraction."

"It is the heart whose nature is a vibration which constitutes the supreme method for achieving the highest non-duality which consists of a universal grace. For the nature of the self-referential character of the consciousness which composes the awakening in the heart is that it is an astonishment brought about by the total fullness of consciousness."

"That reality, which is higher than the highest and the lowest, is called the Goddess, that reality is the essence, the heart, the supreme emissional power of the Lord."

"In order that a sacrifice be successful, one must properly honor the Goddess with fragrant flowers which effortlessly allow for an entrance into the heart; and by flowers are meant all substances—external and internal which nourish the heart because they bestow their own nature within the heart."

"Now as for the supreme, as it is called here, there is a meditation on it. The light, the freedom, whose essential nature is consciousness contains within it all principles, realities, things. This light abides in the heart."

"The knower of truth sees that reality within the heart like a flower within which are all external and internal things, a flower shaped like a plantain bloom. He should meditate with undistracted mind on the union there in the heart of the Sun,

Moon, and fire. This union expands and flames violently in the great firepit known as the heart."

"Just as the large tree is to be found potentially in the banyan tree seed, so this world, both inanimate and animate abides in the seed of the heart."

"This heart which moves in the midst of the lunar stations made up of time—of the all—is present in everything in the form of an undifferentiated self-referential consciousness; one should continually meditate on this seed of the heart as having penetrated into one's own heart, into one's consciousness, which is in the form of the lotus-flower because it plays at expanding and contracting."

"This heart is the abode, the dwelling place, the resting place of all beings. That which is mine, belongs to the perceiving subject. For of all existing appearances beginning with blue and extending as far as the worm, there is nothing whatsoever which may be termed blue, and so on, unless it be penetrated by a portion of consciousness. So, my consciousness attains a portion of the uninterrupted astonishment and then, when it encounters blue, it experiences, 'Blue appears to me.'"

"That which is the space of the Heart which belongs to me, in which are found all beings within the infinite, there the entire universe, whose nature is represented by the sound Mama (mine), has gone, and is completely held. But when it abandons its differentiated nature, the space becomes empty. Then my heart takes on a double nature, which is both differentiated and non-differentiated, supreme consciousness and non-supreme consciousness, and becomes the place of repose, the dwelling place of limits, that is, the 'I.'"

"That which is the stream of manifestation, that is the supreme, which is situated in the space of my heart."

"The tantric practitioner who has penetrated into the heart whose essence is pure existence and potency, who because of the particular efficacy of the practice of the ritual of adoration is capable of remembering perfectly the mantra, thus attains to a very high degree the potency of the mantra which is the reality known as the heart. By the peculiar efficacy of the ritual of adoration he crosses over completely, either by himself or as a result of the clear and pristine lotus-word of the teacher, and obtains the power of the mantra, whose essential characteristic is the heart, and in this way he attains liberation in this very life."

"The essence of consciousness is freedom, and the essence of that is a mass of bliss. It is for this reason that ritual actions directed toward an attainment of a state of identity and absorption should be carried out employing elements that bring joy to the heart."

"When the absorption into the heart is maintained for four periods of forty-eight minutes, then the totality, whose nature is essentially light, attains the condition of day, and the contraction of the night of Maya (illusion) is destroyed. Then the practitioner with this very body becomes omniscient."

Vimarsini, by Abhinavagupta

"I adore the supreme with the priceless goblet of the heart which is full of the ambrosia of bliss."

“This supreme wheel goes out from the heart through the spaces of the eyes, and so forth, and ranges over the various objects of the senses. Because of the wheel’s (chakra’s) rays of light, a form whose nature is of the light of the Moon, Sun, and fire is established in those objects by regular degrees in conjunction with manifestation, maintenance, and dissolution. In this way, as this wheel falls on the various objects of the senses by way of the sense-capacity openings, one should recognize that sensory object as identical with the wheel.”

“Thus, wherever the universal wheel falls, by this methodical practice it falls in its entirety like the universal monarch. In this way, the whole multitude of paths is effortlessly dissolved in the great wheel which is contained in consciousness. Then, even when all this has come to an end and all that is left are latent impressions, one should meditate on the great wheel which revolves and is the overflowing of the true self.”

“He whose heart is completely fulfilled and who does not desire any specific fruit, because of the absence of all limitations, before him the Goddess in her universal form appears.”

“At first abiding in the heart, due to a repose in the mere emptiness, in the portion of the knower alone, in the innate bliss, he experiences a state known as ‘devoid of bliss.’ Then, when the vital breath rises, he experiences in the ‘knowable object’ the bliss that arises from another. In this condition of the bliss that arises from another, he abides at ease in the apana, which is filled with the infinite portions of the knowable, and he is embellished with the Moon of the apana. Having attained the level of the samana, he abides wholly absorbed in the unification of the infinite rays of the knowable objects. He becomes one who is composed of the bliss of Brahman. He is totally dedicated to devouring the limiting forces of the streams of the knowable objects and the means of knowing; he reposes in the fire of the udana and comes to know the great bliss. Then, having entered this repose, and when the great flames begin to abate, the great pervasion which is beyond all qualifications ensues, and this is called the vyana, the unlimited. Then, indeed, the bliss of consciousness occurs which is not strengthened by what is inert. For here indeed there is no possibility whatsoever of a difference which would be formed of the insentient. That is a state where there is no distinction, where everything appears shining on all sides, where consciousness is unstruck and fed by the supreme nectar. There, one does not meet with any realizations in the proper sense of the word at all. This condition taught to me by Sambhunatha is known as universal bliss. The repose in this state may be obtained by employing the pronunciation of the heart. The complete repose in this state corresponds to the attainment of the condition of the supreme. These are the six states which arise from the ascension of the vital breath into our different internal abodes, even if in essence our essential nature, flowing out of the heart, is always one."

Heart Research in Egypt

Knowledge about the cardiovascular system, which led Harvey to the discovery of blood circulation, was achieved only gradually through the ages. It started in Egypt around 3,500 BC, was elaborated by ancient Greeks, was better defined in Alexandria, and, in the West, ceased after the fall of the Roman Empire. This knowledge was preserved in the Islamic world and in European monasteries, and it later advanced with the revival of the anatomical dissection in European universities, paving the way to Harvey's discovery. This review provides an overview about how knowledge about the cardiovascular system developed through the ages.

In ancient Egypt (3,500 BC), the heart was considered the central element of a system of channels distributed throughout the body, transporting blood, feces, semen, benign and malignant spirits, and even the soul. There was a clear notion that the peripheral pulse originated from the heartbeat.

The Heart According to the Greeks

In the Pre-Aristotelian Period, Thales of Miletus (c. 626/623–c. 548/545 BC), paved the way for questions regarding the human anatomy. Medical schools came into existence along with philosophers in the 5th century BC. Alcmaeon of Croton (mid-fifth century BC) believed that the venous system was distinct from the arterial system, although he did not make an anatomical distinction between them. The function of the vessels was associated with wakefulness: withdrawal of blood from veins induced sleeping; but arteries, which brought blood to the brain, promoted wakefulness. According to him, all vessels originated in the head, and their function was to distribute the pneuma (spirit) to the brain.

Empedocles from the city of Akragas in Agrigento Sicily (492-432 BC) had a different view. For him, the heart was the seat of the soul and the center of the cardiovascular system; blood vessels distributed the pneuma, which was internalized by pulmonary respiration. Nonetheless, Empedocles also believed in the existence of fleshy tubes that contained blood and the terminal portions of which externalized in the skin, absorbing and expelling air.

The school of Kos, the main exponent of which was Hippocrates (460–375 BC), with regard to the cardiovascular system in the book *On the Heart*, reported for the first time the anatomical details of the heart, ascribing to the cardiovascular system the transportation of life throughout the body. According to the authors of the book, the lungs surrounded the heart, in the thorax, in order to cool the excess heat produced by incessant cardiac activity. The heart had a pyramidal shape, red color, and intrinsic electric activity. In contrast to the rest of the body, which was nourished with blood delivered through veins, the heart nourished itself from the pure substance created during blood dialysis. The heart housed the mind and the spirit, which predominated over the rest of the soul.

The Sicilian branch of the school of Cnidus, probably with works by Philistion of Locri around 370 BC, also contributed to the anatomical knowledge about the cardiovascular system: the presence of two ventricles was well known, the left being more hypertrophied than the right; the presence of two atria, whose beats were discordant in time with those of the ventricles, was also observed; moreover, the author noted the presence of a vessel connected to one ventricle only, along with semilunar valves.

Aristotle (384-322 BC) believed that the heart was the most important organ of the body and was the seat of the soul. The breath contained only air, the main function of which was to cool the heart. In the same manner, he conceived the brain as a mechanism for cardiac cooling. Aristotle believed that the pulmonary artery and superior vena cava were subdivisions of another great vessel, which he called the 'great vein.' In addition, he described another vessel connected to the medial ventricle, which he named the aorta. Further, he believed that the heart was the origin of all nerves and vessels. According to Aristotle, in comparison with the left ventricle, which had air and more pure blood, the right ventricle contained blood that was warmer and more abundant.

From: Aristotle's *On the Generation of Animals*

"We are justified in seeing the heart as the source of the being's life, shape, and organization."

"Blood and its blood vessels are the original source of life."

"The actual nourishment process of each living thing is involved intrinsically with the entire process of forming the blood. The formation of the blood constitutes 'the final step' of internalizing and transforming nourishment."

"All other parts of the body depend on the heart and have their source, or origin, in the heart."

"Warmth enables digestion and brings about the overcoming, surmounting, and internalization of outside, foreign qualities and find its origin and center in the heart."

"The particular prerequisites for human thought activity are grounded in the polar opposite and painstakingly balanced processes of warmth and cold in the human heart and brain."

"The heart is the center of the perception process of the soul and the sensory environment of the human being. In the heart, these sense impressions are perceived, detected, bound together, and thus first truly felt and understood. The heart is the starting point for all sensory impression."

From: *De Anima*, Aristotle

"The heart is not just the physiological source of life, warmth, nourishment, and growth, but also the center of sensory perception and closely connected with conscious life. It is also the source of sensations. The heart enables, shapes, and manifests the actual soul life in the present moment, while the corresponding processes of sensation and feeling are accompanied by warmth processes. Warmth offers the greatest assistance for the bodily work done to activate the soul. We are dealing with changing, reactive warmth process, focusing on the blood as it moves in and around the heart."

"Memory is seated in the heart. Blood assists with current sense impressions, the associated powers of thinking and imagination, and our processes of sensing, feeling, and sentiment. The heart is also the source of the human capacity for movement."

"According to our theory, life itself, every movement and every perception, depends on the heart. Every stirring of joy, pain, and other sensation originates and ends in the heart."

Alexandrian Period

Better anatomical knowledge about the cardiovascular system appeared later in the works of Herophilus of Chalcedon (325-255 BC) and Erasistratus of Chios (310-250 BC) in the school of Alexandria in Egypt. In the famous school of Alexandria, dissections of the human body were routinely performed. Herophilus's main contribution to the knowledge about the cardiovascular system was his differentiation of the thickness of arteries relative to veins, suggesting that the former were six times thicker than the latter. He termed the vessel connected to the right ventricle 'the arterial vein,' and he observed that arteries were less thick than veins in the lungs. He also believed that only arteries were associated with the heartbeat because the contraction and relaxation movements depended on the heart.

Erasistratus recognized the heart's activity as an impeller pump that contracted due to its so-called intrinsic force. To the contrary of what Herophilus believed, Erasistratus emphasized that arteries did not have active movements of contraction and relaxation, but they were passively filled due to heart contraction. Some authors believe that Erasistratus was the first to describe the valves in veins. With the conquest of Egypt by the Roman Empire, the scientific activity in Alexandria progressively declined, and dissection of human bodies was no longer performed.

Roman Period

In the 2nd Century AD, Galen (130-200 AD), a gladiators' physician in the temple of Asclepius in Pergamon, demonstrated that arteries contained blood, not air, as was the belief until that time. Further, Galen stated that the heart was a muscle with different orientation planes, which permitted its strong and incessant activity. Galen recognized that the left ventricle was more hypertrophied than the right ventricle; he attributed these differences to the presence of air in the left ventricle, and he emphasized the function of the right ventricle in handling blood. Two vessels originated in the right ventricle: one transported blood to the lungs (pulmonary artery), whereas the other transported peripheral blood back to the heart (vena cava). The left ventricle was the source of the great artery (aorta) as well as of other venous structures (pulmonary veins) that transported blood from the lungs to the heart.

Following Galen's period, dissections were performed less often, and anatomic studies were left behind. Galen considered the human body to be the temple of the soul, and his teleological explanations for all phenomena were in concert with the dominant force that had settled in Rome in the 4th Century AD. Because knowledge was supposed to be derived from faith, anatomical knowledge was not considered important. This explains why Galen's erroneous beliefs lasted until the Renaissance, and the functioning of the cardiovascular system was beginning to be understood only in the 17th Century.

Byzantine Period

Oribasius' work (325–403 AD) in Byzantium used magnifying lenses to confirm the anastomosis (connection) between veins and arteries in the kidney's capillaries. He discovered renal circulation: perfusion through the renal artery branch of the aorta and venous return through the renal vein branch of the inferior vena cava.

When the school of Edessa was closed in 489 AD, the Nestorians took refuge in the city of Gondishapur in Persia, founded in 271 AD, taking with them the works by Hippocrates, Aristotle, and Galen translated to Syriac. Greek doctors experienced a similar displacement after the school of Athens was closed by the Eastern Roman Emperor Justinian in 529 AD. These intellectuals also became part of the School of Gondishapur which served as a model for subsequent Persian medical schools. A teaching hospital was constructed and inspired the creation of other hospitals not only in the Islamic world but also in Spain and Portugal. In this manner, medical knowledge acquired in the previous centuries, but forgotten in the Middle Ages in Europe, was preserved in the schools of the Islamic world. When important medical works were translated into Latin, from the 11th century onward, medical knowledge finally returned to Europe.

Summa Theologica, Thomas Aquinas (c. 1225–Mar. 7, 1274 AD)

"The heart is related to the higher cognitive activities, which take place after sensory perception and the development of imaginative images."

"Something takes place in people whenever they perform an act of perception. This is the act of receiving and conceiving the perceived object. This concept designates the sound, and the concept itself is called a 'word of the heart.'"

"This thought process takes place in the individual penetration and unification of the act of perceiving with what is being perceived."

"Sense perception is the tool for the spiritual and intellectual activity of thought."

"The human heart is an organ of knowledge and love, mediating between heaven and earth, thinking and willing, human being and environment."

***Summa Contra Gentiles*, Thomas Aquinas**

"The bodily life of the sense beings exists because of the living breath that streams through the limbs from the foundation of life, that is, from the heart."

"The pure of heart shall look upon God."

"None of the senses perceives itself or its activity. The eye neither sees itself, nor perceives the fact that it is seeing. The knowing spirit, however, recognizes itself; and recognizes that it recognizes itself."

Islamic Period

Rhazis (865-925 AD) disagreed with Galen regarding the presence of bone in the cardiac base. Haly Abbas (930-994 AD) advanced the morphological characterization of the pulmonary artery in two muscle layers, in describing the aorta more precisely, and in describing the coronary arteries in 965 AD. He also suggested a functional communication between the endings of veins and arteries.

Akhawayni Bukhari (983 AD) stated that the heart had four cavities, the pulmonary vessels, and the aorta, all of them with valves that impeded blood reflux. He described the pericardium with anatomic precision. He emphasized that most of the blood received by the right ventricle was transported to the lungs. From the lungs, blood was transported to the left ventricle, from there to the aorta, and from the aorta throughout the body. Thus, Bukhari described a rudimentary lung circulation, emphasizing that the function of the heart was to pump blood and that blood vessels transported only blood, not the pneuma. He also described the coronary arteries with precision.

Avicenna (Arabic: Ibn Sīnā; 980-1037 AD) recognized the cardiac systole and diastole and adopted the cardio-centric model of Aristotle and accepted the presence of pores in the interventricular septum. In his view, the left ventricle was the cardiac chamber that housed the pneuma, and it was the seat of emotions.

The 'Eye of the Heart' in Sufi Tradition

The expression 'the eye of the heart' appears also in the Sufi tradition. Here it represents the opening toward the divine, the eye through which the depth of the heart can be seen and through which the heart can know the supreme divine reality. According to the Sufi description, we can imagine this eye of the heart having two faces: one is oriented toward 'interior,' through which the meditator can 'see' the infinite depths of the heart; the other is oriented toward 'exterior.' This is the eye through which the supreme subject, the inner knower, God, or the witness consciousness is witnessing the world. For Sufis, this place, deep in the Heart, is the symbol of the point of contact with God.

Cultivating the Heart is a fundamental spiritual need that the great Persian Sufi mystic and poet Rumi (Jalāl al-Dīn Muhammad Rūmī; Sep. 30, 1207–Dec. 17, 1273) affirmed:

"There is a candle in your heart, ready to be kindled.
There is a void in your soul, ready to be filled.
You feel it, don't you?
You feel the separation from the Beloved.
Invite Him to fill you up, embrace the fire.
Remind those who tell you otherwise,
that Love comes to you of its own accord,
and the yearning for it cannot be learned in any school."

European Period

Berengario da Carpi (1470–1550 AD) showed the existence of only two ventricles, two atria, and semilunar and atrioventricular valves, thus recovering the knowledge acquired by the ancient Greeks and the Alexandria school and adding to that the existence of papillary muscles as components of the sub-valvar apparatus.

Leonardo da Vinci (Apr. 15, 1452–May 2, 1519 AD) ascribed a functional significance to the atria, showing that the atria contracted when the ventricles dilated. He emphasized that the heart is a muscle, not a seat of spirits or air (pneuma) and presented a detailed picture of the mitral apparatus and described the moderator band of the right ventricle.

Michel Servetus (Sep. 29, 1509 or 1511–Oct. 27, 1553 AD) a theologian trained in anatomy, described pulmonary circulation in a few pages of his *Christianismi Restitutio* (1553), which led to his death at the stake. He believed that the blood in the right ventricle passed through the left side of the heart through the pulmonary capillaries; there were no pores in the interventricular septum. Further, blood mingled with air in the lungs, but not in the left ventricle. He believed that blood passed from the pulmonary artery to pulmonary veins via blood capillaries.

Andrea Vesalius (Andries van Wezel; Dec. 31, 1514–Oct. 15, 1564 AD) of the University of Padua gave the name mitral to the atrioventricular valve, which separates the left atrium from the left ventricle.

Matteo Realdo Colombo (c. 1515–1559 AD) of the University of Padua, correctly described the anatomical position of the kidneys and demonstrated pulmonary circulation. He believed that blood was transported from the right ventricle to the pulmonary artery and from there to the lungs, where it was attenuated; thence, it moved from the lungs, along with air, through the pulmonary vein and to the left ventricle drawing attention to the width of the pulmonary artery. He also described cardiac abnormalities such as the hydrothorax probably secondary to decompensate chronic heart failure, bacterial endocarditis, myocardial infarction, and chronic pericarditis.

William Harvey (Apr. 1, 1578–Jun. 3, 1657 AD) In 1628, he perceived the functions of vein valves to contain blood and direct blood flow. His discovery of blood circulation began the modern age of heart research.

The Christian Desert Fathers

The Desert Father St. Isaac the Syrian (c. 613–c. 700 AD), believed in the 'The Intellect of the Heart.' For him, the heart is not simply a physical organ, but is the spiritual center of the human's being, his deepest and truest self, or the inner shrine, to be entered only through the sacrifice of individuality, in which the mystery of the union between the divine and the human is consummated. 'The eye of the heart' or 'the intellect of the heart,' (called 'nous'), dwells 'in the depths of the soul,' representing the innermost aspect of the heart. Nous is the highest faculty of humanity through which he knows God or the inner essences by means of spiritual perception or direct apprehension. 'The intellect of the Heart' understands Divine Truth by means of immediate experience or intuition.

To protect this sacred ground, the Desert Fathers believed in the 'Guardian of the Heart' who embodies watchfulness and represents spiritual sobriety, alertness, vigilance, and an attitude of attentiveness in which we are almost continuously aware of the heart. This shows how central they held the awareness of the spiritual heart.

Microcosmic Heart, Paracelsus (c. 1493–Sep. 24, 1541)

"The heart is the seed of the microcosm and the sacred island, the first of the seven continents, and within it dwell the 'children of the fire mists' whose reflections are set up in the organs and functions of the outer body. The heart is the Garden of Eden—a place of beauty and felicity. Within it are the springs which, becoming rivers (arteries), pour forth the living waters (blood) for the preservation of the land (body). The 'kingdom of heaven within' refers to the mysteries of the heart. Man is the living Temple of God and the heart is the Holy of Holies of that Mystery Temple. It is the inner room, the sanctuary, the adytum, the very oracular vent in which moves the Deity. It is the cave of initiation, the urn of the spirit. There are seven brains in the heart and also seven hearts in the brain. The seven heart brains are the intelligences of the vital organs, the 'Seven Spirits before the throne.'"

The Perfect Way: Or, The Finding of Christ (1882), by Anna Bonus Kingsford (Sep. 16, 1846–Feb. 22, 1888) and Edward Maitland (Oct. 27, 1824–Oct. 2, 1897)

"Paracelsus knew the mysteries of blood; he knew why the priests of Baal made incisions with knives in their flesh, and then brought down fire from heaven; he knew why Orientals poured out their blood before a woman to inspire her with physical love; he knew how spilt blood cries for vengeance or mercy and fills the air with Angels or demons. Blood is the instrument of dreams and multiplies images in the brain during sleep, because it is full of the

Astral Light. Its globules are bisexual, magnetized and metaled, sympathetic, and repelling. All forms and images in the world can be evoked from the physical soul of blood. The blood then becomes a true elixir of life, wherein ruby and magnetic globules of vital light float in a slightly gilded fluid."

The Theosophical View of G. R. S. Mead (Mar. 22, 1863–Sep. 28, 1933)

"In the human body are at least two 'Trees,' the nerve and vascular systems. The former has its roots above in the cerebrum, the latter has its roots in the heart. Among the trunks and branches run currents of 'nerve ether' and 'life' respectively. The one is the reflection of the other and both are within the human being. Blood has its life and motion from within itself—that is, from the Nephesh, which is the breath of the Elohim. The history of blood is the history of humanity."

Isis Unveiled (1877), Helena P. Blavatsky (Aug. 12, 1831–May 8th, 1891)

"Blood begets phantoms, and its emanations furnish certain spirits with the materials required to fashion their temporary appearances. 'Blood,' says Levi, is the first incarnation of the universal fluid; it is the materialized vital light. Its birth is the most marvelous of all nature's marvels; it lives only by perpetually transforming itself, for it is the universal Proteus. The blood issues from principles where there was none of it before, and it becomes flesh, bones, hair, nails, tears, and perspiration. It can be all neither to corruption nor death; when life is gone, it begins decomposing; if you know how to reanimate it, to infuse into it life, by a new magnetization of its globules, life will return to it again. The universal substance, with its double motion, is the Great Arcanum of Being; blood is the Great Arcanum of Life."

A Sleep of Prisoners (1951)
by Christopher Fry
(Dec. 18, 1907–Jun. 30, 2005)

The human heart can go to the lengths of God.

Dark and cold we may be, but this is no winter now.

The frozen misery of centuries breaks, cracks, begins to move;

The thunder is the thunder of the floes, the thaw,
the flood, the upstart Spring.

Thank God our time is now when wrong
Comes up to face us everywhere,

Never to leave us till we take the longest stride
of soul humans ever took.

Affairs are now soul size. The enterprise is exploration into God.

Where are you making for?

It takes so many thousand years to wake,

But will you wake, for pity sake?

Eastern Wisdom of the Etheric Heart

The Endless Knot

Ancient Hindu philosophy described the heart as an endless knot that goes on continuously forever. They called it the Eternal Knot, Glorious Knot, or Shrivatsa because it was seen as the first and last aspect of human existence. It is said the Shrivatsa symbol appears on the chest of an avatar of Vishnu when he is chosen to be Vishnu's incarnation. This knot creates the immortal spirit of the individual that goes from life to life and never stops the drumming of Shiva that signals spiritual life. The Eternal Knot insinuates that the heart has, in itself, the Drum of Shiva that brings life and ends life. This knot is often found inscribed on the chest of Shiva, Vishnu, and many other gods and goddesses. It is an abbreviation for spiritual life and the human soul evolving into a deity. Through the endless sounding of this drum, human life aligns with cosmic life and the universal spirit is reflected in the resonant response of the individual's heart. This knot was also seen as one of the eight signs of Buddha that indicate spiritual advancement and enlightenment.

The endless/eternal knot, net, or web denotes the auspicious mark emblematic of love and the human heart. It is a symbol of the ultimate unity of everything. It represents the intertwining of wisdom and compassion, the inseparability of 'emptiness' and 'interdependent origination' combined to create enlightenment. It is the symbol of harmony and one of the eight auspicious symbols of Buddhism. It overlaps without a beginning or an end, symbolizing the Buddha's endless wisdom and compassion.

The shrivatsa is an auspicious mark that adorns the breast of Vishnu. Shrivatsa means 'beloved of Shri' and refers to the goddess Lakshmi; the consort of Vishnu. Lakshmi's insignia on Vishnu's breast represents the devotion in his heart for his consort, and since Lakshmi is the goddess of wealth and good fortune, the shrivatsa forms a natural auspicious symbol. The shrivatsa either takes the form of a triangular swirl (vortex), or an upright diamond with loops at its four inter-cardinal corners.

Krishna, as the eighth incarnation of Vishnu, also bears the shrivatsa at the center of his chest. Another name given is 'curl of happiness,' and this curl is shaped like a Greek hooked-cross. Indian and Chinese representations of the Buddha frequently show the nandyavarta or swastika on his breast as a symbol of his enlightened mind.

Another possible derivation of both the endless knot and swastika arose from the S-shaped markings on the hood of the cobra. This in turn gave rise to the nagayantra (serpent mandala), where two or more entwining snakes form an endless knot design or yantra. The endless knot, or granthi, also appears on clay seals from the early Indus Valley civilization (circa 2500 BCE).

In its final evolution as a geometric Buddhist symbol, the eternal knot or 'lucky diagram'; which is described as 'turning like a swastika,' was identified with the shrivatsa-svastika, since these parallel symbols were common to most early Indian traditions of the Aṣṭamaṅgala (The Eight Auspicious Symbols).

The eternal, endless, or mystic knot is common to many ancient traditions, and became particularly innovative in Islamic and Celtic designs. In China it is a symbol of longevity, continuity, love, and harmony. As a symbol of the Buddha's mind the eternal knot represents the Buddha's endless wisdom and compassion. As a symbol of the Buddha's teachings, it represents the continuity of the 'twelve links of dependent origination,' which underlies the reality of Cyclic Existence.

The Box Around the Wish Fulfilling Stone

In Buddhism, the cintamani is said to be one of four relics that came in a chest that fell from the sky [many terma teachings fell from the sky in caskets] during the reign of the first king of Tibet, Lha Thothori Nyantsen. Though the king did not understand the purpose of the objects, he kept them in a position of great reverence. Several years later, two mysterious strangers appeared at the court of the king explaining the four relics, which included the Buddha's bowl and a Mani Stone (cintamani stone) with the Om Mani Padme Hum mantra inscribed on it. These few objects were the 'bringers of the Dharma' to Tibet.

Inside the 'box' that fell from heaven was a Maṇi-jewel (cintamani stone); which is a magical 'Holy Grail' which manifests whatever one wishes for whether treasures, clothing, food, drink, or any other desire. The wish-fulfilling stone grants health and can remove suffering and sickness and life itself can be enhanced. It is the source of the Buddha's teachings and virtues that were given by the Buddhas in the sky—Tushita Heaven.

The Wishing Fulfilling Tree—Cintamani Jewel

Just below the anahata, or heart chakra, is a space called the Ananda Kanda, which means the 'root of bliss, or blissful state.' It is the secret inner altar where the personalized deity is worshipped. It is a center where devotion is intensified. Here is said to be the Celestial Wish-Fulfilling Tree—the Kalpa Taru or Kalpavriksha (Also known as: kalpataru, kalpadruma, kalpa vruksham, kalpapādapa, and karpaga vriksham.). It is one of the beneficial things that was manifested during the churning of the Ocean of Milk during creation.

In this heart cave, one is said to receive what one truly wishes for, if the intention/will is strong enough. In some places, the Kalpa Taru becomes the 'cintamani' or 'Wish-Fulfilling Jewel.' It is still a tree, this cintamani, located on an island in the middle of a beautiful lake, which is itself in the middle of a beautiful garden. It is the Tree of Bounty, able to provide all needs. The Atman, the "I Am," is said to live there. It is sometimes described variously as red or white or pink. It is the spiritual heart.

Heart: Chinese Fire-Energy

The heart is called the King of the organs and commands all of the organs and viscera, houses the spirit, and controls the emotions. In Chinese, the word for heart (hsin) is also used to denote 'mind.' When the heart is strong and steady, it controls the emotions; when it is weak and wavering, the emotions rebel and prey upon the heart-mind, which then loses its command over the body.

Physiologically, the heart controls the circulation and distribution of blood, and therefore all the other organs depend upon it for sustenance. Thoughts and emotions influence the function of various organs via pulse and blood pressure, which are controlled by the heart, where emotions arise. Internally, the heart is functionally associated with the thymus gland, which is located in the same cavity and forms a mainstay of the immune system. Extreme emotions such as grief and anger have an immediate suppressive effect on the immune system by inhibiting thymus function.

Externally, the heart is related to the tongue, to which it is connected by the heart muscle. The color and texture of the tongue thus reflect the condition of the heart. Speech impediments such as stuttering, and mutism are often caused by dysfunction or imbalance in heart energy. Facial complexion, which is a direct reflection of blood circulation, is also a major external indicator of heart function. Fire energy makes the heart the dominant organ of summer, during which season the heart must increase circulation to the surface in order to dissipate excess body heat.

In Chinese medicine, the associated organ of the heart is the small intestine; its element is fire. Long-term memory, thinking, emotions, intimacy, cognition, intelligence, and ideas are all dominated by the function of the heart. The heart is sometimes called 'The Emperor,' or 'supreme controller of all Yin and Yang organs.' The heart houses the body's spirit. The heart dominates sleep; if the heart is strong the patient will fall asleep easily and sleep soundly. If the heart is weak, the patient's mind will 'float,' resulting in an inability to fall asleep, disturbed sleep, or excessive dreaming. The heart's positive psycho-emotional attributes are love, joy, peace, contentment, propriety, insight, wisdom, orderliness, forgiveness, and courtesy. Its negative attributes are hate, guilt, shock, nervousness, excitement, longing, and craving.

Traditional Pulse Diagnosis

Pulse diagnosis is a diagnostic technique used in Ayurveda, traditional Chinese medicine, traditional Mongolian medicine, Siddha medicine, traditional Tibetan medicine, and Unani (Central Asian Perso-Arabic traditional medicine). In Ayurveda, advocates claim that by taking a pulse examination, humoral imbalances can be diagnosed.

Ayurvedic pulse measurement is done by placing index, middle and ring finger on the wrist. The index finger is placed below the wrist bone on the thumb side of the hand (radial styloid). Pulse can be measured in the superficial, middle, and deep levels thus obtaining more information regarding energy imbalance of the patient.

In traditional Chinese medicine, the pulse is divided into three positions on each wrist. There are several systems of diagnostic interpretation of pulse findings utilized in the Chinese medicine system. Some systems utilize overall pulse qualities, looking at changes in the assessed parameters of the pulse to derive one of the traditional 28 pulse types. The traditional 28 pulse types include Floating, Soggy, Empty, Leathery, Scattered, Hollow, Deep, Firm, Hidden, Long, Surging, Short, Rapid, Hasty, Hurried, Moderate, Slow, Knotted, Full, Thready, Minute, Slippery, Choppy, Wiry, Tight, Weak, Regularly Intermittent, Rapid-Irregular, and Stirred. They are analyzed based on several factors, including depth, speed, length, and fluid level.

Other approaches focus on individual pulse positions, looking at changes in the pulse quality and strength within the position, with each position having an association with a particular body area. For example, each of the paired pulse positions can represent the upper, middle, and lower cavities of the torso, or are associated individually with specific organs. For example, the small intestine is said to be reflected in the pulse at the left superficial position, and the heart at the deep position.

The Heart Channel Pathway via Acupuncture Points

The major channel of acupuncture points begins at the heart and emerges via the surrounding blood vessels to pass down through the diaphragm to the small intestine. Another internal branch extends through the throat to the eye, and a connecting channel goes to the tongue. A third branch goes first to the lung before surfacing at the center of the armpit. From here the channel descends along the inner aspect of the arm on the opposite side of the biceps to the lung channel, passing the inner end of the elbow crease. It continues down to the tip of the little finger by the corner of the nail on the thumb side.

The heart meridian has its origin in the heart itself, but does not permeate the heart, rather it permeates the 'supporter of the heart,' the aorta and other major blood vessels entering and exiting the heart. Following the descending abdominal aorta, the descending part of the small intestine, spirally wrapping the small intestine. The branch that passes upwards, surrounding the throat, and going to the 'supporter of the eyes' (the optic nerve), follows the blood vessels passing up into the head, i.e., the carotid artery. The main meridian passes from the 'supporter of the heart,' along the pulmonary artery, to the lungs and thence to the side of the body. The heart and uterus are related: When the menstruation doesn't come, it means that the blood vessel of the uterus is stagnant. The vessel of the uterus, belonging to the heart (meridian), spirally wraps the inside of the uterus. In this case, chi rises-up and presses the lungs from the lower parts. The heart chi cannot pass down smoothly, therefore the menses do not come.

The heart meridian does not permeate the heart itself, rather it permeates the 'supporter of the heart'; which becomes the descending abdominal aorta. This vessel is palpable as the moving chi between the kidneys. The energetic consequences of this distinction are enormously important. We feel that this is making a very direct statement about the energetic nature of the heart, especially about the relation of the heart to the blood. Some authors see the uterus as the place where the moving chi between the kidneys resides. This tends to reinforce the energetic connections that the heart has to this source. Further, it is the superficial trajectory of the supporter of the heart that is the main meridian. This is possibly one reason why many great practitioners have consistently refused to treat the heart meridian directly.

Eternal Para-Bindu Drops

Nada and Bindu are two shakti powers—Naada (Shakti) is seen as a semicircle and sound, while Bindu is seen as a dot, point, or a circle with void inside (Shiva). Bindu is a singularity with no dimension, from which everything proceeds. Nada and Bindu are the progenitors of tattvas, the building blocks of the Universe.

Sakti powers divide again into Nada, Bindu, and Bija. Bindu is Shiva and Bija is Shakti. Nada is the relationship between the two. Nada is action and Bindu is static; Nada is white and Bindu is red.

Sound is contraction and expansion, vibration, and motion. Nada transforms into Bindu which is Isvara Tattva, the origin of the worlds. Bindu's abode is the thousand-petalled lotus chakra in the highest cerebral center of the head. The Bindu should be worshipped like Shiva and Shakti.

Nada and Bindu are all aspects of this Universe, known and unknown. Even gods came from these entities. Nada in its original intent was an act like the union of two entities.

Nada is action where there is a form (Rupa) to the action (Kriya) of power (Shakti), Kriya-Sakti-Rupa. The product in this case is Bindu (Para-Bindu or Supreme Bindu). Para Bindu is a drop, a particle, or a dot. It is light, it is space, it is devoid of decay. Bindu is a compact, super-dense power seed ready for blossoming out into the building blocks of the Universe in an orderly fashion.

Sakti brings about blossoming, actualization and unfolding of the Universe from Bindu. Para Bindu resides in Sahasrara, or the thousand petalled lotus, the seat of Isvara.

Nada is the exciter, and also the excited resulting in creation. From Nada, Goddess creates three Devis and three Devas who possess the Sakti—Will (Jayestha), Desire (Vama), and Action (Raudri) in addition to creation of Fire, Moon and Sun (Brahma, Vishnu, and Rudra). This is known as the creation of sound, the primary creation. The second creation is object creation. The male god comes from female deity; they become couples. Vama creates the Universe; Jayestha maintains what is created; Raudri dissolves.

The Drum of Shiva

According to Hindu mythology, Shiva is the lord of the cosmic dance and the cosmic sound of AUM, from which the entire Universe in generated. Shiva is often depicted with an 'hourglass drum' (damaru) which provides the music for the dance and symbolizes the act of the creation of the Universe through sound. The sounding of Shiva's drum produced the first sound (Nada, the source of creation) in the void of nothingness; its pulse setting up a rhythm to which Shiva began his dance of creation.

Another interpretation of the sound of the damaru suggests that the drum depicts the powers of the rhythm of the heartbeat. If you see your heartbeat, it is not just one straight line but it is a rhythm that goes up and down. The whole world is nothing but rhythms; energy rising and collapsing to rise again. The damaru is also a symbol of sound. Sound is rhythm and energy. The whole Universe is nothing but a wave function, it is nothing but rhythms. It is just one wave (Advaita: doctrine of Hinduism holding that differences in the human condition are illusory). So, the damaru signifies the non-dual nature of the Universe. The drum symbolizes the Universe which is always expanding and collapsing. From an expansion it collapses and then it re-expands, this is the process of creation. Other symbolism suggests the sound of damaru symbolizes the words of the *Vedas*.

The damaru is a small drum with two drumheads, which symbolize the two states of existence--unmanifest and manifest. When a damaru is sounded, it produces dissimilar vibrations which are fused together by resonance to create one sound. The drumbeat is the tuner sound, the sound that fuses the unmanifest and manifest aspects of vibration into one resonance. The sound thus produced by the damaru symbolizes Nada, the cosmic sound of AUM, which can be heard during deep meditation. According to Hindu scriptures, Nada is the source of creation. It is through this drum that the Universe was created, and through it the Universe will be destroyed and renewed again in the endless cycles of time.

The damaru, like all double-headed drums, constitutes a microcosm of the Universe, unites the masculine and feminine principles, and produces sounds with a tremendous dynamic range. By playing a double-headed drum we become co-creators. In such a drum there is balance between male and female forces. Earth and sky, matter and spirit, Shiva (divine masculine) and Shakti (divine feminine) are working together in perfect harmony. With clarity of thought and intent, the drummer becomes a co-creator of all that is needed to benefit all beings unto seven generations.

The damaru was first created by Shiva to produce spiritual sounds by which this whole Universe has been created and regulated. Shiva loves damaru. In the shield shape of some damaru, the triangular upward representation also symbolizes male procreativity (the Lingam), and the downward round representation symbolizes the female procreativity (the Yoni). Symbolically, the creation of the world begins when the lingam and yoni meet at the midpoint of the damaru, and the destruction takes place when they separate from each other. Symbolically, the creation of the world begins when the lingam and yoni meets at the mid-point of the damaru, and the destruction takes place when both separate from each other.

Conclusion

The supersensible nature of the heart has been presented here as the penultimate expression of the human soul and spirit. From ancient teachings to modern research, we have pointed out that no greater sense organ exists beyond the human heart. The modern view that the brain is the seat of the mind and consciousness is simply a partial truth. Without the heart being in coherence with the brain, the brain is only a mirror of the five senses that lacks wisdom without the participation of the heart. Brain-bound thinking leads to cold, dead, materialistic shadow-thinking that will not get beyond superficial knowledge. But heart-thinking, the source of wisdom extracted from experience, is the key to understanding the meaning of life and the reality of life after death. Warmed-up thinking, which comes from the heart, leads to living thinking that Steiner called Moral Imagination. Moral Imagination leads the human heart to commune with archetypal thoughts generated by hierarchical beings (deities) that resonant with the spiritual content of human understanding that transcends the material world. Then comes Moral Inspiration and Moral Intuition that arise from the same spiritual domain that illuminates the true nature of reality.

The heart is not usually viewed as an important sense organ; but in fact, it is the most highly developed organ of perception that has transcendent moral capacities which can evolve into supersensible perception of the spiritual. The heart can sense the outside world through more than is provided by the 'five senses'; and can know and understand much than is considered invisible, or beyond the 'five senses.' The heart can also sense every organ inside the human body and respond to the needs of respiration, circulation, nutrition, and all of other bodily systems. The highly developed heart can assume the autonomic aspects of the cardiovascular system and control circulation, respiration, and many other aspects of maintaining internal equilibrium. The pulse of the heart is the voice of the divine, both inside and outside of the human being. Heart perception is far beyond what science understands about this Holy Grail of human consciousness.

The heart creates the concepts that accompany percepts and colors the individual's world view. Subsequently, that world view is projected onto the world and sets the boundaries for new percepts. When the heart is happy, the world looks lovely. The same sensory input can create a heaven or a hell in the mind of the perceiver, depending on the condition of the heart. Even thinking is changed by the heart as it digests thoughts, feelings, and experiences while tempering them into a personal cosmology. The heart's wisdom is a cosmology that responds to the input of the Cosmos and the internal input of the 'temple' of the human body. We perceive the world and our own individuality through the heart. Thus, the heart is the primal, and ultimate sense organ that evolves into a supersensible organ able to perceive the invisible and the eternal.

This article was started to research the mechanisms whereby sense perception is written into the blood and thus into human memory. We knew that Rudolf Steiner had said that there are three aspects to this process that involved the alchemical understanding of salt/mercury/sulfur as it applies to human blood. The mechanisms of these processes have been presented above in a variety of ways to shed light upon the central pillar of individual human consciousness that drives and controls percepts that can pierce through the delusion of material substance and dispel the illusion of permanence in the physical world. We believe that when this process is fully comprehended, the "I Am" of the individual, the self, will become empowered to directly communicate with the spirits behind matter. We hoped to 'see through' matter to the hierarchical spirits behind substance using the supersensible perception of the evolved human heart.

Once a cosmology has been constructed that aligns the hierarchical correspondences of spirit and matter, the heart becomes able to perceive the Language of the Spirit. Things of this world begin to speak the 'Language of the Birds,' that forgotten language that explains the wisdom inherent in all things. Stones, trees, birds, and all physical substances begin to speak as the heart learns to listen to this language and starts to understand the Sacred Word, Logos, behind all substance, both physical and spiritual. The heart becomes the 'ear' of the Cosmos, the sense organ of the gods that listens and understands the strivings of humans. The heart becomes an antenna to attune to a holy language that contains the 'Lost Word.' Human blood then becomes the vehicle for perceiving and communicating with invisible worlds that interpenetrate the world of matter. The heart becomes a forge where the smithy hammers sense perception into eternal insight and wisdom. The crucible of the heart burns and transforms iron in the blood, to gold in the heart, the mission of the alchemist.

Modern medical research and discovery continually affirm what we can learn from the Ancients. History has shown that physical, material knowledge of the heart can only provide a partial view of what the heart was, is, and will become. To speak of the fifth chamber of the heart or the loosening of the physical heart and the Etheric Heart is shear madness to scientists. But recent discoveries of heart vortex rings and the predictive ability of heart rate variability demonstrate that medical science is still in the beginning stages of understanding the full nature of the heart's capacities. To insinuate that the heart can perceive the invisible or commune with spirits will get you kicked out of medical school. To point in the direction of the auricles of the heart becoming new organs of perception would be judged equally crazy. But the Ancients haven't been wrong yet about the evolving heart and the modern scientific view of the heart is obviously sorely lacking.

The heart is a forge that takes carbon and ionizes it into warmth ether that changes oxygen, nitrogen, sulfur, and calcium into refined substances that bathe the brain and its glands. This steady stream of elements being etherized and ionized into subtle substances that nourish the pineal and pituitary glands was well known about in many spiritual traditions but is totally ignored by science and modern medicine. Science is a new materialistic philosophy of children who won't listen to their parents. Seldom ever does science discover anything that wasn't already known and understood through intuition. As Socrates indicated: "All knowledge is remembered." Perhaps we should take this wisdom and see if what the Ancients have told us might just be something worth remembering and utilizing to heal the weary heart. Then, when the wisdom about the heart that has always been known can lead scientific research, we just might find some of the answers to the mysteries of the heart.

BIBLIOGRAPHY

- Brettshneider, Heinrich, *The Polarity of Center and Periphery in the Circulatory System*, Fair Oaks, CA, 2002.
- Brettshneider, Heinrich, *The Polarity of Center and Periphery in the Circulatory System*, In: *The Dynamic Heart and Circulation*, The Association of Waldorf School of North America, Fair Oaks, CA, 2002.
- Denz H. et al. *Associations between the activation of macrophages*, Haematol, 1992; 48:244-8.
- Dyson, James, *The Mystery of the Blood*, In: *The Image of Blood, The Golden Blade*, 1996, Floris Books, Edinburgh, 1995.
- Hall, Manly P. *The Heart and Blood*, Kessinger Legacy Reprints, 2019.
- Hall, Manly P. *The Occult Anatomy of Man*, Philosophical Research Society, Los Angeles, 1997.
- Harrison, C. G., *The Transcendental Universe: Six Lectures on Occult Science, Theosophy, and the Catholic Faith*, Lindisfarne Press, Hudson, NY, 1993.
- Hauschke, Rudolf, *The Nature of Substance*, Rudolf Steiner Press, 1950.
- Hemsworth, Brüder von Laue, MD, *Life Processes in the Blood Organization,* am Eichhof, 0-75223 Niefern-Oeschelbronn, Germany.

- Hemsworth, Brüder von Laue, MD. *Life Processes in the Blood Organization,* Niefern-Oeschelbronn, Germany.
- Holdrege, Craig. *The Dynamic Heart and Circulation*, AWSNA, 2002.
- Holtzapfel, Walter. *The Human Organs their functional and psychological significance*, Lanthorn Press, 1993.
- *König*, Karl, *Earth and Man*, Bio-Dynamic Literature, Wyoming, Rhode Island, 1982.
- *König*, Karl. *A Living Physiology*, Camphill Books, 1999.
- Lowndes, Florin, *Enlivening the Chakra of the Heart*, Rudolf Steiner Press, London, 1998.
- Marinelli, Ralph; Fuerst, Branko, Van der Zee, Hoyte; McGinn, Andrew; Marinelli, William, *The Heart is Not a Pump: A Refutation of the Pressure Propulsion Premise of Heart Function.*
- Muller-Ortega, Paul Eduardo, *The Triadic Heart of Siva, Kaula Tantricism of Abhinavagupta in the Non-Dual Shaivism of Kashmir,* State University of New York Press, 1989.
- Netter, Frank H. MD, *Atlas of Human Anatomy*, Edition 5, Saunders, 2011.
- Parsell, Charles B., *The Heart As An Organ Of Perception.*
- Pearce, Joseph Chilton, *The Heart-Mind Matrix*, Park Street Press, Rochester, NY, 2012.
- Pfeiffer, Ehrenfried. *Heart Lectures*, Mercury Press, 1950.
- Rohen, Johannes W. *Functional Morphology, The Dynamic Wholeness of the Human Being*. Adonis Press, 2007.

- Rohen, Johannes W., *Functional Morphology*, Adonis Press, Hillsdale, NY, 2007.
- Roitt J et al. *Immunology*, Mosby, London, 1993.
- Salkovskis, *The Art of Perceiving from the Heart*, Salkovskis's Theory on Obsessions.
- Stefanucci Jeanine K. *Follow your heart: Emotion adaptively influences perception.*
- Steiner Rudolf, *A Fragment*, Anthroposophic Press—*Ein Fragment,* (GA 45).
- Steiner Rudolf, *An Occult Physiology,* Rudolf Steiner Press, London, 1983, (GA 128).
- Steiner Rudolf, *Anthroposophie als Kosmosophie Teil*, 29 October 1921, (GA 208).
- Steiner Rudolf, *Macrocosm and Microcosm*, London: Rudolf Steiner Press, London, 1968, (GA 119).
- Steiner Rudolf, *Spiritual Science and Medicine*, Rudolf Steiner Press, London, 1975, (GA 312).
- Steiner Rudolf, *Supersensible Man,* Nov 1923. Rudolf Steiner Press, London, (GA 231).
- Steiner Rudolf, *The Four Seasons and the Archangels,* October 1923, Rudolf Steiner Press, London, 1968, (GA 229).
- Steiner Rudolf, *The Human Being in Body, Soul and Spirit Our Relationship to the Earth,* 1922, Anthroposophic Press, 1989, (GA 347).
- Steiner Rudolf, Wegman I. *Fundamentals of Therapy,* Rudolf Steiner Press, London, 1983, (GA 27).

- Steiner, Rudolf, *An Occult Physiology*, Lecture 6: *The Blood as Manifestation and Instrument of the Human Ego*, March 26, 1911, GA 128.
- Steiner, Rudolf, *An Occult Physiology*, Prague, 1911, Rudolf Steiner Press, 1951.
- Steiner, Rudolf, *Anthroposophic Spiritual Science and Medicine*, Rudolf Steiner, GA 313.
- Steiner, Rudolf, *At the Gates of Spiritual Science: The Three Worlds*, Stuttgart, August 23, 1906, GA 95.
- Steiner, Rudolf, *Curative Education*, Rudolf Steiner, GA 317.
- Steiner, Rudolf, Foundations of Esoterism, Rudolf Steiner Press, London, 1983.
- Steiner, Rudolf, *From Mammoths to Mediums*, June 6, 1923, Rudolf Steiner Press, Forrest Row, Sussex, 2000.
- Steiner, Rudolf, *Macrocosm and Microcosm,* Lecture 9, *Organs of Spiritual Perception Contemplation of the Ego from Twelve Vantage-points. The Thinking of the Heart.*
- Steiner, Rudolf, *Macrocosm and Microcosm*, Rudolf Steiner, Lecture 10, March 30, 1910.
- Steiner, Rudolf, *Man: Hieroglyph of the Universe*, Rudolf Steiner Press, London, 1972.
- Steiner, Rudolf, *Pastoral Medicine*, Anthroposophic Press, Hudson NY, 1987 (GA 318).
- Steiner, Rudolf, *Philosophy, Cosmology, and Religion*, September 10, 1922, CW 21.5

- Steiner, Rudolf, *Supersensible Man*, 5 Lectures at The Hague, November 13-18, 1923, Anthroposophical Publishing Company, London, 1943.
- Steiner, Rudolf, *The Effects of Esoteric Development,* March 21, 1913, The Hague, GA 145.
- Steiner, Rudolf, *The Human Heart,* Dornach, May 26, 1922, GA 212.
- Steiner, Rudolf, *Wisdom of Man, of the Soul, and of the Spirit,* Lecture III.
- Steiner, Rudolf, *Workmen's Lectures,* August, 1922, GA 347.
- Treichler, Rudolf, *Soulways: Development, crises and illnesses of the soul*, Hawthorn Press, 1989.
- Tusenius, Karal Jan, *The Bleeding Wound of King Amfortas*, In: *The Image of Blood, The Golden Blade*, 1996, Floris Books, Edinburgh, 1995.
- Twentyman, Ralph. *The Science and Art of Healing*, Floris Books, 1989.
- Vogel, Heinz-Hartmut, *Warmth and the Heart, The Human Ego Organization*, Wala Publishing, Eckwaelden, 1980.
- Weissmann, L. *How the Immune System Develops*. Scientific American, September 1993.

Videos on The Human Heart

Ralph Marinelli Part One

https://www.youtube.com/watch?v=iKfgeV0ipIE

Ralph Marinelli Part Two

https://www.youtube.com/watch?v=SHAU02d-los

Etherization of the Blood

https://neoanthroposophy.com/2017/02/06/etherization-of-the-blood/

The Heart is Not a Pump

https://www.rsarchive.org/RelArtic/Marinelli/

Two Articles on the Heart

https://neoanthroposophy.com/2017/02/08/perception-as-a-bridge-to-the-spiritual-world/

https://neoanthroposophy.com/2017/02/06/etherization-of-the-blood/

ABOUT DR. RUDOLF STEINER

Rudolf Steiner was born on the 27th of February 1861 in Kraljevec in the former Kingdom of Hungary and now Croatia. He studied at the College of Technology in Vienna and obtained him doctorate at the University of Rostock with a dissertation on Theory of Knowledge which concluded with the sentence: "The most important problem of human thinking is this: to understand the human being as a free personality, whose very foundation is himself."

He exchanged views widely with the personalities involved in cultural life and arts of his time. However, unlike them, he experienced the spiritual realm as the other side of reality. He gained access through exploration of consciousness using the same method as the natural scientist uses for the visible world in his external research. This widened perspective enabled him to give significant impulses in many areas such as art, pedagogy, curative education, medicine, agriculture, architecture, economics, and social sciences, aiming towards the spiritual renewal of civilization.

He gave his movement the name of "Anthroposophy" (the wisdom of humanity) after separating from the German section of the Theosophical Society, where he had acted as a general secretary. He then founded the Anthroposophical Society in 1913 which formed its center with the construction of the First Goetheanum in Dornach, Switzerland. Rudolf Steiner died on 30th March 1925 in Dornach. His literary work is made up of numerous books, transcripts and approximately 6000 lectures which have for the most part been edited and published in the Complete Works Edition.

Steiner's basic books, which were previously a prerequisite to gaining access to his lectures, are: *Theosophy, The Philosophy of Freedom, How to Know Higher Worlds, Christianity as a Mystical Fact,* and *Occult Science.*

ABOUT THE AUTHOR, DR. DOUGLAS GABRIEL

Dr. Gabriel is a retired superintendent of schools and professor of education who has worked with schools and organizations throughout the world. He has authored many books ranging from teacher training manuals to philosophical/spiritual works on the nature of the divine feminine.

He was a Waldorf class teacher and administrator at the Detroit Waldorf School and taught courses at Mercy College, the University of Detroit, and Wayne State University for decades. He then became the Headmaster of a Waldorf School in Hawaii and taught at the University of Hawaii, Hilo. He was a leader in the development of charter schools in Michigan and helped found the first Waldorf School in the Detroit Public School system and the first charter Waldorf School in Michigan.

Gabriel received his first degree in religious formation at the same time as an associate degree in computer science in 1972. This odd mixture of technology and religion continued throughout his life. He was drafted into and served in the Army Security Agency (NSA) where he was a cryptologist and systems analyst in signal intelligence, earning him a degree in signal broadcasting. After military service, he entered the Catholic Church again as a Trappist monk and later as a Jesuit priest where he earned PhD's in philosophy and comparative religion, and a Doctor of Divinity. He came to Detroit and earned a BA in anthroposophical studies and history and a MA in school administration. Gabriel left the priesthood and became a Waldorf class teacher and administrator in Detroit and later in Hilo, Hawaii.

Douglas has been a sought-after lecturer and consultant to schools and businesses throughout the world and in 1982 he founded the Waldorf Educational Foundation that provides funding for the publication of educational books. He has raised a great deal of money for Waldorf schools and institutions that continue to develop the teachings of Dr. Rudolf Steiner. Douglas is now retired but continues to write a variety of books including a novel and a science fiction thriller. He has four children, who keep him busy and active and a wife who is always striving towards the spirit through creating an "art of life." She is the author of the *Gospel of Sophia* trilogy.

The Gabriels' articles, blogs, and videos can currently be found at:

OurSpirit.com
Neoanthroposphy.com
GospelofSophia.com
EternalCurriculum.com

TRANSLATOR'S NOTE

The Rudolf Steiner quotes in this book can be found, in most cases, in their full-length and in context, through the Rudolf Steiner Archives by an Internet search of the references provided. We present the quoted selections of Steiner from a free rendered translation of the original while utilizing comparisons of numerous German to English translations that are available from a variety of publishers and other sources. In some cases, the quoted selections may be condensed and partially summarized using the same, or similar in meaning, words found in the original. Brackets are used to insert [from the author] clarifying details or anthroposophical nomenclature and spiritual scientific terms.

We chose to use GA (Gesamtausgabe—collected edition) numbers to reference Steiner's works instead of CW (Collected Works), which is often used in English editions. Some books in the series, *From the Works of Rudolf Steiner*, have consciously chosen to use a predominance of Steiner quotes to drive the presentation of the themes rather than personal remarks and commentary.

We feel that Steiner's descriptions should not be truncated but need to be translated into an easily read format for the English-speaking reader, especially for those new to Anthroposophy. We recommend that serious aspirants read the entire lecture, or chapter, from which the Steiner quotation was taken, because nothing can replace Steiner's original words or the mood in which they were delivered. The style of speaking and writing has changed dramatically over the last century and needs updating in style and presentation to translate into a useful tool for spiritual study in modern times. The series, *From the Works of Rudolf Steiner* intends to present numerous "study guides" for the beginning aspirant, and the initiate, in a format that helps support the spiritual scientific research of the reader.

Made in the USA
Monee, IL
12 April 2024